Novel Frames
Literature as Guide to Race, Sex, and History in American Culture

Studies in Popular Culture
M. Thomas Inge, General Editor

Novel Frames

LITERATURE AS GUIDE TO RACE, SEX, AND HISTORY IN AMERICAN CULTURE

Joseph R. Urgo

UNIVERSITY PRESS OF MISSISSIPPI
Jackson & London

94 93 92 91   4 3 2 1

Library of Congress Cataloging-in-Publication Data

Urgo, Joseph R.
    Novel frames : literature as guide to race, sex, and history in American culture / Joseph R. Urgo
        p. cm.
    Includes index.
    ISBN 0-87805-530-4 (alk. paper). — ISBN 0-87805-539-8 (pbk. : alk. paper)
    1. American fiction—20th century—History and criticism—Theory, etc. 2. United States—Popular culture—History—20th century. 3. Literature and anthropology—United States. 4. Literature and history. 5. Race in literature. 6. Sex in literature. I. Title.
PS379.U74 1991
813'.509—dc20   91-17627
                                                          CIP
British Library Cataloging-in-Publication data available

FOR

GEORGE DRETAR URGO

CONTENTS

Acknowledgments   ix

Introduction   xi

I   THE RACIAL SELF

ONE **Contemplating the Unthinkable**
     The Myth of Racial Existence
     in Ralph Ellison's America   5

TWO **The Invisible Candidate**
     Network Television News
     Coverage of the Jesse Jackson
     Presidential Campaign in 1988   38

II   THE SEXUAL SELF

THREE *Sanctuary* **and the Pornographic
      Nexus**   77

FOUR **The Body as Popular Commodity**
     Glamour and Pornography   113

III THE HISTORICAL SELF

FIVE **Historical Movement**
     What's Lost in *A Lost Lady*   157

SIX **The Yippies'** *Overthrow*
     What Everybody Knows
     in America   189

Epilogue   223

Index   225

ACKNOWLEDGMENTS

The meaning of this book's structure has been one that has informed the way I think about and teach literature for a long time. But like any conviction, it needed a lot of collaboration in order to move it from an idiosyncrasy to something communicable. I hope that I am not omitting anyone when I offer the following as my intellectual debit sheet.

First of all, I thank Cecelia Tichi for suggesting that I write a book about these ideas—and then providing invaluable initial readings. Many others reacted in profitable ways, and I acknowledge in particular the collegial interventions of Earl Briden, Nora Barry, and Bill Graves. The manuscript was improved significantly by Ann Finlayson's editing. Past teachers, including George Monteiro, Robert Scholes, William G. McLoughlin, George Creeger, and Carol Maturo, will recognize some of my arguments. The methodology of this book originated in my own classroom and I only hope that my students at Bryant College receive as much from my efforts as I do from theirs.

I thank the editors of *American Literature, Studies in American Fiction*, and *Studies in Popular Culture* for permitting me to borrow from works I had published in those journals. I am also obliged to the Network Television News Archives at Vanderbilt University, where my research on Jesse Jackson was completed. And thanks to the Yippies for being so generous with back issues of *Overthrow* and other materials.

Bryant College provided course release time, a research grant, and publication support for this project. I thank Mary Lyons for her belief in the scholar's freedom and Dean Michael Patterson for his material support for that conviction. Daniel Boone at the Koffler Center gave indispensable hard and software guidance. I also benefited from the support provided by Jackie David and her coterie of capable student assistants.

And thanks personally to Lesley Dretar Urgo, who so often points the way, and to George Dretar Urgo, who begins where we finish.

INTRODUCTION

This book seeks to demonstrate that a novel may be illuminated by critical intervention while at the same time provide a means of interrogating the real. A work of fiction is produced within a specific cultural nexus. Yet once it exists, the novel becomes a discrete context within which subsequent productions in that cultural nexus can be understood. In other words, a literary text projects its culture as forcefully as it reflects its sources. This statement is not to be confused with the casual observation that the novelist might possess prescience, or that life may imitate art. More pointedly, it is to suggest that a novel is always "about" much more than its subject matter. What the artist writes about is only part of what the text finally conveys. This book, then, is not a study in sources nor is it on a quest for parallels between fiction and reality. Rather, I am attempting to demonstrate the practical utility of reading literature by making use of ideas projected about American culture by specific novels. The novels, in other words, provide the context for analyzing aspects of the culture which are not written about specifically in the literary texts themselves. To provide a focal point of study, this book centers its attention on representations of the self in various productions of American culture.

Focus: The Self as Object

We no longer speak of character in the singular but now see a wider diversity of legitimate American styles of being. Instead of moving toward a homogenized self, Americans "hang together," to borrow Henry James' term, as a collection of interests with ideological bonds hinged in a variety of beliefs about pluralism, tolerance, and competition. The self, by its postmodern definition, hangs together as a microcosmic mirror of this culture of multidimensionality. Produced by a diverse and stratified social order, the American self is best understood as housing a plurality of voices and interests. What unites Americans into a common culture is this sense of a core multiplicity of being.

At times, the varieties of being in America blur the existence of commonality. A stroll along the walks of a contemporary university, past the African-American house, the ethnic studies house, the women's studies house, the Third World center—these separate addresses would lead one to believe that there is no center here. But each address is, in actuality, a center. Each contributes to the multidimensionality of the culture that all, with differing emphases, seek to describe. We have in America what folksinger Judy Collins calls "many houses / One for every season" of who we are, who we have been in the past (like it or not), and who we would like to become in the future. Elizabeth Fox-Genovese has argued recently that

> to be an American is forthrightly to acknowledge a collective identity that simultaneously transcends and encompasses our disparate identities and communities. Unless we acknowledge our diversity, we allow the silences of the received tradition to become our own. Unless we sustain some ideal of a common culture, we reduce culture to personal experience and sacrifice the very concept of American. (28–29)

The "common culture" to which Fox-Genovese advocates a sort of allegiance is not an easy thing to find. The word "common" may in fact send the seeker off in the wrong direction. The culture is multiple and contradictory, not singular and consistent—and the self at home in this culture is one that can tolerate multiplicity and contradiction. Consider, for the obvious example, the Civil War, the eternal battleground of the Americanist. It was about slavery; it was about industrial expansion, not slavery. Both are true: The war was and was not about slavery. Or consider Thomas Jefferson, archetypal American, author of the Declaration of Independence, slave owner, father of "life, liberty and the pursuit of happiness" and father of chattel slaves. Contradiction is absolutely central to American culture.

Paul Smith finds that the term "individual . . . offers a fiction of cohesion that bears as its symptom a belief in a fully enabled and self-conscious power." Instead, Smith argues that the "individual" cannot "be anything more than a representation of the social formation or of the ideological" (xxxiv, 6). Smith's argument shifts emphasis away from the self as the origin of its own significance to the social order as the source of whatever form of individuation we have. "In the postmodern view," according to Mas'ud Zavarzadeh, "man emerges not as the instigator of meaning but rather as the effect of intersections of meaning-generating signs: in other words, he is seen as the result of cultural overdetermination rather than as a free agent" (5). The self produced by its cultural environment (which is not necessarily the same as its point of origin) will mirror the peculiar qualities of that culture. A diverse, stratified, and embattled social order will produce a multiple, contradictory self known more by its anxieties than by its tranquillity.

Clifford Geertz finds that individualism, or the belief in "the person as a bounded, unique, more or less integrated motivational and cognitive universe . . . organized into a distinctive whole," is "a rather peculiar idea within the context of the world's cultures" (126). Despite overwhelming evidence to the contrary, beliefs in the integral, autonomous self persist as vestiges of a defunct ideological system. It creeps up, as this study demonstrates, in the way that the mass media employ codes of race, sex, and history to project American identity. In the West, as Geertz points out, we continue to imply that the individual possesses an objective existence: self-enclosed, self-interested, and protective of its "inner" self beyond the reach of any but the most intimate, if even to these. The inability to get in touch with this core self is diagnosed as some sort of neurosis, and the inability to share it is called by a number of derogatory terms, from narcissism to frigidity. These ideas are dangerous. They block the emergence of a self liberated from object status.

"Everything outside ourselves, whether we know it in its proper relationship to us, or whether it remains for us apparently without significance and unrelated to our mind and heart," according to Heinrich Zimmer, "actually reflects and mirrors our inner selves" (232). It is not an unprecedented idea, then, this postmodern emphasis on the culturally produced self. Its organicism fits well into the greening trend of American culture by revising the autonomous, conquering hero into an ecologic, networked "site" of values and interests. The self has always been a cagey character: As in a fiction, it is always described, never seen, always evoked, never touched. When the self was considered an integral whole, the critic was called upon to define what the whole object looked like, to define the American "character." The cagey self escaped that project and has now dispersed into fragments. Efforts to piece it together are big business enterprises: self-help, health and beauty, body toning. These efforts are futile, of course, because quite naturally the self is not an object. It can be considered one (it can be considered anything), but as long as it is the self that is making the consideration, it will continue to alter its own image for the benefit of the perceiver. This is the activism of what I will be calling the anarchic self. Turning the self into an object is a reaction to that anarchy, a defense against the terror implicit in multiplicity. Multidimensionality demands that the self be its own subject, its own authorization; it demands that the self not hide its contradictory essence beneath a mask of integrity and consistency. Of course, there is terror before any threshold.

Postmodern challenges to the integral self have been considered by some to be historically progressive, reacting to the modernist's sense of alienation. We no longer feel alienated if there exists no core self to experience that alienation. Ian Angus concludes that "postmodern industrial culture is not a *repression* but a *simulation* of identity. There is no 'alienation' from an original identity to which one can authentically 'return'" (101). Hence, the self feels ambivalent toward any definitiveness, especially toward those definitions that are placed on the individual from without, those that confine the anarchic core to object status. However, instead of seeing this ambivalence as liberational, some have found it frightening. It drove Ralph Ellison's narrator underground before he realized its potential usefulness as a strategy for postmodern survival. The anxiety-stricken invisible one will often look outside itself for definition and attempt to make itself into an object. In this way it achieves visibility in exchange for control over its destiny and in exchange for the terror of anarchy. As an object, the self is defined not from within but from without. Once the self becomes convinced that this must be its fate, it sees that it is adrift among a variety of "simulated" selves, as Angus rightly terms it, from which the self is encouraged to construct an identity. Here mass culture serves its peculiar purpose, to provide models for simulation. The question remains: If one rejects the object status provided by the mass media and clings to an anarchic, invisible core, what then?

Reading Culture

Novel Frames seeks to converge focal points thought perhaps to be too wide for a professional scope. We read widely in order to focus our thoughts. "The condition of reading," according to Robert Scholes, "is the human condition" (69). Scholes means to be more than aphoristic. He indicates a specific kind of reader and a specific kind of reading. He calls it "reading as an intertextual activity," where "reading is indeed never just the reduction of a text to some kernel of predetermined intention but always the connecting of signs in one text to other signs altogether" (11). Why read? Teachers of written literature need to come up with good reasons for reading, especially since students, raised on video, get even more suspicious of teachers than television encourages them to be. Scholes argues that reading provides us with a model for living: the interactive, critical, and productive reader emerges as his model for the political, ethical, and useful member of any collective social order. Scholes's model reader is one with a pen in hand ready at any moment to stop reading and start writing—or perhaps break into some other purposeful action. A link is to be made, then, between what we read and who we think we are.

Luiz Costa Lima calls the fictional "a *discursive* form," and argues that reading fiction "takes on the appearance of a 'game' that does not contain the choice between true and false." He describes this "game" as one "that puts truths into question; that is, it is a game that does not so much expand or apply truths as interrogate them" (53). This is probably the most valuable quality of self-realization offered the reader by the fictional. Fiction *interrogates* the real. Since most interrogation these days is done by the defenders of a reality assumed to be immune to questioning, and since some teachers have taken to drawing up lists of things that everyone should know (not question: know), it is particularly timely that we cultivate Costa Lima's notion of reading. As fiction interrogates the real, it provides the reader not simply with a perspective but with a mode of consciousness.

Some literary theorists, in their zeal as readers, go so far as to suggest that all of life is a fiction. Certainly the power one feels in mastering a text is a power one would like to transfer to mastery of the world. What reading offers us is not mastery, however, but simply a way to consider the culture at large: to consider it *as* a text (or *as* a fiction)—but we ought not to forget that there is a distinction. Blurring the difference between typeface and storefront may serve the purpose of the academic, but none else. Reading does not turn the world into a text, but it does allow readers to bring to their experiences the kind of rigor of thought demanded by a good read. Once having mastered the art of interrogating the text, the reader-human (as Scholes has it) can turn to interrogating the real. Frank Lentricchia has described this reader as an "activist intellectual" who comprises "a culturally suspicious, trouble-making readership" (11). Richard Kearney argues that this activist reader is the source of the postmodern self, "the self as reader and writer of his own life. But it also casts each one of us as a narrator," Kearney explains, "who never ceases to revise, reinterpret and clarify his own story" (395). We seek no longer an integrity of self but a process of self-revision and cultural interrogation. Readers make trouble when they take the critical habits of textual and narrative analysis and assert them over the productions meant to govern, instruct, or define them.

The subject matter of this book centers on ideas about the self as provided by literature and mass media. The works of three American authors, Ralph Ellison, William Faulkner, and Willa Cather, are presented here as literary attempts to interrogate the idea of an autonomous self. I focus on three distinct dimensions of existence: the racial, the sexual, and the historical. Each author under study challenges the tyranny of object status in America and each provides the reader with a mode of consciousness, or a way of thinking about and interrogating cultural methods of self-construction. Most importantly, however, is the fact that each writer provides a way to confront and manage authoritarian efforts that attempt, in the name of hierarchical order, to define and limit the self. All three writers defend the anarchic self from annihilation. To demonstrate that defense, I employ a particular method of juxtaposition.

A Method

The method in this book is plastic. Heinrich Zimmer would have called it the method of the dilettante, of "one who takes delight (*diletto*) in something" (2). The delight taken is in the close scrutiny of things without regard—or perhaps with disdain—for the high structures of disciplinary thought. "Some of us—scholarly specialists—tend to favor certain very definite, and consequently limited, methods of interpretation, admitting only those within the pale of our authoritative influence," according to Zimmer. "But such rigidities can only bind us to what we already know" (5). The worst thing with which the dilettante can be burdened is a memory that is more powerful than the imagination. The anarchic self delights in its ability to create temporary order, but it will not tolerate much of anything for *too* long.

The only idea that this study treats with the kind of reverence reserved for permanence is that the American novel, under close scrutiny, can tell us a lot about the American social order. This does not mean that the novel's subject matter illuminates reality, or that it can substitute for historical or social inquiry. On the contrary, the novel has always been a dubious source of historical accuracy. Rather, what the novel can do is to introduce the kinds of questions one might bring to cultural criticism. In this volume, I am interested in questions raised about representations of the self in various productions of the mass media.

The method employed in this study is that of juxtaposition: to show how the novel can be put to use. The text provides a *literary* context for something that compels interest at the present time. And so I take the kinds of things I can learn from *A Lost Lady* and use them as a critical lens for understanding the Yippies, the political group that publishes the green anarchist newspaper *Overthrow* and also sponsors the history project *Blacklisted News / Secret Histories.* I make this connection with the knowledge that Cather was very interested in history and in the effect that ideas about the past can have on the quality of people's lives. This is not to say that without Cather the Yippies remain unknown or that without Faulkner *Glamour* magazine remains mysterious or that without Ellison Jesse Jackson is incomprehensible. On the contrary, a number of novels could be substituted for the three used here—just as any number of events or mass media publications could be analyzed through the lens they provide. This study is more about literary interrogations than it is about Ellison, Faulkner, or Cather. I am trying here to offer some good reasons to read by demonstrating that reading can save us from turning into data bases.

The first task at hand is to remove fiction from the constraining, disciplinary category of "literature," and to amend the notion that literary study is a self-contained, autonomous enterprise. I do this by demonstration rather than by theoretical argument. To provide some order to the demonstration, I choose three twentieth-century novelists who represent a cross section in the American literary canon (one black man, one white man, one white woman). I use these three writers to illuminate cultural phenomena that I consider typical and important in recent American history. To provide a bit more order, I focus my attention on a single year, 1988. My reading of Ralph Ellison's *Invisible Man* is paired, then, with a reading of Jesse Jackson's 1988 presidential primary campaign. William Faulkner's *Sanctuary* is juxtaposed with a reading of the October 1988 issue of *Glamour* magazine. And, finally, Willa Cather's *A Lost Lady* is read in conjunction with the Spring 1988 edition of the Yippie publication *Overthrow.*

Reading fiction continually juxtaposes the world of the reader with the world of the text. Any reader knows that out of this juxtaposition emerges all we know of truth. We can control our choice of reading material, but we cannot control the social events and experiences that will happen simultaneous to our reading. The truths we find in fiction and the truths we extract from the culture about *the self* will always be largely accidental—and contingent. This makes anarchists of us all, at the core, despite the orderly lives we lead. Our attitude toward those ideas in which we believe will always be, given the multiplicity of things we can believe in, ambivalent. As a people with many houses, we find ourselves in perpetual movement from place to place, metaphysically and in moving vans. In a world of movement, ambivalence is, after all, healthy. We still say "self," and we still say "truth," but we don't mean it. The truths we live by are temporary; they are like plastic toys, little pyramids meant to be played with, thought about, and discarded for the next reading. Reading here is understood as a covert action, as a preparation, but never as an end in itself. To "read" a thing (text, event, self) is to make it true, give it life—once we stop reading, the thing fades into some invisible dimension of self. As long as we read, we contribute to the way things mean, and we discover what we mean ourselves.

WORKS CITED

Angus, Ian. "Circumscribing Postmodern Culture," in *Cultural Politics in Contemporary America,* edited by Ian Angus and Sut Jhally, 96–110. New York: Routledge, Chapman & Hall, Inc., 1989.

Fox-Genovese, Elizabeth. "Between Individualism and Fragmentation: American Culture and the New Literary Studies of Race and Gender." *American Quarterly* 42:1 (March 1990): 7–29.

Geertz, Clifford. "From the Native's Point of View: On the Nature of Anthropological Understanding." In *Culture Theory: Essays on Mind, Self, and Emotion,* edited by Richard A. Shweder and Robert A. LeVine, 123–136. New York: Cambridge University Press, 1984.

Kearney, Richard. *The Wake of Imagination: Toward a Postmodern Culture.* Minneapolis: University of Minnesota Press, 1988.

Lentricchia, Frank. *Criticism and Social Change.* Chicago: University of Chicago Press, 1983.

Lima, Luiz Costa. *Control of the Imaginary: Reason and Imagination in Modern Times,* translated by Ronald W. Sousa. Minneapolis: University of Minnesota Press, 1988.

Scholes, Robert. *Protocols of Reading.* New Haven: Yale University Press, 1989.

Smith, Paul. *Discerning the Subject.* Minneapolis: University of Minnesota Press, 1988.

Zavarzadeh, Mas'ud, and Donald Morton. "Theory Pedagogy Politics: The Crisis of 'The Subject' in the Humanities." *Boundary* 2 XV (1, 2) (Fall 1986/Winter 1987): 1–22.

Zimmer, Heinrich. *The King and the Corpse: Tales of the Soul's Conquest of Evil.* Princeton: Princeton University Press, 1957 [1948].

Novel Frames
Literature as Guide to Race, Sex, and History
in American Culture

I THE RACIAL SELF

CHAPTER I

Contemplating the Unthinkable

The Myth of Racial Existence in Ralph Ellison's America

The master artisans of the South were slaves, and white Americans have been walking Negro walks, talking Negro flavored talk (and prizing it when spoken by Southern belles), dancing Negro dances and singing Negro melodies far too long to speak of a 'mainstream' of American culture to which they're alien.
—Ralph Ellison (S&A, 256)
I ain't done no wrong at all, Just tried to 'fend my little home; I can only weep and moan, White folks got my body, Oh Lord! Have mercy on my soul, Have mercy, have mercy on my soul.
—"The Lynchers" (Adams, 189)

Ralph Ellison's Great American

Ralph Ellison sees Americans as afflicted with a tragic materialism. This materialism leads them to persist in identifying and categorizing one another by their outward, objectified appearance and not by their more complex and varied intellectual existence. The first quotation above captures the essence of something Ellison has been saying about Americans for decades. Black and white, African and European—these differentiations are matters of emphasis, not essence, in American cultural life. White folks, in other words, long ago appropriated Negro bodies and have used them—first in the slave fields, later in such fields of culture as art, music, and literature—to advance American civilization. What remains of the appropriation is the corpse of the purely black or purely white body, and by definition this corpse is certainly, in Ellison's vision, without life or significance. The spirit of a multiracial culture has risen from the body below the lynchers' tree, but Americans insist, nonetheless, that the corpse still lives.

The United States has been a great capitalist, imperial world power, a tremendous producer of goods and services. It has changed the face of the world by its presence and its productivity. Its first product, however, was not the steamboat or the light bulb but the Negro. Extracted as raw material from another continent, Africans were brought to America and hammered, worked, bred, and transformed into a new human object: the nigger/Negro/colored person/black/Afro-American/African–American. Like any product intended for a number of markets, this one has many names and packages. By any trademark, however, the American Negro is a masterpiece of capitalism and marketing. There are masses of people who actually believe that this particular good has a culture and an identity separate from the factory that assembled it, distinct from the mind that planned and executed its production. Racial ideology (the marketing strategy, to continue this analogy, by which the Negro was sold to American history) insists that two cultures exist in the United States—one possessed by the manufacturer of the Negro and another possessed by the Negro itself. George Washington Cable in 1880 called the African in America "a commodity," a being that was captured and stripped of its indigenous heritage and turned into something useful to Americans (169). The process is so fundamental to the American way of doing things as to sound like a parody. American "know-how," as the boosters have put it, created inland waterways, irrigated deserts, connected oceans with canals, put a man on the moon—and produced this object it calls a "black" human being. Long before it put a white man on the moon, the United States had put a black man on earth.

Ralph Ellison has spent his career, in his novel, in his essays, and in his speaking engagements, arguing that the concept of race no longer holds significance in the American democracy but is, rather, a vestige of original racial injustice. At the level of mind, or the level of cultural existence, there has simply been too much exchange between blacks and whites to speak of an autonomous racial existence that has any correspondence to intellectual reality. To speak of the "white mind" and the "black mind" is to indulge in a dangerous illusion, in Ellison's thinking, which serves no purpose other than to suppress, or to negate, complex existence in a pluralized society. "Arising from an initial failure of social justice," in other words, "this anachronism divides social groups along lines that are no longer tenable while fostering hostility, anxiety, and fear" (*GT*, 228). These lines are untenable simply because they are physical categorizations with premodern, archaic meaning. In a postmodern context in particular, racial identification can possess no meaning except to forestall the emergence of a multiple self liberated from its oppressive existence as object.

What Ellison found untenable in 1968 (when he expressed this opinion), scholars have since asserted in even stronger terms. Henry Louis Gates, Jr., for example, reminds us that "race, as a meaningful criterion within the biological sciences, has long been recognized to be a fiction." The fiction persists, and such "biological misnomers" as "the black race" and "the white race" (and "the Jewish race" or the "Aryan race") continue to mean something to cultures indebted to "the dubious pseudosciences of the eighteenth and nineteenth centuries" (Gates, 4). Tzvetan Todorov echoes much of what Ellison attempts to say in *Invisible Man* in his claim that "racism (like sexism) becomes an increasingly influential social phenomenon as societies approach the contemporary ideal of democracy" (371). A democracy, as Ellison has indicated on numerous occasions, does not recognize physical *difference* as politically relevant. Nonetheless, as the physical body ceases to possess legal privileges or handicaps, it begins to assume tremendous social significance. The implications that this phenomenon holds for social existence come to fruition in the plethora of "health and beauty" trade magazines, such as *Glamour*, and the particular ideology they profess. For as Richard Pells has sardonically pointed out, although there are far more important things to watch in the world, most Americans have taken to watching their weight (408), not to mention their cholesterol, their hairlines, and their cellulite. In other words, the body—in its whiteness, its blackness, and even its saggy-bagginess—is the primary source of identity for many Americans even as we begin to realize, as Ellison, Gates, Todorov, and others have argued, that it is irrelevant to who we might be or what we might become.

It appears a weighty coincidence that as courts, Congresses, and proclamations make it more and more apparent that the accidents of physical makeup shall have no influence upon one's legal or political rights, Americans have turned to their physical bodies as their single most common concern. Cholesterol levels, fat content, flat stomachs, and ideal weight have replaced the old, blatant hierarchy of racial and ethnic identity. While a man cannot be overtly barred from a job because of his exterior color, he *can* be barred from a job because of the results of a urine test—the interior color. Or a woman can be told where not to sit because she smokes cigarettes. The democracy speaks with dual purposefulness when it signals, on the one hand, that "race, creed, color [and gender]" shall bear no legal implications but that the ingestion of certain foods and drugs or the general health of the body shall have tremendous social, legal, and economic consequences. Despite the efforts of reformers and the general force of democratic principles, the body remains the object of commercial hierarchies and market colonialism.

Of course, racial difference (like sexual difference) continues to play a major role in the psychic dramas of American culture. "Race" (in quotations) may not exist as a legitimate scientific category, but it does so certainly as a social phenomenon. Appiah claims that racial differentiation is an act which "biologizes" what is essentially "culture, or ideology" (36); in other words, it insists that what is cultural is in fact natural, or that what (as Gates said) is fictional is in fact real. Other students of race have found that racialism, whether proved to be cultural, fictional, or ideological, has an emotional reality not easily overcome.* Winthrop Jordan, in his monumental study, *White over Black,* claims that antiblackness is rooted in the content of Western Civilization's fundamental definition. "Black," even before any European might have imagined there existed a continent of more-or-less black people, "was an emotionally partisan color, the handmaid and symbol of baseness and evil, a sign of danger and repulsion," which served, culturally, as white's opposite (7). Colonizing and enslaving black bodies can be interpreted, historically, as a cultural attempt to overcome and control "baseness and evil." Hence, from the very first confrontation of whites and blacks, bodies (black and white) were considered as objects. "Perhaps

* A distinction is made by scholars between the term "racism" and the term "racialism." Racism refers to the creation of racial hierarchies in which one race is considered inferior to another. Racialism is a broader term, and refers to any attempt to assign specific human characteristics based on racial identity to a person or to a group of persons. Racism indicates a value judgment based on race; racialism indicates a categorical conclusion derived from race.

the object of the stereotype" (or the object of the object itself, the purpose for making a body into a cultural signpost), "is not so much to crush the Negro," claims Ellison, "as to console the white man" (S&A, 41). From the initial discovery of sub-Saharan Africa by the technologically superior Europeans, and indeed, as a product of the entire ideology of "discovery" itself, bodies have shared with continents a tremendous usefulness. Bodies possess value and significance, like ivory or gold, and so they are extracted and made to contribute to the flourishing of the civilized. The "civilized," in this scheme, are those who assign value and significance to what they have extracted. "The dreams of men," in Conrad's phrase, "the germs of empires" (219).

A black body signals a certain "type" of man or woman to a social order that clings to its injustices, one that continually confuses "the black American's racial background with his individual culture" (GT, 105). When a tomato is grown from the soil of an irrigated desert, we call it a tomato, and while we may acknowledge its history, we still eat it. When an African is brought to America and begins to reproduce on American soil, we insist that it is an African-American, something distinct from an American. We do more than acknowledge its history; we insist that its history somehow precludes it from legitimate, unhyphenated existence. A white body signals another type of human being, one seemingly (or mythically) untouched by the other race. Todorov calls this artificial gulf "a racialist, apartheid-like set of beliefs" which insists upon an "insurmountable discontinuity within the human species" (374). Ellison has suggested instead "that most whites are culturally part Negro without even realizing it." Like Gates and Todorov, he labels racial categorization as a "false concept"—but also knows that alternatives to the idea of racial differentiation involve contemplating "apparently unthinkable matters" (GT, 108). For Ellison the problem of race in America is primarily an epistemological one. The situation as it stands is unthinkable; that is, it cannot withstand intellectual scrutiny. The situation, as Ellison envisions it *ought* to be, is also unthinkable; how can race (instead of actual men and women) be made invisible?

Central to Ellison's thinking about race in America is a distinction implicit in his comments above. Human beings possess two identifiable dimensions of existence, the physical and the intellectual. One (the body) manifests itself immediately as an object. The other (the mind) is invisible until objectified—as speech, writing, or plastic art. The two racial groups that have thrived in the American state, historically, are blacks and whites, or, more accurately, those with racial origins somewhere in Africa and those with racial origins somewhere in Europe. These two races have shared the American continent since its appropriation by Europeans and have hyphenated its geographic land mass onto their individual ethnic or racial identities: African-American, Italian-American, Anglo-American, and so forth. Although it is often simple to distinguish a physically black person from a white one, it is often impossible to distinguish the black intellect from the white intellect. It is also impossible—almost always impossible—to distinguish the thoughts of a white person that originate in the historically black physical experience from those thoughts that originate in the historically white physical experience. If a white factory worker claims that he is treated as if he were a slave and refers to his foreman as "a real Simon Legree," or if a black woman becomes an expert in Shakespearean drama—then what sort of thing do we mean by "black culture" or "mainstream white society"?

"Despite his racial difference and social status, something indisputably American about Negroes not only raised doubts about the white man's value system," Ellison asserts, "but aroused the troubling suspicion that whatever else the true American is, he is also somehow black" (*GT*, 111). *He is also somehow black:* In this gritted statement Ellison echoes the full import of his career. The body may be white, but no white body raised and educated and exposed to the complexities of American life in the twentieth century is exclusively, in any cultural sense, white. To insist upon racial exclusiveness (or gender exclusiveness, or ethnic exclusiveness, or, for that matter, historical exclusiveness) is to delimit the cohesive capabilities of the human mind—its instinctive grasp at universality—according to the accident of its physical characteristics. Intellectual history, the arts, and practical experience show clearly that a white body can possess "black" thoughts; a woman may possess "masculine" tendencies; a Spanish scholar may find himself *simpático* with pre-Socratic philosophers. Racism and the insistence upon racial integrity act to define intellectual capacity according to the natural limits of physical existence. Even medical science has proved that one's sexuality, if defined by the genitalia, is merely a contingency. If a stay at the hospital can transform a man into a woman, certainly four hundred years of physical and cultural miscegenation will blur the significance of white and black bodies as cultural indicators.

The narrator in Ellison's *Invisible Man*, in his Prologue, confronts the contradiction of racial identity in America at once. For although invisible man (IM) is colored black, he is culturally black and white. Louis Armstrong's blues meets him as he awakens from an excursion into the "underworld" of racial antagonism.

> *What did I do*
> *To be so* black
> *And blue?*

Armstrong's words ("I know now that few really listen to this music," realizes IM) concern the anguish of having others assume a definitional limit to one's intellectual and emotional horizons because of the color of one's skin—according to what that color traditionally signifies. How can a nation that has amalgamated various distinct cultures continue to insist, in its institutions and in its social forms, that any particular individual "belongs," according to the parlance, to an exclusive racial grouping? IM knows perfectly well (as Armstrong declares later in the quoted song) that he is not colored "black" inside.

> *I'm white inside*
> *But that don't help my case.*
> *'Cause I can't hide*
> *What is on my face. . . .*

As such IM is—as he claims every American is—a walking contradiction. As an object he is highly visible: an American black man. As an intellect, and as a man of emotional content, he is invisible: an American black (*dark, unseen*) man.

Invisible Man reflects, from start to finish, Ellison's sense of the sheer unreality of racial objectification. It is a hurrying novel, hurried in the sense that everyone in it is in some kind of *rush*. IM, of course, is always running headlong from one sense of himself to another, like a child in a hall of mirrors. Phyllis Klotman finds that "running gives shape and meaning to the novel" and that IM "never controls his environment . . . until he stops running" (278, 288). If this is the case, then the novel also suggests that Americans as a whole lack control over their social environment, because they too are depicted as always on the run. Ellison's characters express an urgency for action and an impatience for thought. Bledsoe is most enraged at IM, for example, when he finds that he must discuss race relations with him at an intellectual level, thus revealing to himself and to IM his own hypocrisy. IM was *supposed* to know already, and to have suppressed, what Bledsoe painfully tells him about survival. Things are no different with the Brotherhood, where no one wants IM to think, only to speak. An object can move quickly, it can rise and fall, move and shake—it can lie, speak, and function in a thousand useful ways. But Ellison sees this object-self as merely the "rind." Like Armstrong's face, it masks a more complex existence. The exposure of the heart of the matter will stop the runner in the runner's tracks.

The essence of *Invisible Man*'s relevance as a literary statement about American life in the late twentieth century is located in Ellison's identification of this central contradiction at the heart of racial thought. Although the democracy makes implicit claims about racial and ethnic amalgamation, physical bodies still signal exclusion. Invisibility, then, flows from an intellectual contradiction—and it also flows from ambivalence, the emotional consequence of contradiction. In the novel IM learns to embrace contradiction not as some flaw but as the very stuff of his definition, as the very core of American life. Racism itself, as a mode of thought and guide to action, flows from consistency: It demands that black skin signal an exclusively "black" intellect and style. It is captured in the street saying: "No matter how high you fly, you're still a nigger." The enforcement of this consistency is America's form of racial fascism, and it is deeply embedded in the American psyche. The cast members of the "Cosby" television show, it is commonly argued, act as if they were really white. How are they supposed to act?

Readers responding to Ellison's novel have noted its reliance upon communicating contradiction as "the most faithful representation of human circumstances" (Schaub, 128). Thomas Schaub recognizes that contradiction is the "governing method" in *Invisible Man*, and Thorpe Butler finds it one of Ellison's most important descriptive terms (321). Indeed, in Ellison's imagination of the pervasive nature of contradiction lies the most reliable guide to the novel's force as a representation of American culture.* Others have addressed the workings of Ellison's meditation on ambiguity. Allan Nadel finds that Ellison (like Melville and Twain before him) uses the imagination of what it means to be black as the single most useful key to what it means to be white—black is then the "symbol of humanity" to a culture that defines itself as white (xiii). Similarly, Robert Stepto sees in IM's hibernation a tremendous achievement of freedom (384); Tony Tanner sees in the novel's general form and pattern a challenge to "any 'patterning' of life—whether fictional, ideological, or sociological" (49); and John Callahan perhaps sums up best the most obvious contradiction in the novel, that "Invisible Man's narrative of invisibility is an act of profound visibility" (87). The question remains: What exactly does Ellison's narrator make (or should make) of these boundless contradictions that surround and define him?

The persistence of racial categorization in America does not necessarily add up to an indictment of base cultural meanness. Rather, it may simply be an indication that contradiction—its centrality to the way in which the American mind works—is misunderstood. After all, the culture of productivity that made possible the manufacture of the Negro did not do so separately from its mills, the Constitution's 3/5 clause (that fraction of the slave population that counted in determining a state's representation in Congress), and its assembly lines. An entire system of racial classification evolved in the eighteenth and nineteenth centuries with romantic terminology to mask brutal social implications. The terms were linguistically colorful. A mulatto, for example, signified a person born half-black and half-white; a quadroon had one-quarter black heritage (one grandparent in four); and an octaroon's body derived one-eighth of its origins from African lineage (one great-grandparent in eight). But

* Ellison's social reality is characterized above all else by conflicts and collisions of meaning. The existence of a contradiction signals a situation in which two (or more) irreconcilable explanations carry equal validity. For example, either the narrator is visible or he is invisible—logically he cannot be both. But in a world informed by contradiction, he *is* both, depending upon who is looking and upon the context of that perception. Often, with more than one set of eyes on him, the narrator realizes he is both there and not there. The tension IM often experiences in Ellison's novel is born of the fact that he is consistently perceived in contradictory ways and then forced to act—to respond to a situation where he is both visible and invisible. When he acts, disaster follows. Often, he runs away. Both results flow directly from logical minds confronted with contradiction.

for the purposes of the census the Framers of the Constitution would count any Negro (mulatto, quadroon, or octaroon) as 3/5 of one white vote.

Racial differentiation is neat, logical, rational, and orderly—like Mendel's peas, it can be graphed. Cultural amalgamation, on the other hand, is messy, illogical, nonrational, and uncontainable— "I'm white inside," as Armstrong sings, "but that don't help my case." The personal realization of contradiction does not help when one's culture finds, in contradiction, a sign of illegitimacy. Or perhaps the culture will not tolerate the contradiction. Previous centuries had marvelous names to denote the exotic status of the racially mixed body. In the late twentieth century, anyone who has filled out a federal form asking that one's race be checked off in a box (white, Hispanic, black, Eskimo, and so forth) knows that to check off more than a single box is against the rules ("please check one"). The same mode of consciousness that structures racial identity serves to obscure the fact that historically America has been the continent on which racial exclusiveness is destroyed, not perpetuated. In fact, the American who can avoid multiracial influence is indeed exotic. The popularity of racism, then, serves as an *anti*historical force. It is a method by which history can be assaulted, and, more importantly, it is a method by which historical debts can be canceled. Checking off only one box on the federal form, in other words, perpetuates the mythology that the various races that have produced Americans possess distinct histories. If the races are believed to have discrete pasts, then the inherent intersubjectivity of Americans is obscured. As a result, the federal form, which is meant to serve affirmative-action purposes, evokes the very illusion of separatism that it was designed to confront and overcome. "As for the term 'culture'," Ellison writes, "I know of no valid demonstration that culture is transmitted through the genes" (S&A, 261). Nonetheless, common sense in America persists in identifying cultural membership in the same way it identifies racial traits, as genetic stuff that cannot be bartered and sold—despite a historical record that shows that Americans have always bought and sold (and sometimes stolen) their heritage.

Ellison has explained that at the core of American cultural identity is its mode of racial consciousness. The child who learns that racist categorization extends beyond the accident of skin color in America is mentally brutalized:

> The primary technique in its enforcement is to impress the Negro child
> with the omniscience and omnipotence of the whites. . . . Socially it is
> effected through an elaborate scheme of taboos supported by a ruthless
> physical violence, which strikes not only the offender but the entire
> black community. To wander from the paths of behavior laid down for
> the group is to become the agent of communal disaster. (Ibid., 84)

These "paths of behavior" are, more accurately, paths of thought.
However, they are not simply thoughts on racial caste. Behavior
cannot be enforced until the unlimited capacities of the intellect
have been corralled into group identification. Any attraction to
wholeness rather than physical sameness, to amalgamation rather
than to the enforced narcissism of American culture, is suppressed—turned from the realm of possibility to the world of the
romantic dreamer, the idealist. However, in point of fact, as Ellison
argues, racial exclusiveness is more likely the unreality, or the
dream, and cultural wholeness is the wakeful reality suppressed by
American-style racism. "For the penalty of wakefulness," Ellison
concludes, "is to encounter even more violence and horror than the
sensibilities can sustain unless translated into some form of social
action" (S&A, 84, 92). But the political meaning of any social action,
no less than any social fiction, is easily suppressed. Even IM's declaration that "I believe in nothing if not in action" (13) rings closer to
tragedy than inspiration, given what he's tried and failed to do.

To be "wakeful" is to recognize the brutality behind the rejection
of inconsistency and ambivalence when contemplating racial identity. One thinks of the genocidal quest for scientific racial typification
in nineteenth-century America—the bloodstain that characterizes
American "intellectual" history. To be wakeful is, in fact, to embrace ambivalence and contradiction as the essence of racial identity
in America's multi- and aracial society. IM, through the course of his
memoir, comes to the conclusion that he is an ambivalent being
with a soul rooted in contradiction. Once he realizes this, he can
state that "I myself," paradoxically, "did not become alive until I
discovered my invisibility" (7). To be wakeful is to acknowledge
one's invisibility. Jesse Jackson, in contemplating his electoral campaign in 1984, acknowledged that despite being on the cover of *Time*
magazine twice that year, his candidacy was never considered a national one. "Isn't that a strange phenomenon?" he asked his
Harper's interviewer in 1986. "It's like Ralph Ellison's invisible
man: they look at you but they don't see you" (Jackson, 267). In 1988

Jackson would act to achieve visibility and succeed by plunging into a national nightmare.

Invisible Man does speak, as IM claims, for all Americans on some frequency but not in the ways usually envisioned by critics. The text is no protest novel, for what can it possibly be protesting? It is not a major work of black fiction; to use the categorization is to brutalize the novel itself, to employ the very terminology that the novel resists. And it is not a quest for identity—from where to where, and whose identity is found? Narratively, as Robert Stepto has asserted, the novel is unprecedented in its example "that there is a self, and form, to be discovered beyond the lockstep of linear movement within imposed definitions of reality" (364). Many critics have seen in the novel an uneven quality ("inconsistency of method," for example [Baumbach, 21]), but this is actually Ellison's fusion of form and meaning. The novel does not speak for all Americans "because we are all members of minority groups," even though this is true in the antihistorical sense mentioned earlier, or because we have all, in some sense, "been passed over"—although this may also be true (Whitaker, 391; 392). It may indeed be "an epoch-making novel" (Burke, 350); it may also "link the narrative act to the achievement of identity" (Smith, 27); but neither of these fully explains its status as a clear channel on America's cultural frequency.

The explanation is really more simple. The novel speaks for all of us because its invisible hero is "the most intimate part" (*S&A*, 172) of our history: a bumbling nigger/Negro/colored person/black/Afro-American/African-American who is, at once, us and not us, the heart and the rind of our own bodies, who wants others to tell him who he is but at the same time will reject any identity they give him. He is white inside just as white Americans bear souls colored blacker than any of their deepest coal-black fantasies of the inner city. The novel speaks for us, and Invisible Man *is* us, because the Negro within—within whites *and* blacks, between the Prologue and Epilogue, the troublesome manufactured Negro—will tear the house down and destroy everything, Prologue, Epilogue, analog. Whatever he tries to do—with us, to us, for us—will result in disaster, to himself and to us. "What white Americans do not face when they regard the Negro," according to James Baldwin, is "reality—the fact that life is tragic" (*Fire*, 123). The "reality" speaks, in the novel, to all Americans: that the American apocalypse lies in its racial consciousness, and everybody knows it. However, it is not the racism itself that will ultimately destroy us; it is the knowledge. Doesn't Invisible Man always *know* what he should do? Isn't the solution to his various predicaments always obvious? On this level, at least, the novel is as "realistic" as black and white.

The novel itself, of course, moves without explanation or guide among various levels of "realist" narration: reportage, surrealism, analogy, fable—and it gives each level equal credence, lends to each the same level of narrative authority. The surreal experience in the factory hospital is no less authoritative in its presentation than is the Brotherhood cocktail party. Driving Mr. Norton around is reported in the same tone and cadences as is the stop at the Golden Day. How does the reader know at what level to interpret what she is reading? The Prologue sets a dream sequence off in italics, but no such markers exist with dependable regularity in the main text. The formalistic point is clear: The reader cannot tell what kind of "content" he is dealing with until he has become involved in the narrative itself. The words, like skin, are highly visible; the essential meaning (Louis Armstrong's "I" in "What did I do to be so black and blue") is *invisible*—or impenetrable by formal method, or logic.

American Identities

Invisible Man is not an orderly story—after all, what exactly is it about? A few years in an unnamed black man's life, strutting and jiving from one bizarre incident to the next, beginning and ending in a hole in the ground. The novel is not a story but a postmodern series, or a mosaic of narratives that occur at various levels (or planes or dimensions) of experiential reality. In order to get "the story" out of *Invisible Man*, the reader must provide important (and fictional) narrative links. Some call the novel a memoir, thus grafting onto it a recognizable order. Certainly, if it were not for IM's biographical progression, there would be no reason for the text. But what is the reason for IM's memoir? Ellison has himself been among the noisier authors in literary history. Instead of writing another novel, he has issued a series of footnotes to *Invisible Man*, thus serving only to increase the unruly nature of the original narrative.

Indeed, *Invisible Man* is a fitful novel. The book is often placed in the literary ghettos of "African-American" or "protest" fiction simply because it was written by a black-skinned American and concerns a narrator's experiences as a Negro—something one will quite naturally protest. The categorizations render the novel itself invisible, a curious but not unexpected result. The larger, more encompassing fact is that, if Ellison is correct, all Americans are invisible—made invisible by their various categorizations: race, gender, historical alliance. One of the culture's strongest myths is that it is only through such categorization that visibility is achieved, coded by such terms as racial identity, manhood, tradition. If not for one's group, in this way of thinking, one would be lost in the androgynous melting pot. However, racial, ethic, and gender categorization, as Ellison pleads throughout *Invisible Man*, renders one invisible. What is visible is one's category, one's physical status, one's self as object. The novel, to make this point, violates formal consistency and resists critical categorization: Is it a realistic novel? Is it pure allegory? The novel embraces formal inconsistency as a *style*—of writing, of existence. Only through contradiction is objectification overcome: contraries undermine categories. The variability of Ellison's text is its declaration of wholeness.

Consistency and the rooting out of contradiction are the provinces of the established, not of the radical movements that seek to displace established power. Jesse Jackson's refrain that "in politics, definition is important. If someone can define you, they can confine you," reveals his own oppositional status in American politics. Jackson has challenged as well the "official" definitions of Martin Luther King, Jr.'s career, of his own political candidacy, and of black exposure on network television (Jackson 39, 99, 124). The frame of reference that Jackson shares with IM results in his own "style" of public life, a style often labeled emotional, unpredictable, fitful—and contradictory.

All of IM's major experiences in Ellison's novel are dealt with by his characteristic ambivalence. At the battle royal, he contemplates "the magnificent blonde" and "wanted at one and the same time to run from the room, to sink through the floor, or to go to her and cover her . . . to caress her and destroy her, to love and murder her" (19). At the Founder's statue he wonders "whether the veil is really being lifted, or lowered more firmly in place" (36). He has the same reaction as Mr. Norton when he finds "humiliation and fascination" in listening to the incestuous, remarkable Trueblood (68). His mentor, Dr. Bledsoe, explains that an education, in the South, consists of knowing when and how to lie to white men (139). These are straightforward, literal accounts of contradictory responses and messages. At Liberty Paints, the special "optic white" pigment is achieved by adding *black* drops to the white formula, and by the supervision of Lucius Brockway. "Ain't a continental thing that happens down here," Brockway says, "that ain't as iffen I done put my black hands into it" (218).

In the surreal episode at the paint factory, IM's contradictory experiences are totaled. In terms of race, at least, the only reason white people *exist* as a concept, as a categorization, is because of the black people they have imported, manufactured, and conjured. Without the few drops of Africans in the New World, the Euro-American continent, there would be no such thing as "white" people—not a continental one. This is nothing new or startling. During slavery, whites of all castes were assured of their freedom by the existence of black chattels. South Carolinians went to war in 1861 under the banner "Freedom is not possible without slavery" (McPherson 20). This slogan might be updated as "Democracy is not possible without oppression." In a very real sense the independence of the United States as a whole rested on the internal comparison, made explicit in the Declaration, that free Americans would not be made the slaves of England. For Ellison, the twentieth-century definition of "white people" is steeped in the same type of internal comparison as in the paradox of the optic white formula. The signers of the Declaration themselves, in their tirades against kings and parliament, defined independence as *their* escape from slavery and the establishment of their own right to oppress. (This particular sense of historical contradiction is what sustains anarchist groups in America, including the Yippies.) Whatever twentieth-century "whites" think about "blacks," they owe their existence—politically and culturally, and in many cases, genetically—to those same black drops.

The contradiction is unnerving in a formalist, logical sense. What does Ellison mean, black drops make the white paint whiter? Before getting the job in the factory IM wanders the streets of New York and hears a pushcart man singing a familiar song. The music—here is one consistency in the novel, anyway—jars IM's memory, recalling "the times that I heard such singing at home . . . things I had long ago shut out of my mind." The pushcart man sings:

> "She's got feet like a monkey
> Legs like a frog—Lawd, Lawd!
> But when she starts to loving me
> I holler Whoooo, God-dog!

Cause I loves my baabay,
Better than I do myself. . . ." (173)

The contradictions in the man's expressions of love unnerve IM. He wonders what it means, realizing suddenly "the strangeness of it" as a mode of expression. "Was it about a woman, or some sphinxlike animal? Certainly his woman, *no* woman, fitted that description. And why describe anyone in such contradictory words?" (177)

The answers are revealed throughout the novel, but in particular, they are revealed in the sequences that directly follow the pushcart man: young Emerson, the paint factory, and the hospital. The doctors at the hospital, in their attempt to cure IM and make him a useful member of society, work to let him "live as he has to live, with absolute integrity." In other words, "he'll experience no major conflict of motives, and what is better, society will suffer no traumata on his account" (236). The elimination of "major conflicts"—the removal of contradictory thoughts—amounts to a medically induced "cure": the making of visibility. The cure doesn't take, of course, and despite the hospital machine's electrical force, IM begins to hear "a new, painful, contradictory voice" within his mind. And despite his longing for "peace and quiet," the music will not cease. "If only the contradictory voices shouting inside my head would calm down and sing a song in unison," he could rest, and his visibility would be restored: "Whatever it was I wouldn't care as long as they sang without dissonance" (259). The "peace and quiet" he craves is the tranquillity of visible sleep. Ellison keeps him awake with contradiction.

When in the Brotherhood segment Sybil attempts to seduce IM, he responds with desires "both to smash her and to stay with her" and finds himself "torn between anger and fierce excitement" (416). Facing Clifton's Sambo doll, IM "struggled between the desire to join in the laughter and leap upon it with both feet" (432). In the Epilogue, finally, IM explains what it means to accept contradiction not as immolating, but as enabling. He is thinking about his relation to white-skinned people. "Weren't we *part of them* as well as apart from them" (575)—weren't the connections between blacks and whites as indissoluble as they were nonexistent? In the Epilogue IM claims he can no longer "function under the assumption that the world was solid and all the relationships therein." Instead he realizes "that all life is divided and that only in division is there true health" (576).

IM thus ends, as he says, at the beginning. "I too have become acquainted with ambivalence" (10). Ambivalence, nonetheless, is a socially obnoxious condition, as far as society is presently ordered. Never more hated than when he was honest (572–73), IM's honest self, the contradictory, inconsistent self beneath the orderliness of his objectified life as a black man, can find no place above ground in American society. Above ground, Americans, visible Americans, "seek security" from the "inherited divisions of the corporate American culture." In his essay, "The Little Man at Chehaw Station," Ellison strongly asserts his position that Americans, to achieve visibility, "repress an underlying anxiety aroused by the awareness that we are representative not only of one but of several overlapping and constantly shifting social categories." Instead, we cling to a segment of the corporate culture "which has emerged from our parent's past"—as if, in other words, one could inherit a culture in the same way one inherits a hairline or flat feet. Americans, Ellison claims, are afraid of "cultural wholeness," afraid of the cultural miscegenation that defines them "because it offers no easily recognizable points of rest, no facile certainties as to who, or where (culturally or historically) we are" (GT, 19–20).

Ellison has called this great American resistance a phoniness. "We are all tempted to become actors, and when we forget who we are and where we are from, our phony selves take command" (GT, 69). This phoniness—what scholars have called "masking" in American culture—is endemic to a rapidly changing social order. But "behind the face of things," as young Emerson in Invisible Man insists, is another world. Behind the mask, whether it is the mask of blackface or of an elite white culture, is a denied historical interdependence. And more: behind the mask of the white face is the denial of dependence, Ellison suggests, on the African-American heart of the culture. White Americans cannot ask what they really feel about the black American, as James Baldwin explains, because "such a question merely opens the gates on chaos. What we really feel about him is involved in all that we feel about everything, about everyone, about ourselves" (Notes, 18).

The African experience on the American continent is usually "bracketed," to use Howard Zinn's phrase, within larger, more positive assessments of the nation and the culture. "This is one of the unchanging aspects of our self-evaluation—that we mention the Negro with proper lamentation, and then put him in brackets while we make our total judgment of American civilization" (58). Baldwin refers to this as white America's chronic amnesia (*Just Above*, 138). It is an inversion of the historical record—one way to invert it, anyway—that serves exclusive, white nationalist purposes. The "gates of chaos" would be opened should the intimate reality of the African historical presence on the continent be removed from its brackets and placed in a position to "spoil all estimates about democracy, freedom, and equality in this country" (Zinn, 58). The brackets are entirely possible (and made compulsory by racial exclusiveness) in a culture that finds it possible to "bracket" historical experience into physical categories or bodies of knowledge.

The same disciplinary impulse that brackets *Invisible Man* as "black fiction" or "protest novel" within the larger category of American literature will bracket African-American history within the larger sweep of the continental chronology. Bracketing, as Zinn points out, emasculates and *qualifies* the relevance of the bracketed phenomenon. Mainstream history proceeds, engulfing an army of bracketed concerns (literary, social, gender, ethnic) which, for their brackets, will never achieve parity. The very idea of *discipline* in human knowledge serves to favor the historical masters. The contradictory and the ambivalent, or in the past, the hysterical and the childish, have no place in the discipline demanded by the master. They too are bracketed as certainly part of our history, but not its main direction. Slavery, an institution that lasted 244 years, is implied, by its brackets, to have been simply a misstep in the formation of a nation now two hundred years old. The brackets are ideological. In the actual, psychic experience of Americans, the horrors of slavery and racial oppression inform consciousness. Else why the persistence of fear?

"Far imprisoned in the deepest drives in human society, it is practically impossible for the white American to think of sex, of economics, his children or womenfolk, or of sweeping socio-political changes," Ellison asserts, "without summoning into consciousness fear-flecked images of black men" (*S&A*, 100). What is repressed inevitably returns in nightmare shapes. The "deepest drives" of Americans are objectified into black figures of psychic transaction, to be exchanged and bartered. The refusal to remove the brackets from African history in America is symptomatic of a general refusal to accept contradiction as central to historical movement. Nonetheless, contradiction is at the heart of the American experience on this continent. The independence of the English colonies in America rested in part on an economy based upon Negro slavery. The post-Civil War industrialization and economic capitalization of the United States rested securely upon its transformation from a slave economy—in which the human body had a specific monetary worth—to an economy in which the body had no worth at all and could be expended without capital loss in factories and on share-cropper farms. A higher national standard of living, in other words, proceeded on the backs of a lowered personal valuation. This is not to suggest that the human body was better off under slavery, of course. Even Frederick Douglass acknowledged that $750 (the price he paid to "own" himself) was really the price of his body's admission into the nation of inalienable but not inexpensive rights (246–47). Moreover, Douglass's $750 transaction illuminates on a literal level the invisible force that drives historical development—the ugly fact of the bartered body. Nonetheless, historical development requires transaction (social, political, economic), and transaction demands objects of exchange. An object, furthermore, can have a specific meaning or value, a price tag. As racial object, the white or black body has an unambiguous valuation or currency.

Ellison's IM presents the centrality of historical American contradiction as his chief article of faith. The "hole" in which he makes his home symbolizes his realization that historical progression is an ideological weapon:

> My hole is warm and full of light. Yes, *full* of light. I doubt that there is a brighter spot in all New York than this hole of mine, and I do not exclude Broadway. Or the Empire State building on a photographer's dream night. But that is taking advantage of you. Those two spots are among the darkest of our whole civilization—pardon me, our whole *culture*— . . . which might sound like a hoax, or a contradiction, but that (by contradiction, I mean) is how the world moves: Not like an arrow, but a boomerang. (Beware of those who speak of the *spiral* of history; they are preparing a boomerang. Keep a steel helmet handy.) I know; I have been boomeranged across my head so much that I now can see the lightness of darkness. And I love light. (6)

The world moves by contradiction, verified in the historical contradictions that have produced the present social arrangements of the culture, and verified, repeatedly, in the individual experiences of IM.

The actual plot of *Invisible Man* is repetitive; it continually "boomerangs" back to the same point, that IM is invisible because he refuses categorization. He won't sacrifice his undisciplined, creative, and rather messy self to the rigidities of any system, whether it be the blindfolded boxer, the black college boy, the factory assistant, the Brotherhood spokesman, or the virile Negro lover. "It took me a long time and much painful boomeranging of my expectations," IM declares in the first paragraph of Chapter 1, "to discover that I am an invisible man." When he enters the elevator on his way to the Brotherhood cocktail party, he has the sense that he "had been through it all before" (300). This sense of repetition, the sense that his life is comprehendible more thoroughly in a thematic rather than progressive manner, contributes to IM's epistemological rebellion in this novel. His sense of a metaphysical boomerang is grounded in his personal experiences—over and over again.

Fighting Ras on the streets of Harlem, IM becomes "alive in the dark with the horror of the battle royal" (372), this time playing the role of the earnest boxer who will not let go of the role assigned him by the power brokers. Before Hambro, as he listens to the speech on "scientific objectivity," IM "saw the hospital machine, felt as though locked in again" (505). Hambro, like the hospital personnel, encourages IM to minimize his conflicting motives. "We're scientists," Hambro says. IM's break with the Brotherhood comes after his realization that "discipline" is the virtue by which his own self will be obliterated (or bracketed) to the greater cause of History. "So that is the meaning of discipline, I thought, sacrifice . . . yes, and blindness." And with this conclusion, IM claims, "I had boomeranged around" (476)—to the college and the hospital machine, to the repeated experience, to the *blues* of the novel itself: that the world moves itself and all who partake of it by contradiction. "So after years of trying to adopt the opinions of others I finally rebelled," IM states in the Epilogue. "I am an *invisible* man. Thus I have come a long way and returned and boomeranged a long way from the point in society toward which I originally aspired" (573).

The novel, then, is no tragedy (the categories!). IM reveals no flaw, descends into no more than a metaphysical abyss—and he does that only temporarily. Tragedy has no meaning to a boomeranging people, and tragedy repeated becomes comedy. Robert O'Meally concludes, in fact, that the boomerang makes *Invisible Man* a comic novel. "Time and again," he explains, IM "has been treated not like a man but like an object, which treatment Henri Bergson has termed the essence of comedy" (17). Ellison claims it becomes the blues. Americans, he writes, "might very well be a people whose fundamental attitude toward life is best expressed in the blues. Certainly, the Negro American's sense of life has forced *him* to go beyond the boundaries of the tragic attitude in order to survive. That, too, is the result of his past" (*GT*, 101). IM has a single experience in *Invisible Man* that runs throughout the twenty years spanned in the novel, that emerges out of each successive context. This "boomerang," as he calls it, knocks him repeatedly on the head, trying to enforce "discipline and sacrifice," to have him "experience no major conflict of motives," to "tell the kind of lie they want to hear"—in short, to become a visible man. IM resists and for his resistance he is made to run the same gamut over and over again, until he "reluctantly accepted the fact" of being "clubbed into the cellar" of reality; in other words, he was judged irrelevant, not useful, invisible.

The Functions of Invisibility

The metaphysics of Ellisonian invisibility are more complex than immediately discernible. Invisibility is, first of all, a function of sight. IM is *made* invisible by the refusal of others to see him in the same way that, for example, African-American history is made invisible by progressive theories of history. Whites do not "see" slavery for what it was because it was, according to the history, abolished to the credit of the white mind. Few whites will identify with slaveholders (historians assure us there were really very few of them), or with slave traders, but all whites can identify with emancipators and even with those who fought, not for slavery, but for "a way of life." And so historians speak of the "antebellum" era as if those enslaved were no more than understudies awaiting their cue to enter the historical stage. In IM's case, his invisibility will end— it will become his personal antebellum era—once he takes *his* cue from his (former?) masters and enters "a path of behavior laid down for the group," as Ellison has explained.

Invisibility, contrary to common parlance, is the result of a *failure* to conform; conformity, on the other hand, produces visibility. This is the paradoxical nature of Ellisonian existence. Conformity brings about the visibility of a stereotype, of the self as subject, recognizable in quantitative terms, predictable, functioning, and rewarded. This visibility is achieved, however, only by making the self in its multi-dimensional wholeness invisible. Holistic contradictions are called anxieties; ambiguities are termed neuroses; and each is rightfully controlled in response to cultural demands that the self become visible and effective. One result is the widespread popularity of the idea that the self that outwardly conforms is inwardly crazy. In fact, to be considered "crazy" is a compliment in the culture of objectified selves. It means that somewhere beneath the object something survives. When IM delivers a graduation speech which "shows that humility was the secret, indeed, the very essence of progress," he is "praised for [his] conduct." "Not that I believed this," he adds, "I only believed that it worked" (17). IM's pragmatism here indicates his enslavement, his visibility. "He believes in that great false wisdom taught slaves and pragmatists alike," according to the Vet at the Golden Day, "that white is right" (95). A visible slave, IM as the pragmatist concerns himself with doing what works, conforming to the pattern that assures visibility, success. He tries to do this in college, with Lucius Brockway, and with the Brotherhood. In each case, his visibility is maintained as long as he stays on the path. Each time he veers off, he invites communal disaster and becomes invisible, clubbed into a hole by "reality."

IM's grandfather encourages him to be *visible* (not invisible) by yessing and grinning his way to survival. Bledsoe instructs him to cultivate connections and power, to "stay in the dark and use" what power he has to his advantage, maintaining a visible front of conformity and submission (145). The Vet tells him to "play the game but don't believe in it" (153). All three of these major influences upon IM's character instruct him to cultivate a pragmatic detachment in which his visible self is unconnected to his invisible motives. Each instructs him to wear a mask, to consider his real self as a veiled and secret possession. They encourage him by assuring him that his intellectual self *is* invisible—that no one is interested in it, that it is solely a private matter. "You're hidden right out in the open," the Vet tells him. "They wouldn't see you because they don't expect you to know anything, since they believe they've taken care of that" (154). The grandfather, Bledsoe, and the Vet want IM to suppress the contradiction inherent in a visible, public front and an invisible, true self and use it to his advantage. IM rejects this, forcing his invisible self to share the stage with his visible self, presenting himself *as* the very contradiction his role models have suppressed. Neither slave nor pragmatist, IM claims wholeness: He is slave and master, idealist and pragmatist, black and white *at the same time*.

The contradictory essence of IM's being is exemplified best by the gloss that invisibility places on the idea of racism as it is examined in the novel. Invisibility functions two ways. First, IM is "invisible" to many whites (such as the bumped man in the Prologue) who see only race when they contemplate a black body. In this function, the individual black man or woman is made invisible by the sheer power and force of the productive categorization, "Negro" in the white mind. Because "black man" and "black woman" have such resonance as social and cultural icons, whoever happens to *be* the particular black man or woman encounters tremendous and often insurmountable difficulties in asserting his or her self from under the weight of the racial categorization. In *Invisible Man*, IM's role in the Brotherhood exemplifies this function of invisibility. "What was I," IM thinks in a moment of insight, "a man or a natural resource?" (303). In the Brotherhood he was clearly the latter, his status as *black man* was his inclusive identity.

The second function of invisibility as a gloss on racism directly contradicts the first. Here the person of color is made invisible because the white interlocutor *refuses* to acknowledge the racial differences between them. Claiming to be freed of "racial" thinking, the white eye in this second function denies that race plays any role whatsoever in its contemplation of the black face in front of it. This denial, however, erases the consequences of the historic antipathy between the races—in fact, it makes racial categorization *invisible*, leaving the individual black person without historic precedent or context. The result of this function of invisibility, the invisibility favored by the Equal Employment Opportunities Act (as compared to affirmative action programs, which operate according to the first function of invisibility) is to absolve the present generation from the burden of historic injustices in a particularly American act of cleaning the slate. IM's role in the Brotherhood exemplifies this function of invisibility as well. His speech at the arena was judged "incorrect" by the committee for its reversion to Negro folk and sermon cadences—IM was chastised for bringing to visibility the historical traditions that produced his mind.

In one sense, then, invisibility refers to the blinding force of race, in which the individual self is obscured by the force of the racial categorization. On the other hand, invisibility refers equally to the obliteration of those same categories in the name of individual autonomy—so that historical context is denied by a blinding insistence upon the irrelevance of categorical injustices. However, to be properly understood, these two functions of invisibility must be recognized as existing and operating *simultaneously*. They are, of course, contradictory. In the Brotherhood, IM is recruited *because* he is a Negro man and a good speaker. He is recruited to be the "Negro spokesman" for the organization. When he is recruited, his individuality is irrelevant—no interest is shown in his particular self (indeed, he is given a new name) but only in his racial category. However, when this racial identity becomes inconvenient for the Brotherhood, when IM's racial background leads to his employment of an African-American preaching style in his speeches, the relevance of that same racial category is denied. The Brotherhood intelligentsia is quite capable of insisting, at the same time, that racial identity is important and that racial identity is irrelevant.

Hence the contradiction embodied in the very idea that is the soul of *Invisible Man*. It would be horror enough if IM could divide culture between those who employ the first and those who employ the second function of invisibility, but he cannot. He cannot divide and comprehend because all Americans practice the two forms simultaneously. There are occasions when the insistence on the all-inclusive function of race is inescapable. The bumped man sees only an arrogant black man; Sybil sees only the virile black assailant; Jack sees only the articulate black speaker. There are occasions as well when the denial of race as an inclusive categorization is equally inescapable. Lucius Brockway sees only a union sympathizer in IM's report of the meeting; young Emerson tries to show IM that more powerful connections than race can affect his future; Hambro speaks of the subordination of racial identity to scientific socialism. IM is confronted with the two contradictory forms of racism throughout the novel, the two forms that make him invisible twice over. He is invisible because he is defined inclusively by his race, and he is invisible because his race is irrelevant to his definition.

Ellison's treatment of racial objectification in *Invisible Man* depends upon the simultaneous existence of the contradictory functions of invisibility. The legal structure in the United States proclaims at once, for example, that discrimination according to race will not be recognized as legitimate and that historic imbalances owing to racial discrimination must be amended in the future. The first form of invisibility insists that every person of color is primarily representative of a particular history and set of social myths and traditions, and the second form of invisibility insists that that same history and those same myths and traditions be denied particular relevance to the individual. IM must be aware, at all times, when he exists in a situation defined by the first function, and when he exists in a situation defined by the second. Ralph Ellison, in the complexity and contradictory nature of his projection of racial behavior, locates an ambivalence at the heart of America's great racial division. Because of this cultural ambivalence, solutions proceed at cross-purposes, and progress resembles cross fire.

With Sybil, for example, IM thought at first his race was invisible to her—only to learn that her apparent "problem . . . with certain aspects of our ideology" (409) was a mask for her more urgent problem with racial and sexual mythology in America (516–22). After refusing to participate in Sybil's masochistic fantasy (and at the same time assuring her that he did participate), IM boomerangs to the night of the battle royal, to his forced participation in another white, staged pornography. He later has as much difficulty ridding himself of Sybil as he did in discarding the nigger bank. "*I am invisible,*" he insists as she clings to him (and labels him "Anonymous brute 'n boo'ful buck"); he is made invisible before the dark shapes that haunt her sexuality. Sybil is, to echo F. Scott Fitzgerald, a "genius" racist, quite capable of holding two contradictory ideas simultaneously: that IM is an advanced thinker and that IM is a "black bruiser" capable of raping her. Sybil propels into IM's mind a series of boomerangs, back to his first entry into Harlem, and toward a renewed sense of time being "fluid, invisible" (532). Through her he becomes cognizant once again of the "fluid" or contradictory essence of racial existence in his country.

IM must recognize and sustain a vision of the cosmos around him that will provide a context for his contradictory simultaneity in order to come to an acceptance of himself as both ambivalent and whole. His characteristic reaction to contradiction is, as formal logic demands, rejection. If one idea conflicts with a second idea, two solutions are possible. Either one or the other idea is rejected as erroneous, or the two ideas are reconciled. In either case, a resolution is found. This is the Hegelian process of thesis, antithesis, and synthesis. IM's experiences, however, negate the Hegelian model. Instead, IM's world resembles one in which the dominant model is thesis, antithesis, thesis, antithesis, thesis, antithesis—one boomerang after another *without synthesis.* Can one synthesize the two functions of invisibility? A man is defined by his race *and* his race is irrelevant. No synthesis possible; one must accept contradiction as resolution.

The reason the issue of racism is so alive—and the reason IM knows *he* is alive, in the sense of being socially significant and poised, as he says in the Prologue, for action—is that it is contradictory. Mundane contradictions, such as the light is red/the light is green, are of course false. But this does not preclude the existence of a *true* contradiction: The man is visible/the man is invisible; race is central/race is irrelevant. The distinction is really no more elusive than that between mundane consistency, or petty tyranny, and what some call integrity. Brendt Ostendorf locates in Ellison's "dialectical, combative, antiphonal, and always dialogical" writing style the essence of his radicalism. "It rejects all closed systems that speak with a single voice" and rejects "any systems of thought that are too rigidly schematic" (101, 105). In rejecting the logical imperatives that result in oppressive social structures, and by embracing an ontology that defines reality by its contradictions, IM is well on his way "underground"—that place to which we relegate the secret existence of contemporary dissent.

IM formulates a philosophic understanding of contradiction throughout the novel, but especially in his exposure to Rinehart. Through Rinehart IM articulates the core of this understanding, his metaphysical invisibility (just as Rinehart remains, for all his influence on IM, invisible to him). IM had been prepared for Rinehart and for the lessons he would learn from Rinehart on several occasions. After the factory hospital episode, IM concludes that "I could no more escape than I could think of my identity" (243)—a defining contradiction which he rejects. Munching on the regressive and unscientific yams, IM experiences the exhilaration of "no longer [feeling] ashamed of things I had always loved" (266), but he will reject this conclusion when he joins the Brotherhood shortly thereafter. At the Brotherhood cocktail party, when the incorrect Brother asks him to sing some antebellum spirituals, he wonders whether there should be "some way for us to be asked to sing" without compromising his dignity (314). In all these cases IM finds himself defined not by his consistencies but by his contradictions, what might be called the essential core contradictions of his being. These would include his love of baked yams but not his love of the South and the apartheid he fled, his knowledge of and connection to the old slave songs, but not his nostalgia for slavery, and his attraction, recall, to Sybil, but not to a desire to play the role of rapist.

The difference between those who accept contradiction and those who reject it is exemplified in IM's estrangement from Brother Wrestrum over Brother Tarp's leg iron. Wrestrum objects to IM's placement of the leg iron on his desk ("Because I don't think we ought to dramatize our differences" [392]), but IM finds it an appropriate and useful item, slipping it over his knuckles and suggesting its use as a weapon. Wrestrum finds the reminder of slavery regressive because it contradicts his role as a prominent Brother. IM finds the reference to slavery useful. It is a dramatic example of the resilience of history, of how the world *moves*, as he states in the Prologue, by boomerang and contradiction. The example is a resonant one. During Jesse Jackson's 1988 presidential campaign, discussed in detail below, an imbroglio followed Jackson's reference to slavery as a way to understand his place in the Democratic party. In both cases, Jackson's and IM's, some auditors considered the reference to slavery counterproductive, and others saw it as an essentially true contradiction. The slave is master; the leg iron becomes a weapon: History is a boomerang heading for those who had the power to throw it.

The realistic, reportorial style of the yam-eviction-Brotherhood membership sequence is followed directly by the surreal, dreamlike style of the Rinehart-Ras-race-riot episode. In each series of events, the two levels of narrative have identical purposes, which is to convince IM of the truthfulness of his ambivalence. Eating yams and discussing leg irons cannot be read and understood, however, on the same level as donning dark glasses and hat and *becoming* someone else, or throwing a spear through another man's cheeks. When *Invisible Man*'s reader gets to Rinehart and Ras, he enters a surreal world in which "consistent reality," as a metaphysics, is denied. Like the earlier episode at the Golden Day, Rinehart and Ras signal the end for IM: allowing himself to serve the white power structure by accepting a "realistic" definition of racism.

By putting on the dark glasses and fancy hat, "by dressing and walking in a certain way," IM achieves a high degree of visibility. "I was recognized at a glance—not by features but by clothes, by uniform, by gait" (485). But this visibility also assures his anonymity.

"No one paid me any special attention, although the street was alive with pedestrians. . . . If dark glasses and a white hat could blot out my identity so quickly, who actually was who?" (493). IM makes his self into an *object*—something with cultural visibility and individual anonymity, an object that transforms his social categorization into the essence of his being. The glasses block the transcendental "window" to his soul, asserting his self-imposed objectification, so that those who even attempt to look closely see themselves reflected, insulated from deeper penetration.

Dressed in this street uniform, IM is soon mistaken for Rinehart, the man of multiple selves, the contradiction incarnate in *Invisible Man*. Rinehart does not play various roles (runner, gambler, extortionist, lover, Reverend), but *is* all these roles—just as he "is," finally, IM. "He was a broad man," IM says of Rinehart, "a man of parts who got around." Not a "whole" man but *a man of parts*, a pastiche. The universe, as IM has experienced it, he says, is a "seething, hot world of fluidity, and Rine the rascal was at home" in it. He is "at home" in it because he has modeled himself after it, accepting its "fluidity" and contradictory nature as integral. His integrity, in other words, hinges on his harmony with the contradictory. "It was unbelievable," IM concludes, "but perhaps only the unbelievable could be believed. Perhaps the truth was always a lie" (498). To understand Rinehart—that is, not to be offended or amused but *instructed* by him—is to grasp the essential, ontological contradictions of the self in nature and in history. The universe is a great liar, a "seething fluidity" in which phenomenological observation defies scientific evidence, in which the invisible are made visible by accepting their invisibility, in which men and women strive for consistency as evidence of careful thought. "Perhaps," as IM observes, "the truth is always a lie" because the truth, in the orthodox sense, demands consistency. The truth about Rinehart, in any case, is an elaborate guide to survival in the anarchic ("seething fluidity") universe of social existence in Ellison's America.

Rinehart's example brings together all of IM's major experiences in the novel. In a temporary euphoria he realizes that he could "agree with Jack without agreeing" (507), something his grandfather would recommend, an example also of playing the game, as the Vet would say, without believing in it. Boomeranging as well to the yam-eating incident, IM claims, "I began to accept my past." But this time the various examples gel, and IM sees the costs involved in "being" Rinehart. "Well, I *was* and yet I was invisible," IM concludes, finally accepting "the fundamental contradiction" that made him alive. His past, for example, all the separate incidents in his memoir "flickered through my head and I saw that they were more than separate experiences. They were me; they defined me" (507–08). IM is, in other words, a man of parts: separate parts, contradictory parts. Out of this comes his metaphysics of a shifting (and shifty), boomeranging universe.

> And that lie that success was a rising *upward*. What a crummy lie they kept us dominated by. Not only could you travel upward toward success but you could travel downward as well; up *and* down in retreat as well as in advance, crabways and crossways and around in a circle, meeting your old selves coming and going and perhaps all at the same time. How could I have missed it for so long? Hadn't I grown up around gambler-politicians, bootlegger-judges and sheriffs who were burglars; yes, and Klansmen who were preaches and members of humanitarian societies? Hell, and hadn't Bledsoe tried to tell me what it was all about? I felt more dead than alive. (510)

IM remains "more dead than alive" as his metaphysics forces him underground. To accept what many would call society's aberrations—"gambler-politicians" and "bootlegger-judges"—as society's *rule*, to see contradiction and multiple truth not as exception but as definition is, IM claims, frightening and immobilizing. To become Rinehart would mean to abandon any hope of changing the social order or to address the horrors of racial objectification in America. "I felt that somewhere between Rinehart and invisibility there were great potentialities," but these are underground matters—not officially accepted, perhaps subversive. In any case, the revelations force IM into his hole, illuminated yes, but unseen.

In his hole IM knows, finally, that if he wishes to hold on to something akin to a social vision, he must prepare not for permanent invisibility but for purposeful action—in essence, he must prepare for visibility, but on his own terms. Contrary to what the Vet told him, he realizes that one cannot "play the game" without playing the game. "By pretending to agree," he says of his Brotherhood role, "I *had* indeed agreed" (553). The outward form *is* the inward essence while the outward form is being played. Accepting visibility of form or conformity, while insisting upon an inward skepticism or disbelief, is to accept the invisibility of that inward self, that essence. To accept an outward, object status while claiming to be "pretending" is simply not possible, not even in the world of possibility. In IM's formulation, you are what you pretend to be, even if you are that pretension only for a short time. The effects of your play, in other words, cannot be masked behind what you think you "really" are. IM's grandfather was indeed the traitor he confessed to be. The Epilogue pleads for the reader to accept the ethos of invisibility as a way to maintain integrity, but not as a permanent means of escape. IM suspects that it will not be believed. "You'll fail to see it though death awaits for both of us if you don't" (580). "Seeing it" results in the seer feeling more dead than alive, and not seeing it means that death awaits. Ellison speaks here, in this contradiction, of more than one form of death: one as a prelude to action, the other as a surrender.

In the dream sequence of castration that follows IM's final "plunge" into the manhole, Ellison makes one final attempt to clarify his metaphysics—his stand, that is, on what is and is not "true" to his self. IM has just discarded all the outward forms of his identity: papers, diploma, letters. Critics often refer to this scene as IM's final liberation from the "official" identities assigned him by his culture. IM tells his former masters, in the dream sequence, that he is *"through with all your illusions and lies."* However, Jack orders him to return, or *"we'll free you of your illusions all right."* IM refuses, and Jack fulfills his promise by castrating him. *"Now you're free of illusions,"* Jack states. The narrator then acknowledges that it feels *"painful and empty"* to be free of illusion.

Social existence is no more possible without illusions than is masculinity possible without the genitalia that define or signal it. Ellison's "illusions," by definition, are the markers by which the culture locates meaning. They are very real things, closer in essence to the semiotic notion of the sign than to what an "illusion" signifies in common speech. The human race knows male, as it knows each sex, by its physical manifestations. It also knows its social order by *its* signs, by its illusions. Those illusions, in Ellison's novel, cannot be simply removed without destruction, or social suicide.

The illusions of racial identity—and the illusions of sexuality, which concern us later in this book—are not window dressing to American culture; rather, a culture's illusions, the way in which it makes the invisible visible, are at the core of its definition. Like the male testicles, to follow Ellison's analogy, these illusions are as vulnerable to mutilation as they are powerful and sustaining to the culture. Racial difference, for example, understood as an illusion, signals the rich diversity of the American social fabric. This illusion, when mutilated—that is, when it is either denied *or* overly exaggerated, made "invisible"—results in cultural paroxysm. Denying racial difference mutilates the socially vital illusion of historic racial identity; exaggerating racial differences mutilates the socially vital illusion of what Ellison has called "the blending and metamorphoses of cultural forms which is so characteristic of our society" (*GT,* 125). To do *either* is murderous to the social fabric. Both make the individual invisible, and an invisible man, IM assures us, is an irresponsible man.

"When one is invisible he finds such problems as good and evil, honesty and dishonesty, of such shifting shapes that he confuses one with the other," IM concludes, "depending upon who happens to be looking through him at the time" (572). To counter this anarchy, IM reminds himself and the reader again of the centrality of illusion. "The mind that has conceived a plan of living must never lose sight of the chaos against which that pattern was conceived" (580). All illusions (or "plans of living") are both true and untrue: true because they do in fact introduce order into chaos, untrue because they are merely one of many possibilities. In fact, they become *permanently* untrue when it is forgotten that all "plans" and all illusions originate in chaos and must also return to chaos for regeneration. Rinehart, the man of possibilities, demonstrates this principle. If Rinehart were to "settle down" and become a full-time preacher, he would be a false one, untrue to his own integrity. In his hole, IM demonstrates this principle as well. If he stays in his covert hole, he is irresponsible—and so he stays, as he says, only to prepare for a more overt action.

An uncontradicted truth, according to the metaphysics of *Invisible Man,* is a false truth. (Here Ellison's debt to Faulkner, one of his literary "ancestors," is clear.) A Negro who is not "white inside" or a white man whose soul is not black is certainly a "visible" man, but he is also culturally emasculated. Contradiction signals vitality, integrity, and that sense to which IM refers throughout the novel as being alive or awake. Denying contradiction invites death by confusing illusion itself, or the way in which value is assigned to a phenomenon, with the illusion of consistency. But this death—or this conformity, this *visibility*—is only another name for the objectification by which racism flourishes in American culture. A sense of integral contradiction puts to rest the dis-ease of racism in America by bringing to visibility the hidden, multidimensional essence of all Americans. But for the present, those tuned in to the frequencies over which true contradictions are broadcast as existential realities find themselves, along with invisible man, in a hole—metaphysical, political, or otherwise. And for all the light that IM brings to this condition, with his 1,369 light bulbs and his relentless narrative, the hole remains a black one, an essential ambivalence of color. Into this black hole are cast those who walk Negro walks, talk Negro talk, and, as illuminated in the next chapter, those who take the Negro course into the national race for political power. Anything, in other words, that reminds American culture of its black essence will be "clubbed," or buried in that hole unseen by Monopolated Light and Power.

WORKS CITED

Adams, C. L. *Tales of the Congaree.* Edited by Robert G. O'Meally. Chapel Hill: University of North Carolina Press, 1987.

Appiah, Anthony. "The Uncompleted Argument: Dubois and the Illusion of Race." In *"Race," Writing, and Difference* (see Gates, ed., below), 21–37.

Baldwin, James. *The Fire Next Time.* New York: Dell, 1964. (Cited as *Fire.*)

———. *Just Above My Head.* New York: Dell, 1979. (Cited as *Just Above.*)

———. *Notes of a Native Son.* New York: Bantam, 1964. (Cited as *Notes.*)

Baumbach, Jonathan. "Nightmare of a Native Son." In *Ralph Ellison* (see Bloom, ed., below), 13–27.

Benston, Kimberly, ed. *Speaking for You: The Vision of Ralph Ellison.* Washington: Howard University Press, 1987.

Bloom, Harold, ed. *Ralph Ellison: Modern Critical Views.* New York: Chelsea House, 1986.

Burke, Kenneth. "Ralph Ellison's Trueblooded *Bildungsroman.*" In *Speaking for You* (see Benston, ed.), 349–59.

Butler, Thorpe, "What Is to Be Done?—Illusion, Identity, and Action in Ralph Ellison's *Invisible Man.*" *CLA Journal* 27, no. 3 (March 1984): 315–31.

Cable, George Washington. *The Grandissimes: A Story of Creole Life.* New York: Penguin, 1988.

Callahan, John F. "Frequencies of Eloquence: The Performance and Composition of *Invisible Man.*" In *New Essays on Invisible Man,* (see O'Meally, ed.), 55–94.

Conrad, Joseph. "Heart of Darkness." In *Three Great Tales*. New York: Vintage, n.d.

Covo, Jacqueline. *The Blinking Eye: Ralph Waldo Ellison and His American, French, German, and Italian Critics, 1952–1971, Bibliographic Essays and a Checklist*. Metuchen, N.J.: Scarecrow Press, 1974.

Douglass, Frederick. *Frederick Douglass: The Narrative and Selected Writings*. Edited by Michael Meyer. New York: Modern Library, 1984.

Ellison, Ralph. *Going to the Territory*. New York: Vintage, 1987. (Cited as *GT*.)

———. *Invisible Man*. New York: Vintage, 1989.

———. *Shadow and Act*. New York: Vintage, 1972. (Cited as *S&A*.)

Gates, Henry Louis, Jr. "Introduction: Writing 'Race' and the Difference It Makes." In *"Race," Writing, and Difference* (see Gates, ed.), 1–20.

———. ed, *"Race," Writing, and Difference*. Chicago: University of Chicago Press, 1986.

Jackson, Jesse. *Straight from the Heart*. Philadelphia: Fortress Press, 1987.

Klotman, Phyllis R. "The Running Man as Metaphor in Ellison's *Invisible Man*." *CLA Journal* 13, no. 3 (March 1970): 277–88.

Jordan, Winthrop. *White over Black: American Attitudes Toward the Negro, 1550–1812*. New York: W. W. Norton, 1977.

McPherson, James M. "The War of Southern Aggression." *New York Review of Books* 35, no. 21–22 (January 19, 1989): 16–20.

Nadel, Allan. *Invisible Criticism: Ralph Ellison and the American Canon*. Iowa City: University of Iowa Press, 1988.

O'Meally, Robert. *The Craft of Ralph Ellison*. Cambridge, Mass.: Harvard University Press, 1980.

———. "Introduction." In *New Essays* (see O'Meally, ed.), 1–23.

———, ed. *New Essays on Invisible Man*. New York: Cambridge University Press, 1988.

Ostendorf, Brendt. "Ralph Waldo Ellison: Anthropology, Modernism, and Jazz." In *New Essays* (see O'Meally, ed.), 95–121.

Pells, Richard H. *The Liberal Mind in a Conservative Age: American Intellectuals in the 1940s and 1950s*. New York: Harper & Row, 1985.

Schaub, Thomas. "Ellison's Masks and the Novel of Reality." In *New Essays* (see O'Meally, ed.), 123–56.

Smith, Valerie. "The Meaning of Narration in *Invisible Man*." In *New Essays* (see O'Meally, ed.), 25–33.

Stepto, Robert. "Literacy and Hibernation: Ralph Ellison's *Invisible Man*." In *Speaking for You* (see Benston, ed.), 360–85.

Tanner, Tony. "The Music of Invisibility." In *Ralph Ellison* (see Bloom, ed.), 37–50.

Todorov, Tzvetan. "'Race,' Writing and Culture." In *"Race," Writing, and Difference* (see Gates, ed.), 370–80.

Whitaker, Thomas R. "Spokesman for Invisibility." In *Speaking for You* (see Benston, ed.), 386–403.

Zinn, Howard. *The Politics of History*. Boston: Beacon, 1970.

CHAPTER 2

The Invisible Candidate

Network Television News

Coverage of the Jesse

Jackson Presidential

Campaign in 1988

Run, Nigger run! De Patter-
rollers'll ketch you.
Run, Nigger run! It's almos'
day. Dat Nigger run'd, dat
Nigger flew, Dat Nigger tore
his shu't in two.
All over dem woods and
frou de paster,
Dem Patter-rollers shot; but
de Nigger got faster,
Oh, dat Nigger whirl'd, dat
Nigger wheel'd
Dat Nigger tore up de
whole co'n field.
—"Run, Nigger Run!"
(anonymous slave song,
Randall, 5)

Make up your mind. There
is nothing more powerful
than a made-up mind. Run
toward freedom! Don't
stand still! Run! Steal away

What Does Jesse Want?
On July 17, 1988, CBS news correspondent Betsy Aaron opened her report on
the Evening News by asking whether
Jesse Jackson would play the role of
spoiler in Michael Dukakis's inevitable
nomination as the Democratic Party's
presidential candidate. The competition for the Democratic nomination
was over, but as Aaron pointed out,
Jackson was "grabbing all the attention" while sights should be set on Dukakis. Trouble between Dukakis and
Jackson could detract from the momentum of the clear first choice among
Democratic candidates—in effect,
Aaron concluded, Jackson's continued
challenges to Dukakis could weaken
the nominee's candidacy. Jackson, according to Aaron, "keeps saying he's
earned consideration and inclusion,"
but it was not clear what he meant by
this claim. Aaron's CBS colleague

to freedom! Run! . . . Take the chains off your ankles, but don't shift them to your mind. Run! . . . Run from the outhouse to the statehouse to the courthouse to the White House. Run!
—Jesse Jackson, 1983
(Jackson 22)

Run, Jesse run!
—1988 Jackson campaign slogan

Bruce Morton echoed her report, saying that it is difficult to know what Jesse Jackson wants. One thing was clear, in Morton's eyes, however: Jackson could not stop running. "You can end a campaign," Morton concluded, "but how, if it is in your blood, do you end a crusade?"

Aaron and Morton might have chosen perplexity to inform their story line, but in Atlanta, on the streets outside the convention hall, clashing mobs were less confused. CBS anchor Susan Spencer followed Morton's comment about Jackson's crusading with an introduction to Peter Van Zandt's report about Atlanta street fighting. "The two camps inside the hall worked for resolution," Spencer announced, "but violence erupted outside the hall as white supremacists clashed with anti-Klan demonstrators, who in turn clashed with the police." The people, as mobs are sometimes called, understood perfectly what Jesse wanted. Van Zandt's report featured street film: skinheads marching, white supremacists waving United States and Confederate battle flags, a banner proclaiming "Hands off South Africa/Defend Apartheid," and plenty of pushing and shoving and clubbing. According to Van Zandt, a KKK march was planned but canceled because of threats of anti-Klan counterdemonstrations. On camera, one Klan member, with burning eyes claimed that the police "said that they could protect them but they couldn't protect us. We got just as much right as they have." The police attempted to keep peace outside the convention hall by forming barricades. "Police didn't allow the two opposing groups to get near each other," Van Zandt concluded.*

CBS news presented a compelling parallel in this July 17 broadcast. Inside the hall, according to the report, the Jackson and Dukakis factions of the Democratic Party were having difficulties coming to terms—no one knew what Jackson wanted, and no one knew

---

* Research on network television news was completed at the Vanderbilt University Television News Archive in Nashville, Tennessee, under the auspices of the Mellon Foundation.

what Dukakis would give him. Outside the hall, the broadcast showed, the rift between these elite political forces was played out bluntly and physically. Keeping the two popular forces apart was in the interest of the police, the state, and the community. Allowing them to clash would result in race battle, chaos, and the breakdown of law and order. But considering the looks in the eyes of the racists and the determination in the eyes of the anti-Klan protesters, the police clearly had their hands full. Inside the hall, a parallel racial conflict was being enacted. Although the elites inside battled without making physical contact, they nevertheless sent encouraging messages to the street. In other words, Dukakis's political "problem" with Jackson was the elite articulation of the white-supremacists' "problem" with blacks. The CBS evening newscast captured the simultaneous enactment of street images and racial confrontation in the Convention hall. Jackie Judd, on ABC news, July 17, sent a clear message: The Dukakis campaign did not want to appear as if it were being led by Jackson. The aim of Dukakis was to maintain control; after all, he was about to become the party's official leader. And, one could say, he had "just as much right" as Jackson had to be there.

Who exactly was Jesse Jackson in the 1988 presidential campaign? How was it that on March 2, early in the Democratic primary season, ABC News anchor Peter Jennings could claim that Jackson was "a much different man" from his 1984 persona? In Rebecca Chase's report, which followed Jennings, Jackson was shown speaking to an enthusiastic Texas crowd. "It is real, this ability to inspire, to excite, and Jesse Jackson thinks it's his greatest gift," Chase went on. "But who is Jesse Jackson?" The following night, on NBC, Tom Brokaw introduced two reports on Jackson with the blunt appraisal that Jesse Jackson was "the best-known candidate in either party." Well, which was it? To ABC, Jackson had changed since 1984 and was still an unknown: "But who is Jesse Jackson?" At the same time, another network saw him as the "best-known candidate" in America. The answer is really quite simple. Jackson, in 1988, became Ralph Ellison's invisible man: visible as object, invisible as man; useful as speaker, threatening as power.

Jackson is most clearly seen as an Ellisonian phantasm in the coverage of his campaign by the three major news networks, ABC, CBS, and NBC. On television Ellison's invisibility becomes formulaic. The television camera films objects: It covers space in two dimensions and employs a visual shorthand in order to characterize those objects. It knows nothing of subjectivity and cannot film the inner self or capture an ambiguous image. In a presidential campaign, set roles are available to the contenders—winner, loser, long shot—and a candidate becomes visible by fulfilling the criteria for the part. In a news story about a youthful drunk-driving death, for example, the parts may include the formally posed high school photograph of the victim(s), the inarticulate grieving parents, the pedantic alcohol counselor, and the "get tough" legislator. Any major variations—such as nonchalant parents or a laissez-faire politician—would strike the viewer as so inappropriate that the news people would be unlikely to use the segment—and thus the player would be rendered invisible. Jackson's initial problem, in 1988, was his own invisibility. Because his bid for the Democratic nomination possessed an unprecedented plausibility, his "inner" self was the site of serious debate. Jackson was certainly visible as a black American, talking about injustice and seeking increased power for "his people." But what more did he want and why did he want to be the president of all the people? The camera could capture his objective self, but his objective self was not behaving according to any criterion known to the camera.

Rebecca Chase (ABC News, March 2), in attempting to come to grips with *who Jackson is,* touched on a number of the salient points of the candidate's invisibility. She cut directly from her question about his identity to film clips of civil rights marches in the 1960s. Her voice-over explained Jackson's strained relations with Martin Luther King's family and others from the civil rights movement "who will have nothing to do with Jesse Jackson." Some black people, including powerful black people, do not like Jackson. From here Chase got to her theme: "the charisma, the contradictions, of Jesse Jackson." How was it that some blacks would respond with enthusiasm when he spoke and some would find fault with him? Chase brought on camera a number of anonymous black faces to criticize Jackson. She concluded her report by calling Jackson's campaign "a remarkable achievement" for someone who had never held elected office. Since no comparable report could be put together regarding a white candidate, this report could be viewed as racist. It was now clear *who* Jackson was and was not. As an object, he was the Black Man Running for president, but as an individual, he was as enigmatic, as contradictory, and as *unimaginable* as Ellison's narrator.

Throughout the 1988 campaign, television journalists had profound difficulties realizing and reporting Jackson's identity. Social scientists have commented extensively on the structure of television news, a structure that relies heavily on thematic continuity. Doris Graber, for example, finds that in presidential campaigns television news "casts" candidates in particular dramatic roles. "To conserve their limited time, television newscasts create stereotypes of the various candidates early in the campaign and then build their stories around these stereotypes by merely adding new details to the established image" (197). These created images become powerful points of reference, as candidates are then "judged according to the assigned role" (181). A candidate dubbed "front-runner," for example, who fails to win each succeeding primary will be seen as in decline. Similarly, if a candidate labeled "long shot" happens to place first or even second in a major primary, he will be seen as having accomplished a dramatic turnaround.

Candidates and their organizations, of course, attempt to influence the media's power as typecaster, but once an image is established, it is almost impossible to overturn it. Even Jimmy Carter, cast as "outsider" and "long shot" in 1975, became not an "insider" but simply the outsider who won, the long shot who led the pack (Arterton, 118; Patterson, 138). Casting candidates in dramatic roles is of a piece, moreover, with the basic structural principle of all television news: the story. Journalists call their material by this name, referring to getting "the story" and covering "the story" when they mean to describe events, persons, or crises that may or may not be narratives. The point is that television news presents what happens in the world as bits and pieces of stories—and as one would expect, the better the story, the stronger the coverage. David Atheide sees this process as one in which the newscaster predefines "what is important about an event" and uses this definition "as the basis for a story." The significance of an event is then shown by "constructing a narrative account with a beginning, middle, and end"—and this Aristotelian structure is what Atheide calls "the news perspective" (73). Once the story is cast, it serves to prefigure subsequent events. The story, in other words, determines the way subsequent facts and developments are presented. "Thus, newsmen seek evidence which supports the story line" (Atheide, 76). Because of this reliance on thematic narratives, Paul Weaver finds television news "far more interpretive than a newspaper news story." In television news, facts and details (or substance) are secondary to the "general trends, situations, and dynamics of the campaign" or of the established story. "Thus the tendency of TV campaign reporting is to disregard the surface of events in preference to explaining *what's really going on underneath*" (Weaver 68—my emphasis). What's really going on is, to quote young Emerson in *Invisible Man*, what lies "behind the face of things." Behind the apparent facts lie the invisible stories that explain reality. What's really going on is the *story*—if details or developments contradict the story line, they must, to save the narrative, be explained away or somehow negated.

Television news, then, even with its pictures, is essentially an oral form. It resembles oral forms of narrative most clearly when it endeavors to cover an ongoing event, such as a presidential campaign. (Other, more isolated events, tend to be presented as oral/pictorial headlines.) In covering a primary election season and subsequent national campaign, television news exemplifies many of the characteristics of an oral tradition. It is repetitious (how many times *did* Jesse Jackson "make history" in 1988?), it is moralistic, thematic, and heroic. Its narrators claim that the story itself possesses an autonomous existence—in other words, the story is "got"; it is not created. Television journalists do not create their stories; very few of them even control the writing of their stories. Instead, they "participate," as literary historians say of preliterate narrators, in the tradition of getting the story told. As in any repetitious form, specific content is selected to reinforce the primary pattern (or rhythm) of meaning. Once the story is established, it becomes more important than the journalist (any correspondent can "fill in"), more important than the hero (who can also be replaced), and more important than any minority view, divergent viewpoint, or political commentary— to name a few of the categorical strategies by which television marginalizes pluralism. The necessity of maintaining thematic unity, in other words, will result in the suppression, or muting, of details and developments which do not "fit" the pattern of what's really going on. And because of television's visual component, the heroic characteristics of its peculiar oral form are magnified beyond even the formalistic, heroic quality of an epic narrative.

If primitive epic forms emphasized and glorified heroic action by making it larger than life, the *technological* epic form of television news does more by providing a heroic, graphically represented dimension to the everyday existence of those lives considered newsworthy. Life for the viewer may be chaotic and without a clearly defined thematic content, but not so the newsworthy. In fact, to *be* newsworthy in this context is to possess a story, especially a televisable story. Finally, because of its heroic emphasis, television news is, above all, moralistic. Moral superiority and moral failing are what make and break the political lives featured on the television news. This is why newscasters deal in personality and not issues. It is not that journalists are sensationalist, but that their medium is tied to epic movements, not issues and ideas. In an epic narrative, heroes have feelings, not convictions; they respond to cosmic strains and universal movement, not material, political controversy.

Herbert Gans has noted the reliance of television news on symbolism and has described the role of the TV journalist as the manager of "the symbolic arena, the public stage on which national, societal, and other messages are made available" to viewers (298). Television news is a prime example of postmodern communication because it *refers* to real events without fully defining or explaining them. (If viewers want to know more, they read the newspaper or the weekly newsmagazine.) Storytelling and symbolic communication are, of course, endemic to the structure of the television medium itself (Hofstetter, 188; Sperry, 297), just as symbolic representation is indispensable to epic forms of narrative. In casting world and national events as stories peopled by narrative "types," television news reporters are simply expressing what students of narrative structures have found to be "basic to modern discussions of both history and fiction." That is, reporters are presupposing "a notion of reality in which 'the true' is identified with 'the real' only insofar as it can be shown to possess the character of narrativity" (White, 6). In other words, "getting the story" is essentially indistinguishable from "getting reality." To report on Jesse Jackson, then, the newscaster must find out first of all who Jackson is (or how to cast him), and what Jackson wants (or what his story is). The persistence of these two questions reveals Jackson's invisibility. Like Ellison's narrator, Jackson's story moves among multiple *levels* of narration—the surreal, the historical, the realistic—and makes him, like IM, a bundle of narrative contradictions.

Who was Jackson in 1988? Black man, preacher, spoiler; spokesman for the poor, the dispossessed, and the working class; great speech maker, rainbow coalition leader, Chicagoan, Southerner, Democrat, civil rights leader, voter registration promoter, news hound, and above all, nomination Runner and—Rinehart? Dennis Murphy on NBC called him "the superstar of black politics" (March 3), casting Jackson as a cross between Michael Jackson and the 1970s macho cinema figure, Shaft. His NBC colleague, Bob Kerr, said watching Jackson campaign was "like watching a rock star" and that his appeal worked like "magic to those who feel left out" (April 13). But Kerr's report carries more than a hint of condescension, for rock stars are not statesmen, and no one wants a magician for president. In May, when Jackson's nomination hopes were eclipsed, Murphy found Jackson acting more like a "preacher" than a candidate, but no longer a superstar (May 7, NBC).

Jackson played a number of roles in that aspect of the primary campaign known as the horse race. The "horse race" is the term social scientists use to describe the characteristic electoral focus of the newsmedia, which is on the popularity ranking of each candidate, and not on complex issues or political philosophies. The horse race is the favorite and by far the easiest "story" to use in covering a campaign. It provides a convenient and continuing structure to the electoral "race," and allows reporters to compete with one another for the prestige that comes with "calling" the outcome (Arterton, 47; Iyengar, 128). At first, Jackson was upgraded from his 1984 status as "outside agitator" to his 1988 status as "bona fide candidate" by Richard Threlkeld at ABC. However, Threlkeld, tuned in to what is "really going on" in the campaign, pointed out that despite anchor Peter Jennings' having called Jackson "the most exciting speaker on the trail" and a man with "days in the sunshine ahead of him," the "accepted wisdom," according to Threlkeld, "is that he cannot be nominated" (February 15). In characteristic TV fashion, Threlkeld does not say by whom such wisdom is accepted, much less in whom it originates—but the message is clear. Despite the excitement and the legitimacy, the real story is one of a failed candidacy owing to some tremendous, invisible counterforce ("cannot be nominated"). Young Emerson played the same role in *Invisible Man*, the white face willing to reveal the secrets of power in America to the ambitious black runner.

This particular story, that of the unelectable candidate, continued to lead Jackson news reports even as the man began to gain support around the country. Anchor Tom Brokaw reported on NBC News, March 11, that Gary Hart had withdrawn but "Jesse Jackson, on the other hand, is on a roll." However, "more and more, the question is, can Jesse Jackson be elected president?" Reporter Dennis Murphy followed Brokaw's introduction with an analysis of Jackson's supporters, "a populist coalition of blacks, women, and workers." This "coalition" did not appear to leave out many voters unless one knew what "workers" meant in the Jackson story. Brokaw followed Murphy's report with a live, electronic interview with Jackson and made the code explicit. He asked Jackson directly whether Jackson was or was not "too radical" to be elected. Here Brokaw exemplified a major motif in the Jackson television story. Nothing the candidate would do in the campaign would shake the "unelectable" story line from his bid for the Democratic nomination, although the specific reasoning would change as the details of the campaign shifted. Newscasters claimed that he was unelectable because he was not white, he was too radical, or (in the New York campaign) he was anti-Semitic. When Jackson did not do well in the Wisconsin primary, falling off the "roll" he had been on, NBC reported that it was because he suffered from a "surge in expectations." It seemed that people realized he might win if they voted for him, so they refrained (April 6). In this twist to the story, Jackson was so unelectable that if voters found themselves electing him, they would reverse their mistaken proclivities. History may only move in one direction at a time. No newscaster wants to be hit with an Ellisonian boomerang, especially not on his own ground, television.

Television news is about one thing in general and a multitude of things in detail. In detail, first of all, the news concerns an endless series of events and people. These change from day to day, week to week, and season to season. In general, however, the news is about just one thing: the news, the *idea* of news, and especially, the people and the institutions that assemble and report the news. Ultimately, the news is about newscasters. In the oral tradition referred to earlier, the story was said to take precedence over the storyteller. The teller of the oral tale in primitive cultures was known to partake in the story itself as he or she recited it. Gradually, however, as oral tradition gave way to written forms of discourse, the storyteller asserted control over the story by writing it down, by claiming authorship. With literacy comes authorial proprietorship. Once an author establishes a reputation, readers read not the story but the author. The literary critic, for example, specializes in Faulkner or Ellison or Cather—not in any particular story.

Newscasting has followed a similar, if greatly truncated, line of development. The early days of the self-effacing correspondent, or of the newscaster who held sheets of paper in his hand and *read the report*, had given way by the 1980s to "ABC World News Tonight *with Peter Jennings*," "CBS Evening News *with Dan Rather*," and so forth. A story in any newscast, furthermore, is seldom reported without the appearance of the reporter and his or her name on screen for a number of seconds. By structure and format alone, then, it would appear that television news is about the newscasters first, and the details of news second. This fact became exceptionally clear during the initial reports of rioting in Beijing in 1989, when Dan Rather of CBS interrupted prime-time television with no information. The big story here, he said, was that there was no story—that Chinese officials would not allow reporters to get the story.

Covering Jesse Jackson, then, put reporters to a test. Charges of racism would inevitably follow any blunt treatment of the *obvious* story: the novelty of a black face in the crowd of presidential candidates. Journalists initially attempted to deflect this test by claiming that Jackson's candidacy was a test for the nation as a whole. However, the test was fixed from the start. Because he was "unelectable," his candidacy would "prove" a racist element in America. When Jackson began to do well in primary elections and caucuses, the "unelectable" story was in jeopardy. To defend the story, reporters began to speculate on a backlash. So the story of Jackson's campaign, while making good potential copy (excitement, historic drama, charisma), also created problems for the actual subject matter of newscasts, the reporters.

Casting Jackson as a historic object never quite worked, because one cannot be an object both of history and the news. History exists in the past, and newscasters are powerless to create it. The guardians of history are the historians, and when television needs one, it finds one in a prestigious university to provide an on-camera remark. But still it is difficult for television newscasters to use historical materials (especially if there exists no footage) to inform their own stories. A university professor explaining a historical point is hardly an event. History is not newsworthy because, quite simply, it is not news—it has already happened. In other words, casting Jackson as "historic" was another way to cast him as "unelectable." History exists in the past, and in a presentist medium like television, the past exists as set pieces, as bits of information, but not as powers in the present. Consequently, reports of Jackson's historic status were usually coupled with signals of Jackson's invisibility. "History will record," according to CBS's Betsy Aaron, that "Jesse Jackson, a black man," came in second in the primaries in 1988. This is what "history" will say, but what will *CBS* record? Despite history, the big question remained, according to Aaron: "What does Jesse want?" (June 7). If Jackson were not invisible, of course, the question would be ridiculous. If he were visible it would be obvious that the man wanted to be the president or vice president, or hold some position of national power.

Invisibility, however, precludes *any* single answer. And furthermore, historic figures cannot "want" in the same way that present political figures "want." John Chancellor, in his June 7 commentary on NBC, rephrased the popular question. "What does Jesse *need*," he said, is the more pertinent question. According to Chancellor, "Jesse"—in 1988 Jackson was everybody's brother—needed to stay politically visible, get voters to the polls, and remain politically influential. Even by the time Jackson had made it clear that he had "earned the right to be seriously considered" as Dukakis's running mate, the question persisted. Connie Chung at NBC reported on June 11 that Jackson's "list of wants is long and specific" while Jackie Judd, on ABC, asked not only "What does Jesse Jackson want" but "what will he get?" Nothing Jackson could do would answer this question. In the end, however, the network news story concluded that as a historic figure Jackson wanted what *all* of history wants from the present, recognition. Peter Jennings, on ABC's July 18 broadcast, claimed that Jackson got what he wanted—"our attention. There simply has not been a time when a man who was defeated in the primaries and the caucuses has continued to be so close to the center of the stage—mind you, there's never been another campaigner like Mr. Jackson." What Jackson wanted was to be visible, but nothing he could do in the 1988 campaign would alter his status as the invisible candidate.

Historic figure, unelectable candidate, preacher, coalition builder, spoiler—all of these Jesse Jacksons were pursued by the unanswerable, contradictory question, "What does Jesse want?" On July 15, Bruce Morton claimed on CBS that Jackson's various roles acted to negate one another. Jackson, according to Morton, "wears a couple of hats: his interest as a black leader, the preeminent black spokesman, may nudge him one way; his interest in being a mainstream kind of Democrat, a power in the party after this election is over, may nudge him in another." One can be a *black* leader or a *black* spokesman, but not if one also wants to be a *mainstream* Democrat or a *power* in the party. Jackson is torn only because he is black—and blackness equals contradiction, which equals invisibility. If Jackson *insists* on being a black man, by Morton's logic, then he cannot have a future in the party. Presumably, an African-American can someday be elected president in the United States, but not one who insists on being as black as Jesse Jackson.

As Black as Jesse Jackson

The main story employed to make sense of Jesse Jackson's campaign was as clear as black and white—and it was established early in 1988, in Iowa. Although the form and structure of TV news is oral, its power to convince us of its stories lies in the illustrations provided by its pictures. Social psychologists have found that in television news, "pictures dominate the news viewers' recall" and that "the visual dimension overrides, sometimes even blots out the audio dimension" (Patterson and McClure, 86–87). For this reason, television news is capable of profound distortions and epistemological reversals, such as trivializing complex events and dramatizing trivialities. During the Paris Peace Talks between the United States and North Vietnam in the 1970s, for example, audio reports of high level, complex negotiations were undermined by the only available pictures: laughing and waving diplomats getting in and out of limousines. Complex diplomatic procedures are always carried out behind doors and away from cameras. On the other hand, a triviality—such as a slip of the tongue on the campaign trail—can be dramatized immensely by good repetitious visual coverage. President Ford's slip regarding Poland's political status in the 1975 television debates—which was initially unnoticed by viewers and listeners alike—became a "big" issue once the film clip of the gaffe was turned into a major event.

Iowa, as it turned out, was the perfect place to introduce the story of the black man running the white race. "Jackson is out to make a point" in Iowa, according to Tom Brokaw on NBC, January 11. "If he can win in Iowa, he can win it all." Iowa footage is then shown, a line of black cars against a purely white background of snow and January

Iowa sky. As voice-over in this scene, the newscaster says, "Can Jesse Jackson get white votes? That's all there are in Iowa." Jackson is then shown standing in an Iowa farm crowd, and the reporter makes the point clear: "In places like these, Jackson is often the only black face." The camera then cuts to the reporter's face: "Can a black man become president? That's the question that Jesse Jackson is asking white Iowa to confront." At a high school rally, NBC's camera zooms in on a lone black girl in the audience. At another rally, Jackson is seen kissing a black baby with whites looking on. "In short," the report concludes, "he is calling on the voters of this state to send a message."

The other two networks followed the same story line, but resisted the naturalistic use of the countryside. On January 12, ABC led its broadcast with a white man introducing Jesse Jackson as "Brother Jesse Jackson." CBS insisted that "Jesse Jackson's message these days is, 'I really am electable' "—and CBS enforced this theme by running film of Jackson holding and kissing a three-year-old white girl. All three networks pursued this thematic principle in January 1988, the dramatic story of the individual black man testing white America's belief in equal opportunity. The uniformity of the networks' coverage demonstrated Doris Graber's finding that news services typically select "the same kinds of stories" and emphasize "the same types of facts, despite the wealth of diverse materials available to them" (190). Indeed, in January, when Jackson attempted to changed the newscasters' story line, his input was effectively muted when reporters presented evidence against his story and for theirs.

On January 16, in Iowa, ABC carried three successive reports about racial issues on its evening broadcast. The middle report, from the Iowa debates, consisted of a flip clip of Jackson with the reporter's voice-over: "The Reverend Jackson suggested that his race would not be a factor in his campaign." The voice-over fades into the Jackson clip, and the candidate is shown proclaiming that "If I am the best candidate . . . I expect to gain [the voters'] support." However, this particular angle contradicts the established, epic TV news story about the prominence of race, and the two reports that sandwich Jackson's statement served to undercut his point—or at least to make him appear cagey. The first report would seem to have no other purpose than to counter Jackson's claim by "priming" viewers to regard race as an unavoidable point of contention. In 1987, the

town of Forsyth, Georgia, received national attention wh
Klan march resulted in street violence between anti-Kl
strators and the KKK. ABC sent cameras back to Forsyth i
cover what turned out to be an entirely peaceful march. The
the report was that the racial violence that characterized the
march in 1987 was *absent* in 1988. Because the 1988 event
drama, the 1988 report centered primarily on what occurred i
syth *last* year and, by implication, what did not happen this
Here, again, the lack of a story became the story. Since racial
frontation was expected, its absence amounted to an event.

The report that followed Jackson's was a bit more substantive. It concerned the Jimmy-the-Greek Snyder scandal, in which the odds maker, according to the report, "said that blacks were bred for superior ability" during slavery, which accounted for certain characteristic physical features of the race today. Snyder, on camera, pointed out that "the slave owner would breed his big black woman, so that he could have his big black kid, see. . . . The black is a better athlete to begin with because he's been bred to be that way," and for this reason many blacks excel in sports today. The "story" here was not the relative accuracy of Snyder's historical observations, which went without comment in the report, but the fact that Jesse Jackson "seemed to accept [Snyder's] apology" when Snyder called him. Jackson might claim that his race was invisible in the campaign for the Democratic nomination, but TV news possessed a national network of source material with which to contradict his claim. Jackson insisted on one kind of invisibility, in which his racial background would contain no significance, and the networks insisted on another, in which his race was the sum of his existence.

ABC followed up on the story the next day, on January 17, with its sports reporter Ray Gandolf covering it as a "scandal." The scandal, however, did not concern the historical horrors of slavery, but the news scandal of Snyder's possible loss of prestige, and the need for him to apologize to the man who, according to the TV news campaign story, *represents* victims of racism and personifies racial "tests" in America, Jesse Jackson. Gandolf led this story for ABC, but the network sent a black correspondent, Kenneth Walker, to cover the volatile issue. In any case, the issues of slavery and forced breeding, racism in contemporary sports, or Snyder's motives for making the comments in the first place, were all made secondary to

ramatic apology issued by the white man to the black candi-
. No mention is made of the germ of truth in Snyder's remarks,
t as no reference is made to Jackson's own slave heritage.

Jackson, who said race would not be an issue, was, according to the
"facts" in the news, simply wrong. In the story of the 1988 campaign, Jesse Jackson's role was not simply one candidate among
many, not Long Shot or Preacher-Candidate, but Black Man Running
for nomination. In his book about the 1984 Democratic primary
campaign, Adolph Reed found that the Jackson phenomenon "was a
ritualistic event—a media-conveyed politics of symbolism, essentially tangential to the critical debate over the reorganization of
American capitalism's governing consensus" (1). In 1988, the television networks would cling to this story of the Black Man Running.

By the time of Super Tuesday in March, all three networks had the
Jackson story solidified. Dan Rather at CBS opened the February 29
broadcast with the headline "The Politics of Race, 1988" and over-
saw a series of reports on the South. Bruce Morton went to a Jackson,
Mississippi, radio station to film a local disc jockey playing "Run,
Jesse Run," a record, the DJ says, that gets "lots of requests" lately.
But, asks Morton, "will whites vote for a black candidate?" In Flora,
Mississippi, the CBS cameras show black men in overalls with looks
of blank indifference milling about outside the New Deal Market in
the town square. Film clips of decrepit outlying farms are also in-
cluded. Morton gives the depressing statistics about black illiteracy
and unemployment, with the clear implication that *this* is the black
South. But what does Jackson have to do with this? Is race an issue
("The Politics of Race") only because "Jesse" is on the run? Is Jesse
Jackson responsible for, or to, Flora, Mississippi? The pictures from
Flora are offered in response to Morton's stock questions: Will
whites vote for a black candidate? Will they vote for Flora?

To maintain the illusion of reportorial objectivity, newscasters do
not insist upon their interpretations; rather, they simply find someone who will voice the idea, preferably (but not necessarily) on camera, that needs to be conveyed. This practice is among the "strategic
rituals" of objectivity, the "routine procedures," according to Gaye
Tuchman, which are in fact "formal attributes" that "protect the
professional from mistakes and from his critics" (677–78). Bob Faw,
CBS correspondent in Texas on March 7, opened his story with a clip
of James Clark, speaker of Alabama's legislature, saying, "Blacks
support black candidates and whites support white candidates.

That's the way it is, and that's the way it will be for a long time." Alabama may be a long way to go for a lead-in to a Texas story, but space and time possess little meaning on television. Faw cuts directly from Clark to his own comment that "the difference this time" is that Jackson *is* gaining white support. But, asks Faw, is a backlash possible if Jackson is perceived to be gaining "crossover" votes? To answer this, Faw returns to Alabama. "The time has not arrived," says Clark, for a black candidate to win the nomination. To seal the story, Faw cuts to an anonymous black face: "What's holding him back is his race," says the black commoner. Having echoed and returned to the master theme, Faw then continues his Texas report, which features Jackson claiming that poverty is a class issue, not a race issue: "A new born baby who is hungry—it doesn't matter what color it is." But by this point, Jackson has been undercut. This story is not about class, but about race. In fact, on February 29, ABC reported that Jackson's "populist message" might not work in the South because today, in the South there are "more haves than have-nots." This is not Jackson's story, but television's, not Jackson's campaign, but television's. And from the corporate perspective of network news, an industry not merely dependent upon capitalism but symbolic of its workings, the class story is simply untenable.

The news story of the Black Man Running led to a variety of spin-offs. Lesley Stahl (CBS) asked on April 5 whether Democrats could attack Jackson without being accused of racism. When is it racism and when is it politics as usual? However, Stahl's is typical of many television reports on "race" topics, because it reports only the possibility of racially based *conflict,* but it does not report content. What is the substance of the attacks and are they in fact justified? In any case, when racial conflict did erupt in the campaign, television was there. On May 10, ABC correspondent James Wooten reported how racist remarks made directly to the candidate in West Virginia "led Jackson to complain bitterly about what he saw as covert racism from the Democratic hierarchy throughout his campaign." On camera, Jackson is pictured explaining that he was called a "nigger" by a white West Virginian. "Well," Jackson says, "I am not a nigger." No reportorial comment follows this statement, which falls into the same category as Richard Nixon's famous "I am not a crook." After all, what is a nigger and to whom is the candidate offering his denial? Jackson continues, on camera, explaining that Americans have an obligation not only "to not use the code words" of racism but "to eradicate the unfounded fears that people have" of other races. The Black Man Running, if he stops in one place long enough to be seen, will inevitably be called a nigger by some American convinced that only as objects do his compatriots possess real space. That West Virginia man who used the epithet surely knows himself as a "cracker" or "hick" or whatever the local West Virginia term is for peasant. In any case, Jackson's line of thought about covert racism, code words, and irrational fear is not pursued by the newscasters.

When the Black Man Running insisted that race was not an issue in his campaign, he was contradicted by television news reports. Eventually, as television reported the epic, he would give up insisting that he was "not a nigger"/Negro/colored person/black man and declare his "true" identity. In July 1988, Jackson became the descendant of slaves. He became a man in whose consciousness is imbedded images of forced labor and systematic injustice. Reporters had refused to make his race invisible; their reports cast Jesse Jackson as an invisible man beneath that role of Black Man Running. In July, when it was clear that Jackson would not be the nominee and that he would also not be Dukakis's choice for vice-president, he removed the "race is irrelevant" mask he had worn for the cameras. In a grand example of an Ellisonian boomerang, Jackson found himself—candidate, statesman, diplomat, coalition leader—back in the cotton fields of his slave ancestry.

Finally before the cameras in blackface, the original question about his candidacy is answered. However, when "Jesse" is black, he is *too* black for TV. When Jackson accepts the role of Black Man Running, he takes on the cast of Freedman on the run—and this time he is knocking at the door of the Democratic Party's big house. According to Tom Petit (NBC), "What he wants is a clear cut role in the Democratic Party free of ancient [sic] stigma." Petit cuts to Jackson's controversial historical analogy: "It is too much to expect that I would go out in the field and be the champion vote picker," Jackson explains, "and bale them up, and bring them back to the big house, and get the reward of thanks, while people who do not pick nearly as much votes, who don't carry the same amount of weight amongst the people, sit in the big house and make the decisions." John Chancellor's commentary, later in the broadcast, would signal the newscasters' fear of the very story they had insisted upon: "So it came as a surprise to me to see how emotional he's become in the last week or so—emotional and sometimes almost out of control. For Jesse Jackson that's unusual. It may be he's come to the end of a road, and he doesn't know what to do." When Jackson finally agrees, on camera, that this *is* a race story, that he is the Black Man Running, the nigger/colored person/Negro, the product of slavery, in pursuit of the master's house—then the network newscaster blanches. But you can't trust a field nigger, and Chancellor knows it. As for Jackson's "emotional" outbursts? Chancellor concludes his commentary wise to the trickster: "It may be calculated," he admits.

Chancellor's final comment indicates an attempt to explain Jackson's behavior in a more favorable light. After all, appearing "emotional" on television—consider Edmund Muskie's tears in New Hampshire in 1972—is not something that television is able to convey without irony. Television does quite well with irony itself; the gap between what can be portrayed in pictures and what is actually occurring in front of the camera gives rise to ironies of many kinds in any given newscast. However, a sincere show of emotion, because it originates in the *invisible* space of inner ambiguity, presents a challenge to the telecaster. Staged emotion is easy: The close-up shot of the human face "presses" inward in a gesture meant to give the illusion of capturing the inner self. But when that inner self emerges on its own, naked as it were, it always appears, on camera, to be an "outburst"—the sudden, inappropriate, embarrassing display of what is meant to remain beyond sight. In Ellison's terms, the display is rooted in irresponsibility: an intrusion of the invisible man into the visible sphere of objective existence. By showing emotion, by presenting his invisibility, Jackson made his bid for subjective existence. But this is something the television camera renders ironic because the camera does not know anything about subjectivity. The camera must make Jackson into an object in order to see him, and viewers, raised on television, must recognize that object in order to believe that they know who he is and what he wants.

By introducing the field-nigger analogy, Jackson verified the role cast for him by the media, but he also stepped out of the style with which he was to play that role. His role was the Black Man Running who *insisted* that race was irrelevant. In this way, he was a "good" black man because he embraced his invisibility by conforming to a role provided him by the white media. Successful black Americans, while they may have black faces, leave their slave pasts behind them and become, as the Louis Armstrong song so central to *Invisible Man* laments, "white inside." In fact, the blues song suggests that the American Negro who successfully appropriates the white mind finds the sight of his own face jarring: "What did I do," in other words, "to be so black and blue?"

Anthony Walton, reflecting on the racial scandals of the 1988 campaign, found that he had to renew his own double consciousness as an educated black American. "I must battle, because I am black, to see myself as others see me; increasingly my life, literally, depends upon it" (77). Jackson may well have *thought* he had a chance at the nomination, or the vice-presidential slot, simply because he was immensely popular, articulate, and charismatic. He was caught, however, in the trap of Ellison's dual invisibility. When Jackson insisted that his race was invisible, the networks proved him wrong by casting his candidacy in racial terms and by priming audiences to see Jackson as a racial object. When the candidate finally embraced the role, making his race and his slave heritage public and significant, the networks countered once again, claiming slavery to be an "ancient" stigma and accusing Jackson of emotionalism. Hence, the two parties change places, and the networks begin insisting that race (at least racial history) be invisible. This is the trap of invisibility that serves to disenable public figures like Jesse Jackson from emerging as visible, powerful political actors in the United States. In 1859, Jackson might have run from "patter-rollers" trying to incarcerate him in physical chains. In 1989, Jackson, still running, found himself prisoner of the news media, the "pater-rollers" of the public conscience—captured in the metaphysical language of invisibility. The Black Man Running is an eternal and highly visible American figure, but he is not permitted a resting place in American political culture. If he stops running, he is made invisible, "clubbed" by reality, in Ellison's phrase, driven into a hole.

Television reporters were appalled when Jackson stepped out of his submissive role as invisible candidate. Betsy Aaron on CBS included the "cotton picker" speech in her July 14 report and claimed that Jackson had made the vice-presidential issue "both personal and political." Brit Hume, on ABC, who consistently trivialized Jackson's campaign, reported on July 19 that Jackson's meetings with Democratic Party officials had proved that he had arrived "where he insisted he should be—at the table with the big shots." The fear, though, that Jackson would get to the "table," the intimate places where whites exchange the secrets of their power, was the subtext of the entire Jackson phenomenon on the news. It can be seen in two continuing motifs in the "story" of Jackson in 1988: the secret, off-the-record admissions of fear of Jesse Jackson by party officials, and the personification of racial fear in the figure of Willie Horton.

Jesse Jackson's Foil: Willie Horton

Newscasters have a ready supply of violent images for use in political campaigns, and so the metaphors of disruption and threat applied to Jackson's candidacy may in fact be unremarkable. In addition, journalists regularly quote secret, off-camera sources, and so the practice in Jackson's campaign of assigning racial fears to "high level" and confidential officials may also be nothing unusual. However, long before Willie Horton was introduced as a campaign issue, before his angry, nightmarish face and his violent, purposeless crimes were made familiar to television viewers, a similar role was provided to Jackson by newscasters. In effect, audiences and newscasters alike were primed to make the thematic connection between Jackson and Horton before anyone thought of the two men as symbolically interchangeable.

On February 22, for example, Ken Bode reported for NBC that "Jesse Jackson is preparing a political ambush in the South" on Super Tuesday. However, despite some optimistic pollsters (quoted on screen) who say Jackson has a shot at the nomination, the "conventional wisdom," Bode concludes, "is that Jesse Jackson cannot be nominated—and that is not likely to change. The question after super Tuesday may be, Who is going to tell him?" Who is going to tell him the "truth" about his role in America and what will happen when he stops being a "good" black man and becomes a you-know-what?

NBC on April 2 characterized Jackson's campaign as "emotional," not intellectual, because the candidate claims to "love" the American people. CBS reported the same story on April 4, pointing out that Jackson is "campaigning on emotion" when he advocates "love and respect for one another" in his speeches. Similarly, Jackson's campaign was often analyzed as a "crusade," with its connotations of unreliability and irrationality. Jackson was often presented as a live wire, difficult to predict, and potentially unruly. "With Jesse Jackson, you're never sure what he will do next. . . . Has he finished his personal crusade?" (NBC July 18). Crusaders, of course, are unelectable, and worse, they are disruptive to the civil, democratic process.

When Jackson would win, or nearly win a primary election, thus defying his role as unelectable Black Man Running, his victory would likely be reported as "shocking"—as it was in Michigan by CBS on March 27. Susan Spencer said that Jackson's victory "once again put the party in chaos," because, presumably, Jackson was not supposed to win. Sam Donaldson at ABC reported that party leaders were "in both awe and fright" after Michigan, and reporter James Wooten claimed, "Now that he's also attracting whites, the hierarchy sees him as a threat to the party's future." Paul Kirk, the Democratic Party chairman, on camera, claims simply that if Jackson wins, he will be nominated. But Wooten undercuts the "official position" with the "secret wisdom" that cannot be quoted. "Despite his remarkable successes . . . there are still serious questions about the willingness of white voters to support a black man for the American presidency." White voters are forewarned: A vote for Jackson is a threat to the party. Furthermore, white voters are reassured: Most will not vote for the black man.

All three networks thus effectively made "secret" racism legitimate in their coverage of the high water mark in Jackson's campaign following the Michigan victory. The story was consistent on ABC, CBS, and NBC. Democratic Party officials would be shown, typically on camera, claiming that if Jackson wins, he wins, and the system will support him. Then the reporter would claim, as Bruce Morton did on CBS, that "off camera, a lot of Democrats say, 'we have a problem'" (March 28). On March 30, Brit Hume at ABC covered Jackson's meetings with Democratic Party leaders ("an extraordinary attempt to get to know one another") and featured film clips of Jackson having breakfast with white power brokers. According to Hume, the white men with the friendly faces around the table "were careful to hide their personal fright" that Jackson would be their nominee. Perhaps, as E. Franklin Frazier has remarked about black voting in the South of the 1920s, "the closer a Negro got to the ballot box the more he looked like a rapist" (quoted in Adams, lxi). What exactly informed the fears of white power brokers in 1988? What these television reports suggest is that liberal messages of integration and racial harmony, when voiced by powerful whites, are simply hypocritical—the fact is that they do not mean what they say. On the streets, of course, this particular type of television news story would only make racist attacks legitimate among classes of people who do not see the need to hide their antipathies.

Once Jackson's momentum began to wane, "the fear," according to Sam Donaldson, that Jackson would win subsided (ABC April 6). But this did not put an end to Jackson's role as troublemaker. As Clint Wilson points out, the media is quite adept at presenting blacks and ethnics "as people who either *have* problems or *cause* problems" (107). Jackson's next troublesome role would be that of the extortionist. On April 20, ABC's Brit Hume reported that party officials will give Jackson *anything* short of the vice-presidential spot in order to keep him satisfied, but also to keep him off the ticket. In early June, NBC presented Jackson as "still running" in hopes of maintaining his power base. Two days later, on June 5, NBC made the implicit Jackson "threat" a bit more clear with a report on Jackson's "half-brother, Noah Robinson." Robinson is shown wearing an orange jumpsuit, handcuffed between two policemen. "At times they have been close, at times estranged—whatever, today Robinson was arrested. He was charged with being an accessory in the stabbing and wounding of a woman last December." Of course, "accessory" can mean just about anything. What the story suggests, nonetheless, is that violence-and-violent-crime is a half-brother to Jackson—and that Jackson is somehow close, even if estranged at the present time, to such behavior. No follow-up on Noah Robinson's case was aired during the campaign season.

The next day, Brit Hume reported that Jackson's "rhetoric has become a puzzling mixture of promise and threat" at this point in the campaign. At the same time, CBS reported on Michael Dukakis's "problem" with Jackson, and NBC reported that Jackson was "threatening a convention fight" over various platform and procedural policies. In June, despite Jackson's on-camera denial that he is "proceeding in an atmosphere of threat" (CBS June 15), newscasters, especially at ABC, continued to characterize him as an ominous presence. Jackie Judd had him "whipsawing Dukakis" on the vice-presidential issue (ABC June 12); Peter Jennings characterized him as "an unpredictable" politician (July 8), as opposed, for example, to a resourceful one; Brit Hume observed that "Jackson still has the ability to make news, and if he chooses, make trouble" (ABC July 14). John Chancellor chose the image of murder to characterize Dukakis and Jackson: "Metaphorically . . . they seemed ready to murder each other" on the eve of the convention (NBC July 15). But ABC capped the story of the unpredictable, fearsome Jackson on the day after his speech at the Democratic National Convention.

Jennings saw him as a trickster: "It is a little hard at times to tell for whom Jesse Jackson is campaigning" (July 20). Brit Hume followed Jenning's statement with a report concluding that "with Jesse Jackson there is always more to determine, something more to wonder about. . . . This man operates on pure instinct."

Ralph Ellison has claimed that the American of African descent, because of his facelessness in the culture, can never achieve a defined or visible public role. In his words, "the democratic assumption that Negro citizens should share the individual's recognized responsibility for the welfare of society [is] regarded as subversive" (*GT*, 175). From the start of his campaign, Jackson's candidacy was never cast in terms of what Jackson might attempt "for the welfare of society." Instead, his candidacy was seen as a test of *white* attitudes toward race—so much so that a vote for Jackson was considered, by extending the television newscasters' logic, to be a vote against racism (or for an end to racism). In no instance and in no report, however, was a vote for Jackson construed as a vote for any particular political agenda having to do with the state of the nation, and seldom was Jackson's own political philosophy taken as anything but a ploy for the Black Man Running to get votes. This cast to Jackson's campaign continued right into the Convention Hall, where Jackson's insistence that his constituency retain a voice concerning the future of the party was interpreted as yet another "subversive" act, to apply Ellison's formula. Television's coverage of Jackson's subversive role, his threat to party order, his status as troublemaker—all this did nothing less than prime Americans who watch TV to accept the connection between Jesse Jackson and the obscure figure of Willie Horton.

On December 27, 1987, CBS carried a story about Boston prison furloughs because petitioners in that city were trying to get the program on the ballot. Richard Schlesinger's report featured what would become the two stock images of the black slasher/rapist: Willie Horton's photograph, the mug shot that would eventually haunt white American imaginations in 1988, and the photograph of Horton in custody, being led away to the prison that would not hold him. Anthony Walton describes Horton's appeal:

> George Bush and his henchmen could not have invented Willie Horton. Horton, with his coal-black skin; huge, unkempt Afro, and a glare that would have given Bull Connor or Lester Maddox serious pause, had

committed a brutal murder in 1974 and been sentenced to life in prison. Then, granted a weekend furlough from prison, had viciously raped a white woman in front of her [husband], who was also attacked. (52)

According to Walton, a middle-class professional man of African descent, the symbol worked even on him. "I thought Willie Horton must be what the wolf packs I had often heard about [in New York City], but never seen, must look like. I said to myself, 'Something has got to be done about these niggers'" (52).

CBS in December 1987 could not know to what use Horton's image would be put in the campaign. The report showed the suburban home of the victims Angela and Cliff Barnes, and showed Cliff Barnes claiming that Horton "enjoyed" what he did to them. The sentencing judge is also featured, who remembers Horton as being "devoid of conscience." Horton clearly was unpredictable. Allowed out of prison, he proved to be, in a sense, an instinctive rapist, not worthy of white trust. With equal clarity, Horton represented a threat to white America—and, as Walton points out, a threat to African-Americans who have made peace with whites. Horton would come to symbolize all the hidden, "secret" fears aroused by the Jackson campaign. What *does* Jesse want?

The television medium's chief power lies not in creating news, as its critics often claim, but in setting the national agenda. Television news functions by *referring* to reality, not by creating it. As such, television news is "a powerful determinant of what springs to mind and what is forgotten or ignored" (Iyengar, 114). The news "primes" viewers by "attending to some problems and ignoring others" and by "defining criteria underlying the public's judgments" (33, 117). However, television news is far less successful in changing minds than it is in *reinforcing* accepted ideas or stereotypes. "Television coverage simply reminds [viewers] of what they already know" (93). Because of this function, television news operates most successfully on the symbolic level. In fact, TV newscasting does some of its most damaging work in its projection of racial symbolism.

Donald Kinder and David Sears, in psychological studies of racial thinking, have found that racism is primarily informed and reinforced *not* by actual threats of violence and confrontation but by "symbolic resentments" (427). In their study of voting trends in the Los Angeles mayoral races of 1969 and 1972, in which one candidate was black and the other white, Kinder and Sears found that "in every single case, affect toward the specified racial threat has more effect on voting behavior among the least vulnerable respondents" (424). In other words, white racial antipathies were more strongly reinforced by the perception of distant threats than they were by the presence of black people near to them. Kinder and Sears call this "symbolic racism." It "has less to do with any tangible and direct impact of racial issues on the white person's life" and more to do with "stereotypical symbols of blacks' violation of traditional values, which are in the media and informal communication all the time" (416). Kinder and Sears suspect that symbolic racism may be the most powerful form of racial prejudice today because it relies not so much on actual confrontation as on media images, which convey and offer legitimacy to oral traditions and folk stories that each race tells about the other.

In its role as medium of American collective consciousness, television news, according to Clint Wilson, has looked for "common themes, ideas, and interest areas" with broad appeal. This means that "the content of the mass media reinforced, rather than challenged, the established norms and attitudes of the society" (40). The figure of Willie Horton, who would become the synecdoche for both black American anger and white American retrenchment in 1988, possessed the kind of mass appeal that encouraged TV news in its most regressive tendencies. NBC, however, picked up the furlough story on January 21 and attempted at first to avoid racial stereotyping. Cassandra Clayton reviewed the Horton crimes, showed the photographs, and interviewed the mother of Horton's original victim. Clayton then pointed out that Horton had been on nine unremarkable weekend furloughs prior to the one that gained him notoriety. She then interviewed prison officials and convicts, who testified to the overwhelmingly positive role played by the furlough program. Officials claim it helps convicts adjust; prisoners say it provides an incentive to rehabilitation. Nonetheless, the presentation made by Cassandra Clayton, a correspondent somewhat aptly named, would not quite get the story.

Horton would not return to the nightly news until June 22, when George Bush began to make him a campaign issue. Bush, on camera, is shown by NBC denying that "all convicts can be rehabilitated." Lisa Myers reported that "Bush again brought up the case of Willie Horton," and then repeated the litany of Horton's offenses. Film clips showed the Barnes couple, and Myers' voice pointed out that

Horton raped her and slashed him "twenty-seven times." Is there a connection here to Jesse Jackson? His status as "threat" and his reputation as an "unpredictable" politician was already well established by June. Has Jackson rehabilitated himself since his radical days, at the 1968 Democratic Party Convention, when he too wore an Afro and looked angry? All three networks, on occasion, ran file footage of the youthful Jackson of 1968 when attempting to cover his political career. If the black Jesse Jackson wants the White House, whose house do other black men covet? Bush is beginning to attack Dukakis for being "soft" on the likes of Willie Horton at the same time that Dukakis is said to be getting tough with Jesse Jackson. By July, the same language used to describe the slasher/rapist will be transferred (metaphorically and sometimes literally) to the candidate/crusader.

On June 26, only two black faces appeared in the CBS Evening News—Horton's and Jackson's. The newscast opened with Jacqueline Adams's report on Bush's latest use of the Horton image at a speech to a group of policemen. Horton's custody photo and mug shot are shown, as are the Barneses in their suburban home. Dukakis spokesmen are given time to defend the furlough program. The newscast cuts next to a report on the rejection of "controversial Jackson planks" by the Democratic platform committee. Jackson's face is then shown in a story about *his* effect on whites. If "pictures dominate the news viewer's recall" (Patterson and McClure, 86), then CBS has merged the two images effectively here. Jackson won some of his demands, according to the second report, but "hasn't decided yet whether to pursue a platform fight." Horton, too, presumably got what he wanted when he was on the run.

Michael Dukakis was portrayed in the media in June and July as fighting off two black images. On the one hand, he was accused by George Bush of being responsible for the rape and assault on a white couple by a black man because of his liberal—read "soft" or "coddling"—ideas about race and rehabilitation. On the other hand, he was depicted as being "hounded" by Jackson on platform issues and on the vice-presidential decision. On July 17, NBC carried Dukakis's statement that "every team needs a quarterback, and that's the nominee," which was his way of insisting on his control over Jackson. Later in the broadcast, Lee Atwater (the Bush campaign manager supposedly responsible for the use of the Horton materials) bluntly claimed on camera that his aim was to show Dukakis as "a Jackson liberal." Dukakis was portrayed by television newscasts as being cornered by images of black attackers. The same man, in other words, who could not control Willie Horton was now seen as incapable of keeping Jesse Jackson in line. Is Dukakis the man suited to be the nation's Cliff Barnes, head of household, the man in the White House? The Republican Party's use of Horton was indeed an act of racist political genius.

Jackson and Horton are thus each made into objects affecting Dukakis's political future. In this way, television news displays its historic tendency to define "news" as "events of consequence to the majority audience, which meant Whites" (Wilson 137). By implying, furthermore, that Dukakis's political problems were being caused by black faces, the news perpetuated dangerous stereotypes of conceivable African-American roles in politics. This is not to suggest that the networks, or even TV journalists, are or were racist. Such an explanation could be easily addressed and the problem remedied quite simply by a change in personnel. The actual cause of such distortions, on the other hand, is structural. "Routine news procedures," according to Atheide, "do not permit new insights into how the social world works" (185). Deadlines and story patterns, as opposed to critical inquiry, demand that stereotypes be perpetuated in the name, ironically, of clarity. How often is the criminal interviewed concerning his crime? The story of Dukakis—who, having "won" the nomination, is now the hero of the next epic-campaign— is well underway in July, and he is depicted as fighting off his formal (and formalistic) opponents. Jackson and Horton have no narrative choice but to be cast as his antagonists.

The line concerning Jesse Jackson's Convention Hall speech was that, as Brokaw put it, "he lit up the hall" (July 20). Dan Rather referred to Jackson on the same day as "the man who brought the house down." Again, Jackson was not the only American black man on the news. Later in the CBS broadcast Horton appears. Lesley Stahl covers "the politics of crime" for CBS, the network that had earlier done "the politics of race" in a story about Jackson (February 29, discussed above). Politics, after all, is politics. Stahl's report includes Cliff Barnes describing what it was like to watch his wife, Angela "being violated and beaten." They are once again portrayed in their home, the house that *Horton* brought down. A film clip of the middle-class, suburban Maryland ranch-style structure is shown while Stahl explains, "Horton broke into the Barnes home, bound and stabbed Mr. Barnes, and raped his wife." Stahl explains that Bush intends to make Barnes and Horton "household names" in the campaign in order to undermine Dukakis. Stahl does include facts about California furloughs, including one man who escaped and killed a policeman while Ronald Reagan was governor. But this, like Cassandra Clayton's report, is really not a part of the story. Stahl returns to the main point, the Horton symbol, and its thematic relevance. The Barnes couple will make a campaign commercial for Bush because, as Angela Barnes says in the final word, "I'm so mad at this justice system—there's no justice, no justice." Who brings down *your* house? And who is the quarterback, who is in control?

By the time the presidential campaign was underway in September, Jackson and Horton were indistinguishable as symbolic messages on television. The merger was accomplished in June and July. Horton had surfaced as an "issue" and as a presence on television just as Jackson was making "demands" that he be considered as the vice-presidential nominee. In July and July, when Jackson was presented as "hounding" Dukakis and causing "trouble" among Democrats, Horton surfaced as Bush's most successful campaign ploy. By the time the presidential campaign was underway in September, the Jesse Jackson issue was "still unresolved" in the Dukakis campaign, according to CBS reporter Betsy Aaron (September 15). Aaron uses two clips to explain the nature of the "relationship" between the two men. Clairbourne Darden, a white Atlanta pollster, makes the connection clear: "The Democrats are walking a tightwire with this. The Jesse vote, or the black vote, is absolutely mandatory for the Democrats. . . . *But let Jesse out, and put him on the front stage,* and he will defeat the Democrats singlehandedly" (italics added). The analogy is unmistakably Hortonian. Aaron's report then cuts to Tyrone Brooks, a Georgia state representative, a black man who had worked for Jackson in 1984: Conservative white voters will go and see Jackson "but they will never vote for him—and they really don't want to see Jesse that close to the President of the United States. That's the fear in white America."

By September 22, in any case, the story was clear. Horton's tale had gone from an obscure story of violence and a potential campaign liability for Michael Dukakis, in December and January, to "the symbol of everything George Bush finds wrong with Michael Dukakis" in September (ABC). Although reporters would continue to point out that other states had furlough programs, thus assuring their objectivity, Bush continued to get coverage of the "story" of Willie Horton—the mug shot, the custody shot, the Barnes house, and the Barnes couple themselves. In October, ABC would conclude that "Willie Horton has become a campaign burden for Michael Dukakis" (October 7). It was clear in October that Jesse Jackson was also a burden to Dukakis. On October 20, for example, NBC's Ken Bode reported that for a time Dukakis's organizers were afraid that "Jesse Jackson would scare away Reagan Democrats." But Jackson is still considered unpredictable. "Jackson makes his own schedule, goes where he wants to," according to Bode, and will not take direction from Dukakis's people. So too, Horton, who went where he wanted to go, and "would not take direction" from *his* patter-rollers. Bode then comments on Jackson's opinion of the use of the Horton story by Bush. "Jackson thinks there has been a subtly racist component to the Bush campaign" because Horton is "a scare tactic." CBS carried Jackson's comments on October 21, which were made in response to the "revolving door" political advertisement. According to Bruce Morton, "Bush has scored big" with this commercial, which Jackson claims possesses "racial overtones . . . scaring white voters with pictures of black criminals."

"Scaring white voters with pictures of black criminals." Patterson and McClure have found that TV ads during political campaigns are overwhelmingly effective—not in changing people's minds, but in capitalizing on existing fears and biases. In other words, television advertisements may provide the final push to voters who are "leaning" one way or another or who are apathetic, but still plan to vote (113). By covering television campaign ads and the reaction to them as "news," TV newscasts emphasize the importance of knowing the content of the advertising spots. Horton's angry face served to remind white Americans of just what it was that Jesse Jackson "wanted" by evoking historical, psychic American connections between African-American ascendancy and white sexual paranoia, property fears, and fears of eventual black domination. Winthrop Jordan has traced these fears to the initial confrontations of Europeans and Africans on the African and American continents. Furthermore, the reminder acted to indict Dukakis, again at the level of symbolic (or perhaps stereotypical) meanings, of coddling this source of danger. In 1978, at a meeting of the Associated Press, Jackson spoke of the "decision makers in both the program and news departments of television" who are almost exclusively "white and male with a suburban and an economic middle- to upper-middle class mentality or perspective—'bias' if you choose" (Jackson, 318). The producers and the people who "cast" TV news are the neighbors, as it were, of Cliff and Angela Barnes, suburban dwellers who live with nightmare shapes of black criminals, assailants, and rapists—nightmare shapes personified on the nightly news in the figure and fate of men like Willie Horton. As Jackson faded into Horton in 1988, the meaning of Ellison's claim that racial typification in America is "a major cause, form, and symbol of the American hierarchical psychosis" (GT, 336) becomes clear. The shape of defeat, disorder, and social chaos in America is a black one—at the ballot box and at the back door.

Throughout the fall campaign, while Bush was holding up Horton's photograph on television, or while reporters were reiterating the details of the crime, or even while the Democrats would object to Bush's "injecting racism" into the campaign (ABC October 23), no network report attempted to make Willie Horton into anything but a symbol of black encroachment on white power and position in America. Horton remained highly visible—the incarnation of white racial fear—but completely invisible as a human being. "When they approach me," according to Ellison's invisible man, "they see only my surroundings, themselves, or figments of their imaginations— indeed, everything and anything except me" (3). Network television "approached" Horton the same way—through his criminal acts, through the Barneses' fears and resentments, through the photographs taken by the police and by themselves. Who was Horton if not a figment, or a symbol, in television's technological imagination? The images of Horton and Jackson would continue to intertwine in 1988. October news reports featured charges of racism by Democrats, and Jackson would be asked to comment. The results of the charges and denials had nothing to do with political issues, of course, but simply accomplished the Republicans' goal: to make household words of Horton and the Barneses—and to link Horton to Jackson and both to Dukakis. By October 30, ABC found newsworthy a letter sent to Maryland voters, shown in full-screen, which asked: "Have you heard of the Dukakis/Willie Horton team?" The question was highlighted on the screen, and the page carried photographs on either side of its text, one of Dukakis and one of Horton. This story followed directly ABC's report that Dukakis had accepted the term "liberal" to describe his political leanings. The same pair of stories was carried by NBC, where Bob Kerr characterized the campaign as a form of "psychological warfare."

A week later the campaign was over. At the end of November, the Black Man who ran was shown on NBC at the White House, invited there by George Bush. According to Andrea Mitchell, "they talked about the Willie Horton issue," and George Bush assured Jackson that "there was no racial intent" (November 30). Intentions, though, are irrelevant. Bush's use of the Horton materials demonstrated that his hand was indeed on the pulse of American society.

Trying to Talk About a Black Person

Blackness and whiteness are, to invoke Ellison's term, untenable. Casting human bodies as black or white with categorical significance leads to unimaginable convolutions of thought. To insist that Jackson is the black candidate implies that the adjective is paramount to his mind and his political identity—as it would be if he were, say, the Communist Party candidate or the anarchist candidate. To insist that he is the black candidate, in other words, makes Jesse Jackson, as a political actor and as an autonomous human being, invisible. However, to *deny* that he is the black candidate is to make his particular heritage invisible. To deny blackness is to erase the fact that it is most certainly significant whether one has black or white skin in America, or whether one is descended from the American slave or slaveholding caste. This is, of course, Ellison's discovery of the essential contradiction of racial categorization. What the contradiction amounts to for the network newscast is a crisis of representation and narration.

Scholars who study narratives have found that the impulse among human beings to tell stories is tied to their need for moral judgment. The demand for "closure," for example, "is a demand . . . for moral meaning." In fact, "in any account of reality, [if] narrativity is present, we can be sure that morality or a moralizing impulse is present too" (White, 20). The story of the Black Man Running, which began in the snow-covered fields of all-white Iowa and ended in the Barneses' white, suburban home, has a profoundly moralistic meaning. According to the television news story extracted here, Jesse Jackson had tried to make himself visible by being *the candidate*—impassioned, determined, claiming to transcend racial categorization. He did become visible, but not on these terms. Plunging into the paradigm of Ellison's invisible man, Jackson was first given an identity by the news*casters*—historic, black, unpredictable. He was then given an identity by his own party—spoiler, extortionist, demander. Finally, he was given an identity that must have astounded even him, despite his experience in American political life. He was given Willie Horton. Bommerang.

The invisibility of either Jackson or Horton without the other is undeniable. They complete, in a sense, a "set" in American racial thinking: the ambitious black man and the criminal black man, the historic pathbreaker and the eternal housebreaker. One man wants white votes and positions of power, and so has to be placated; the other wants white bodies and property, and so must be incarcerated. Both are running—one toward authority and state power, the other away from authority and power—and both achieve visibility when they are "caught": as Black Man Running or as rapist. The confluence of Jackson and Horton was exemplified repeatedly in 1988, but the clearest, and perhaps most inadvertent example came in the interview of Lloyd Bentsen by Dan Rather on CBS Evening News, October 26. In the dialogue between the two very powerful white men, the interchangeability of Jackson and Horton as symbols, their essential symbiotic relationship in the American mind, is unmistakable.

Dan Rather, in the live interview, questions Bentsen closely about the "racist element" in the presidential campaign. Bentsen responds by condemning the use of the Horton materials. According to Bentsen, Lee Atwater's aim was to make Americans "think that Willie Horton is Mike Dukakis's running mate." Dan Rather then asks bluntly, "Senator, yes or no: George Bush, the man, a racist?" To this Bentsen says no, but explains that instead of allowing the inflammatory material to be used, Bush should "root those things out." Specifically, Bush should not allow, according to Bentsen, "this *idea* of using Willie Horton over and over again . . . running the black photograph over and over again. I just think that's not the way to run a campaign." However, Bentsen never says exactly *why* the Horton material is inappropriate, or why Lee Atwater would want to make Horton appear symbolically close to Dukakis. Either the connection is self-evident or so inflammatory as to be unspeakable, unutterable. One function of the contradictions inherent in racial invisibility is that it is simply not possible to "utter" race without invoking racism. Bentsen, at this point, is playing it safe, assuming that "we" know what he's getting at.

Dan Rather, however, will not settle for ambiguity in this interview. The CBS anchor responds by asking whether the charge of Republican racism is not in fact opportunistic. Bentsen vehemently denies this. Then Rather makes the connection already solidly embedded in the "story" of this campaign: It isn't opportunism, Rather concedes, "it's something you feel deeply about. If that's the case, can you tell me how many times, since the Democratic Convention in July, that you appeared on the same podium with Jesse Jackson?" Bentsen was not going to make this connection visible—but Dan Rather, who, along with his colleagues in television journalism, has acted to create the visible story line that "casts" Horton as Jackson's foil. If you do not like the way Bush treats Horton, in other words, tell us first how you have treated Jackson.

Rather's question is not a complete nonsequitur, because the narrative context has been established by the television news. To the objection What does Jesse Jackson have to do with Willie Horton? viewers need only have been watching TV news since June or July. At first, during the primary season, there was only one black national figure in the running, Jesse Jackson, the Democratic wild card. Newscasters did not know what he wanted. By November, a second Democratic liability had emerged, Willie Horton, the rapist. What Horton wanted and what Horton did was made quite clear. To Dan Rather's question, Bentsen stumbles, "Well, I don't know," he says, and says that "next week" he and Jackson are scheduled to meet. Dan Rather then interrupts to get the "story": "I think the point is this: I don't find a single time since the Democratic National Convention that you've appeared" with Jackson in public. By this time, however, Bentsen has regained his composure. His answer signals the ultimate invisibility of Jesse Jackson, Willie Horton, and all Americans cast as "black":

> Well I was— Let's choose what we're talking about here. If you're trying to talk about a black person, I have been with Willie Brown a couple of times. I have been in the black churches. I was leading a rally in a black church in Little Rock the other night. I was doing one in St. Louis the other day, and I'm appearing with Jesse Jackson this week in California, and did a national hook-up with him just last week. (smile)

Bentsen's smile speaks volumes. The man believes that he has scored a victory here, outwitting Dan Rather's aggressive questioning. The logic of the exchange (which ends here; after this response, Rather asks about Dan Quayle) corresponds to the logic of Jackson's story on television news in 1988 or the logic of invisibility. George Bush is using racist tactics, says Bentsen, because he wants to link Dukakis with the evil black man, Willie Horton. But how about you? counters Rather. If Horton is really Jackson, how do you get along with him? Well, answers Bentsen, if you mean to talk about black people, I get on with them just fine. Willie Brown, Willie Horton, Jesse Jackson, black congregations, *any black person*—it doesn't make any difference (smile).

And this, finally, is the moral of the story, Run, Jesse, run! But don't think you will ever be free of your illusions. White Americans, after all, hold you as among theirs. When the news is cast on the nightly frequencies of television, the Black Man Running "seems rather to exist," to borrow Ralph Ellison's formula, "in a nightmarish fantasy of the white American mind as a phantom" (*S&A*, 304). But perhaps no American racial illusion is more cherished than that of the angry figment, Willie Horton, certainly akin to "one of the most irresponsible beings that ever lived" (*Invisible Man*, 14) who stalks white fears of home and body. The final illusion, though, is that Jesse, Willie, and every black person in the television story is one and the same. And when this black illusion bumps against any of its white counterparts, in the polls or in suburbia, average Americans or national political candidates, all of them become white victims. The contrast, as the story goes, is America's racial problem: black faces against the white backdrop of Iowa in January, American civilization, invisible and murderous. At the end of *Invisible Man*, Ellison's narrator acknowledged that some will find his "rave" about his invisibility so much "buggy jiving" (581). Perhaps equally so these ravings of the Horton/Jackson displacement. What is an invisible man and who are an invisible people? With Jesse Jackson at the door of power in American politics, the mirrors that project his invisibility cast Willie Horton as the intruder. This buggy jive entered the television frequencies in 1988 and made legitimate once again the untenable American belief in racial autonomy as something of unutterable cultural and political significance.

WORKS CITED

Adams, C. L. *Tales of the Congaree.* Edited by Robert G. O'Meally. Chapel Hill: University of North Carolina Press, 1987.

Atheide, David L. *Creating Reality: How TV News Distorts Events.* Beverly Hills, Calif.: Sage, 1974.

Arterton, F. Christopher. *Media Politics: The News Strategies of Presidential Campaigns.* Lexington, Mass.: D. C. Heath, 1984.

Cohen, Akiba A. *The Television News Interview.* The Sage CommText Series. Vol. 18. Newbury Park, Calif.: Sage, 1987.

Ellison, Ralph. *Going to the Territory.* New York: Vintage, 1988.

———. *Invisible Man.* New York: Vintage, 1952, 1989.

———. *Shadow and Act.* New York: Vintage, 1964, 1972.

Gans, Herbert J. *Deciding What's News: A Study of CBS Evening News, NBC Nightly News, Newsweek, and Time.* New York: Pantheon, 1979.

Graber, Doris A. *Mass Media and American Politics.* 2d ed. Washington D.C.: Congressional Quarterly Press, 1984.

Hallin, Daniel C. "The American News Media: A Critical Theory Perspective." In *Critical Theory and Public Life,* edited by John Forester, 121–46. Cambridge, Mass.: MIT Press, 1985.

Hofstetter, C. Richard. *Bias in the News: Network Television Coverage of the 1972 Election Campaign.* Columbus: Ohio State University Press, 1976.

Iyengar, Shanto, and Donald R. Kinder. *News that Matters: Television and American Opinion.* Chicago: University of Chicago Press, 1987.

Jackson, Jesse L. *Straight from the Heart.* Philadelphia: Fortress Press, 1987.

Kinder, Donald R., and David O. Sears. "Prejudice and Politics: Symbolic Racism vs. Racial Threats to the Good Life." *Journal of Personality and Social Psychology* 40, No. 3 (1981): 414–31.

Patterson, Thomas E. *The Mass Media Election: How Americans Choose Their President.* New York: Praeger, 1976.

Patterson, Thomas E., and Robert D. McClure. *The Unseeing Eye: The Myth of Television Power in National Politics.* New York: G. P. Putnam's Sons, 1976.

Randall, Dudley, ed. *The Black Poets.* New York: Bantam, 1971.

Reed, Adolph L., Jr. *The Jesse Jackson Phenomenon: The Crisis of Purpose in Afro-American Politics.* New Haven: Yale University Press, 1986.

Sperry, Sharon Lynn. "Television News as Narrative." In *Understanding Television: Essays on TV as a Social and Cultural Force,* edited by Richard P. Adler, 295–312. New York: Praeger, 1981.

Tuchman, Gaye. "Objectivity as Strategic Ritual: An Examination of Newsmen's Notions of Objectivity." *American Journal of Sociology* 77, No. 4 (January 1972): 660–79.

Vanderbilt University Television News Archive, Nashville, Tenn.

Weaver, Paul H. "Is Television News Biased?" *Public Interest* 26 (Winter 1972): 57–74.

Walton, Anthony. "Willie Horton and Me." *New York Times Magazine* (August 20, 1989): 52–53, 77.

White, Hayden. "The Value of Narrativity in the Representation of Reality." In *On Narrative,* edited by W. J. T. Mitchell, 1–24. Chicago: University of Chicago Press, 1981.

Wilson, Clint C., and Felix Gutierrez. *Minorities and Media: Diversity and the End of Mass Communication.* Beverly Hills, Calif.: Sage Publications, 1985.

II THE SEXUAL SELF

CHAPTER 3

Sanctuary and the

Pornographic Nexus

Now I can stand anything,
she thought quietly, with a
kind of dull, spent
astonishment; I can stand
just anything.
—*Faulkner,* Sanctuary

Pornographic Culture

Pornography is a myth of power: It establishes a degree of control over one's sexual universe not inherently or naturally existent. It brings human love and its physical expressions, secretions, and demands under intellectual control, submitting the erotic compulsions of the body to a system of authority and order. It places eros, as the Rolling Stones sing it, "under my thumb." Susan Griffin, in her study of pornographic structures in Western culture, asserts that "eros does not accept the order of the world which the ego needs to believe. And it is for this reason," Griffin concludes, "that erotic knowledge is dangerous to culture" (261). As cultural products, human beings are hierarchically ordered, socially defined, and authoritatively placed. As erotic products, human beings are anarchic, fluid, and continually self-displaced. As if recognizing the threat to its own need for order and definition represented by sexuality, culture acts to provide the anarchic compulsions of the body a set of guidelines and structures. These guidelines and structures are known by the euphemisms "socially acceptable," "decency," "decorum," and so on. By these guidelines and structures a degree of power and control is established by culture over the body. However, as power corrupts, throughout history cultural power is recognized more by its abuses than by its abdications. The French Revolution had its Terror, the American revolutionists had their slaves. What is commonly known as "pornography" in the popular mind is simply the abuse of a cultural system of power over physicality—of control over the body. We recognize as pornographic those points at which cultural productions, or cultural representations, go "too far" in their assertions of bodily submission to authority and domination.

The very effort to control or make systematic the sexual dimension of the self provides entry into the notion that the self cannot be objectified. Carole Vance argues that "sexuality may be a particularly unpromising domain for regulation" in human affairs simply because sexuality has no objective existence. It "remains fluid and everchanging," according to Vance, "flexible, anarchic, ambiguous, layered with multiple meanings" and resistant to adult, social ideas about order and control. "The connection of both sexual pleasures and fantasy to infancy, the irrational, the unconscious is a source of both surprise and pleasure" (22). It is also a source of discomfort and fear for those who seek adult order in every aspect of their lives. When people talk about sex, the level of discourse immediately changes and resembles the talk of children, flipping from seriousness to fantasy and metaphor, evasion, and embarrassment. When people engage in sexual activity, they risk the loss of their cultural sense of objective existence. As Muriel Dimen explains, the sexual dimension of human existence "lies between things" and is "intrinsically ambiguous. . . . Sexual experience entails loss of self-other boundaries, the endless opening of doors to more unknown inner spaces, confusions about what to do next, or who the other person is . . . or where one person begins and another ends. This is sometimes painful, always unsettling" (144–45). It is especially painful and unsettling to a culture intent on the fixed categorization of bodies.

Sexuality evokes the child within the self—the child that knows something about itself other than a specific, nuclear existence and believes it is "connected" to its environment and to the people it depends upon for love and sustenance. The child must be taught or socialized into believing that boundaries exist between it and those it is drawn to. Everything Carole Vance says about sexuality places it in opposition to an understanding of the self as an object readily identified and categorized. Sexuality, then, must be "controlled" so that its anarchic, fluid essence does not overrun cultural representations and definitions of human existence. If Dimen's notion that sexuality threatens "self-other boundaries" concerning "where one person begins and another ends" is accurate, then the culture that objectifies persons, that defines them as beginning and ending within camera-ready borders, must provide extraordinary resources to counter the sexual with its own structures of order.

In his 1932 novel, *Sanctuary,* William Faulkner examines sexuality in American culture in the notorious novel about rape, abduction, prostitution, sexual fantasy—and, in particular, in the creation of Temple Drake and Popeye Vitelli. Temple Drake is, to borrow from Ralph Ellison, an invisible woman: a phantasm with no subjectivity, no autonomous, perceived self. She is a *seen* object, visible as "coed" or "jelly" to the town boys outside the college and to Gowan Stevens, as "whore" to Popeye, and, finally, as "daughter" to the courtroom jury, but she is never allowed to represent herself. The narrator of *Sanctuary* often describes her as a young animal, sexually vital and in constant danger. Margaret Miles has explained the social function of such representations, which is "to stabilize assumptions and expectations relating to the objects or persons represented." According to Miles, an art historian, "Consistent, cumulative, and continuous representations of an object cause that object to 'disappear' in its complex and perhaps contradictory 'reality,' subsumed in [the orderliness] of the standardized representation" (10). This is precisely what Faulkner demonstrates with Temple Drake. She is made invisible by acting in complicity with a culture that encourages her to become a phantasm—a sexual fantasy in this case—by cultivating the arts of "glamour" and of physical attraction (her "scant dress" and "painted mouth"). Having once mastered the arts of sexual seduction, Temple also becomes vulnerable to rape and, as a consequence, develops a "need" for the protection of the same men who represent a source of danger to her. In the opening scene to *Sanctuary* two men stare belligerently across a spring at one another. One carries a book and is a lawyer; he will be Temple Drake's ineffectual protector. The other carries a gun and is a bootlegger; he will become her (ineffectual?) sexual violator. At the end of the scene, the two men walk together to the farmhouse where Temple's ordeal will eventually take place, having completed their standoff in a draw.

Griffin characterizes Western culture as existing in an adversarial relation to the body. In Griffin's scheme, the culture, in its dominant expressions and representations, is "pitted against the body" for its survival. In pornography we witness this cultural agenda at its most base and least subtle. The adversarial relation between body and culture can be understood—and is often understood in cultural productions—as identical to the adversarial relation between females and males within the culture. In this schema, "culture" is a male domain (as males wield power and are responsible, in preponderant degree, for the production and maintenance of cultural forms and structures), and "the body" is a female domain (as female beauty and physicality are privileged, displayed, and considered emblematic of cultural value, and propagation). However, in this schema the female symbolic function is problematic—for while it is privileged and displayed, it must also be controlled and dominated. The male-symbolic function is equally problematic. The culturally dominant, pornographic, and primarily male consciousness must exclude from itself that part of the total human experience "which pornography calls 'feminine.'" And according to Griffin, what is symptomatic of pornography is "precisely what society in reality does" (55, 660). The effect of this schema is to produce sensually crippled human beings, or human beings whose sensuality is severely handicapped by their culture. The pornographic self identifies its sexuality solely by its physical gender—by its genitalia—and not by the intersubjective wholeness of the erotic dimension of human existence. Males who suppress the feminine elements in their consciousness and females who are compelled to fear the masculine element in theirs are the casualties of a cultural system of pornographic sexual exclusiveness.

The binary opposition characteristic of pornography, where female equals bodily pleasure and male equals cultural control, is an unnatural one, in Griffin's analysis. Because bodily pleasure is anarchic, disruptive, and disorderly, its expressions are fiercely controlled and regulated to secure a productive and hierarchial social order. The result, however, is a twofold damage to human beings. First, as a result of the binary equations, the female in Western culture is suppressed as the embodiment of disruptive eros; second, as a result of this suppression, complete bodily knowledge is prohibited to males in Western culture. Pornography, then, acts to assert the conscious, rational power of culture over the sensual, irrational compulsions of erotic existence. The result is a schism of self-understanding, introducing tension and ambivalence to what should, by any logic, be among the body's most natural functions. "For to choose to follow out the separation of consciousness from sexuality, of culture from nature, or of self from self, is quite simply to choose death" (Griffin, 231). The death chosen is the death of the sensual self, the choice idol of the hyperconscious, rational, controlled self—the triumphant Western mind.

The myth system of pornography, then, is no aberration in Western culture, but rather exists as a distillation—or a popular expression—of the underlying logic of the culture as a whole. Western culture, for example, has been historically patriarchal and dependent to an extraordinary degree upon the authority and performances of its male component. Politically, culturally, economically, in all facets of living, males are placed under more pressure to succeed than females—and as a result, their successes are privileged above those of females. In popular sexual parlance, the language of masculine potency, penetration, and performance exist as synecdoches, or emblems, for the more inclusive role of males in the culture at large. In the power mythology of pornography, a great deal of attention is given to the display of powerful and sexually capable males, serving, logically, a compensatory function for fears of poor performance, general failures, and the like. As with any expression of power, however, the underside of this mythology is ugly. There is a point at which compensation for masculine anxiety becomes degrading to its represented objects, and pornography thrives by the trademark of its excesses. It is the point at which fantasies of sexual power take the form of violence, usually sexual violence against women (or against "unmasculine" men) that pornography is recognized as a cultural expression of evil.

Feminist critics of pornography condemn the entire genre as, in Laura Lederer's terms, "the ideology of a culture which promotes and condones rape, women battering, and other crimes of violence against women" (19). Andrea Dworkin, recognizing that terrorism is the nuclear era's chief expression of power, has judged that terrorizing women is the essential characteristic and purpose of pornography, with the male playing the role of the terrorist. "He chooses how much to terrorize, whether terror will be a dalliance or an obsession, whether he will use it brutally or subtly" (16). Nearly all feminist comment on pornography identifies the male's subject status, and the female's object status, as reflective of cultural power structures. Susan Brownmiller examines the reductive roles assigned to women in pornographic story lines, the standard plots that turn virgins into nymphomaniacs (394). Susanne Kappeler, following the logic of feminist criticism in the 1970s and 1980s, has concluded that this subject/object division provides pornography its ideological and narrative core. She examines "the view that human status equals male status" in pornographic logic, "and it is natural to see the status of women as a form of dehumanization" (153).

To be fully human in Western culture, Kappeler argues, is to achieve "subject status," whether one is male or female. Subject status demands, for its achievement, "supremacy over another, not intersubjectivity." In Western culture, males and females are encouraged by social structures to share the will to become full subjects: to achieve a degree of power over others, who are understood as the objects of one's power and selfhood. Subject status is achieved through competitive interaction with others and through the abandonment of intersubjective models of human interaction. The degree to which one abandons intersubjectivity, in this cultural system, is the degree to which one is powerful and fully human.

Pornography is a bald, popular expression of the cultural imperative that suggests that power, pleasure, and "the feeling of life" are located in authority, performance, and domination—in full, independent subject status. Gender relations, according to Kappeler, form the basis of all power relations in the culture. A man's understanding of these relations "is at the very bottom of his understanding of himself, it informs his understanding and organization of society, and it informs his semantics, his symbolism of it" (154). Women who achieve power in the culture either identify wholly with the male subject, remaking themselves in the masculine image, or face continual reprisal in the form of silencing, ridicule, and other means of cultural abuse. Men who refuse subject status or insist upon intersubjective alternatives are assigned object roles of powerlessness and cultural exclusion.

Kappeler's intersubjectivity, Griffin's erotic knowledge, Dworkin's terrorist paradigm, Vance's paradox of the "pleasure and danger" of female sexuality—all these studies of pornographic structures and scenarios present pornography as an authoritarian expression of power and control. Against this agenda of pornography stands an alternative that is silenced or suppressed. Intersubjectivity, eroticism, or anarchic, undefined relations between the genders or within any one gender, or among persons in general, is antithetical to pornography, and antithetical to the culture as a whole. Ambiguity, ambivalence, and intersubjective models of knowledge are considered lesser or inferior modes of consciousness in a culture that rewards authority and order. Precision of thought, seemingly valuable in itself, becomes a source of danger when used as a model for physical precision, or when used to compel precision, definition, and accountability in the habits or compulsion of physical life. Dominic LaCapra identifies the analytic method itself, which "provides clear and distinct ideas which define boundaries and confine ambiguity" as the root of oppressive power structures. When the "polar opposites or dichotomies" of analytical thought are mistaken for the "conditions of knowledge and projected onto the world as defining separate disciplinary or life activities," LaCapra argues, they take on "the operation of a logic of surveillance and control if not domination" (152).

The subject/object structure of pornography, then, reflects a larger, cultural structure of binary oppositions that inform Western analytical thought and which then, in turn but not inevitably, inform Western culture's social arrangements. Adding to the alternatives of intersubjectivity and erotic knowledge discussed above, LaCapra suggests the alternative of "an open or unfinished dialectic." LaCapra identifies this unfinished dialectic with Derrida's logic of supplementarity. This alternative, according to LaCapra, "attempts to think through dichotomies and double binds and to prefigure a more creative interplay among aspects of the world." Nonetheless, power is power in the world, and "creative interplay"—like intersubjectivity and erotic knowledge—"recognizes that structures of domination may always be regenerated, and thus insists upon the role of recurrent critique" (153). The price of any such alternatives to culturally hegemonic practices has always been, it seems, eternal vigilance.

In all thinking about "dichotomies," or about "binary oppositions," the thinker is confronted with the validity of the one opposition that seems to be fixed and irrefutable: that of sexuality. If male and female are eternally separate, then from what natural phenomenon can we take the idea of intersubjectivity as a viable model for critical thought? The answer is to question the validity of the sexual divide. It may be that, while the male and female genitalia are naturally distinguishable at birth, nothing that follows, nothing that goes by the name of masculinity or femininity, can be so readily and "naturally" distinguished.

The Feminist IX Conference, "Toward a Politics of Sexuality," held at Barnard College in 1982 issued the following statement in a concept paper, which articulates the objection to ideas about the natural in connection to the sexual:

> Feminist work on sexuality starts from the premise sex is a social construction which articulates at many points within economic, social, and political structures of the material world. Sex is not simply a "natural" fact. Although we can name specific physical actions (heterosexual or homosexual intercourse, masturbation) which occurred at various times and places, it is clear that the social and personal meaning attached to these acts in terms of sexual identity and sexual community has varied historically.

From this observation comes the conference participants' stress on "the historical and cultural construction of sexuality. Without denying the body, we note the body and its actions are understood according to prevailing codes of meaning" (Vance, 444).

The conference position does not contradict Griffin's idea that there is something "natural" about sexuality, which culture oppresses, but sharply refines it. Whatever is natural in the sexual dimension of existence is only known, or communicated, on cultural grounds. The conference position here is of a piece with the overall postmodern questioning of the "natural" as a sphere somehow immune to critical analysis. For centuries, the claim that something was natural meant that it was beyond reproach or irrefutable. Lawrence Buell has found that, in American letters, images of nature have always been employed to express alienation. However, the same representation, such as the one figured in a "retreat to nature," can mean a number of contradictory things. A pastoral retreat may be "a means of expressing alienation," or it may be "a means by which alienation is mediated" (19, 23). In essence, then, nature means nothing naturally—but it can mean anything culturally. Cecelia Tichi has found that, at the turn of the twentieth century, cultural changes in the workplace—new technologies and new machinery, for example—resulted in an altered perspective on "the natural." Writers at the turn of the century began to employ machine-age metaphors to describe nature, mixing "American flora and fauna with pistons and gears and engines" and blurring "the perceptual boundary between what is considered to be natural, and what is technological." And as for the human body, Tichi observes, "the language of the automotive machine was appropriate" in order to describe the inner workings of the body as made of parts, power levers, cylinders, and so forth (34–35). Today such images may sound quaint, but only because they have been supplanted by figurations more "appropriate" to the present era, such as erotic "zones," physical "systems" and "syndromes," and the like.

As a result of postmodern examinations of the cultural uses of natural space, sexuality has been provided a historical dimension of its own, and sex has become recognized as a constructed phenomenon rather than a natural dimension of life. As Gayle Rubin points out, "human sexuality is not comprehensible in purely biological terms. . . . The body, the brain, the genitalia, and the capacity for language are all necessary for human sexuality." The institutional forms of sexuality, the language used to express and comprehend it, and the outlets available to it, are cultural. "Moreover," Rubin concludes, "we never encounter the body unmediated by the meanings that cultures give to it" (276–77). It seems, then, that idea of "human nature" as something fixed and eternal is now archaic. Louis Mink has argued that historians must abandon the idea that "human nature . . . is everywhere the same" and so must abandon the use of objective standards of historical assessment. It is clear to Mink that "human nature is infinitely various and self-created" and that there is no such thing as a universal, natural self that can be fixed or formulated as a point of reliable historical reference (104).

If there is a human nature, then, it is an anarchic phenomenon, and nothing definitive can be said about it. Any attempts to corral it or categorize it, to objectify it or make it visible, inevitably put the mind on the path to pornographic representations. The view that "the natural" is beyond control and beyond objective representation, that "sexuality" is opposed to all efforts to understand or delimit its functional expression or reception, places all efforts to depict the sexual as *meaning* something under suspicion. Any use of sexuality to communicate a power relation, to sell an automobile, or to accomplish anything—even the pleasure of the viewer—must be understood as pornographic if "pornography" is to be a matter of ideology and not simple preference. "No matter how sex is played out or with what gender," in other words, "Power is the heart, not just the beast, of all sexual inquiry" (Hollibough, 406). The way in which we depict sexuality—the way we talk about it, the way we "get it" or "give it"—reveals more about political relations than anything having to do with orgasm. Even the current demands for "safe sex" transcend the AIDS epidemic and can be understood as symptomatic of cultural anxieties over the disappearance of private space. In a consumer social organization, of course, one would need cultural protection or a product—the condom—in order to have sex "safely."

Radical opponents of pornography, along with serious critics of all cultural forms of domination and oppression, find themselves thus wholly outside the main structures of social interaction and exchange. Starting with a condemnation of pornographic exploitation, with the sense that something is *wrong* with the images and plotlines of pornography, the critic of pornography follows a path to a radical critique of the culture as a whole—from its structures of power, control, and achievement to its mode of thought and critical analysis. The conclusion that pornography is no isolated or perverse form of sexual expression but is in fact a *characteristic* articulation of cultural paradigms—that it represents not the culture's refuse but the very sustenance upon which the culture thrives—is no assimilable position. Rather, it is as antisocial, upsetting, and disruptive as is, according to Griffin, erotic knowledge itself. It produces an ambivalence toward the culture as profound as that which characterized Ellison's *Invisible Man*—it is, in fact, the ambivalence of the slave. Some recognition of this ambivalence must account for much of the anger and frustration that characterizes analyses of pornography and discussions of pornography in the popular media. It certainly accounts for the anger and frustration at the heart of the single most effective literary treatment of pornographic structures of thought and action, William Faulkner's *Sanctuary*.

Opponents of pornography are varied and often act at cross-purposes. Those who consider the form solely as a perverse genre, solely as a form of sexual representation, seek only to control and limit its dissemination and availability—a particularly revealing response from a culture that has as its purpose control, order, and limitation. Advocates of limited availability would certainly find the analyses of Griffin, Kappeler, or Dworkin excessive, identifying in these radical critiques of sexual representation the same degree of danger to their own position that the radicals themselves find in pornography. The battle lines within the antipornography camp cease to divide simply and neatly over sexual representation, then, and come to demarcate a sexual dialectic of cultural defense and cultural revolution, with each position recognizing in the other the root of social, if not human evil. Against either side of the division, of course, stand the defenders of pornography—but who are *they*?

The question of defining what is and what is not pornography ultimately becomes an issue of interpretation—an aesthetic issue. And, as with all aesthetic issues, the definition owes as much to the interpretive method employed as it does to the problematic text or image in question. And furthermore, interpretive and aesthetic issues are, ultimately, revealed as power issues—dependent upon subtextual (or extratextual) issues such as who is funded, who is published, who decides, determines, and interprets. William Faulkner's *Sanctuary* serves as the focal point for a host of problems in pornographic representation, problems that continue to generate critical interest in the novel. What Faulkner accomplishes in *Sanctuary* is neither a clear denunciation of pornography nor any sort of defense of pornographic sexuality. Rather, the novel may be situated at the intersection of main lines of thinking about pornographic representation.

Pleasure and Danger

The narrative in *Sanctuary* is an angry one—as cold, mechanical, and distant as is characteristic of any pornographic text. Similarly, the representations of human beings that appear in the text are often degrading, mechanical, and, in Faulkner's word, "cheap." In an Introduction to the novel, Faulkner himself expressed anger toward the novel, referring to its premise as "a cheap idea" and to its plot as a "horrific tale" (*Sanctuary*, 337, 338). Nonetheless, prior to the literary canonization of Faulkner following his Nobel Prize, *Sanctuary* was the only Faulkner title that consistently sold in the mass market. In 1948, when most of Faulkner's novels were out of print, the New American Library paperback edition of *Sanctuary* sold 470,000 copies; by 1954 it had gone through thirteen printings and sold over 1 million copies (Schwartz, 58). Hence, when Faulkner received the Nobel Prize for literature in 1950, the popular reading public in America knew him primarily as the "corncob man" who had written *Sanctuary*. This reputation was the direct result of the way in which his books had been marketed.

The Signet Giant combined edition of *Sanctuary* and *Requiem for*

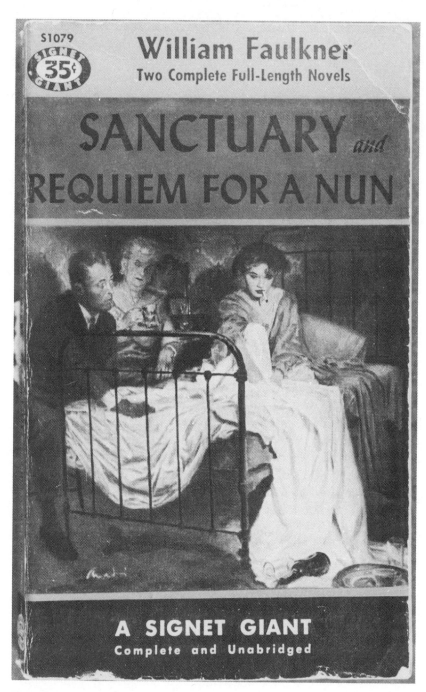

Figure 3.1

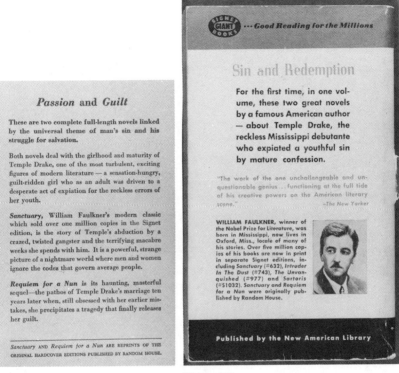

Passion and *Guilt*

These are two complete full-length novels linked by the universal theme of man's sin and his struggle for salvation.

Both novels deal with the girlhood and maturity of Temple Drake, one of the most turbulent, exciting figures of modern literature — a sensation-hungry, guilt-ridden girl who as an adult was driven to a desperate act of expiation for the reckless errors of her youth.

Sanctuary, William Faulkner's modern classic which sold over one million copies in the Signet edition, is the story of Temple's abduction by a crazed, twisted gangster and the terrifying macabre weeks she spends with him. It is a powerful, strange picture of a nightmare world where men and women ignore the codes that govern average people.

Requiem for a Nun is its haunting, masterful sequel—the pathos of Temple Drake's marriage ten years later when, still obsessed with her earlier mistakes, she precipitates a tragedy that finally releases her guilt.

Sanctuary AND *Requiem for a Nun* ARE REPRINTS OF THE ORIGINAL HARDCOVER EDITIONS PUBLISHED BY RANDOM HOUSE.

SIGNET GIANT BOOKS ···*Good Reading for the Millions*

Sin and Redemption

For the first time, in one volume, these two great novels by a famous American author — about Temple Drake, the reckless Mississippi debutante who expiated a youthful sin by mature confession.

"The work of the one unchallengeable and unquestionable genius ... functioning at the full tide of his creative powers on the American literary scene."
—*The New Yorker*

WILLIAM FAULKNER, winner of the Nobel Prize for Literature, was born in Mississippi, now lives in Oxford, Miss., locale of many of his stories. Over five million copies of his books are now in print in separate Signet editions, including *Sanctuary* (#632), *Intruder In The Dust* (#743), *The Unvanquished* (#977) and *Sartoris* (#S1032). *Sanctuary* and *Requiem for a Nun* were originally published by Random House.

Published by the New American Library

Figure 3.2   Figure 3.3

a Nun, published in 1954 and reprinted into the 1960s, describes "William Faulkner's modern classic" as a story of "abduction"—"a powerful, strange picture of a nightmare world where men and women ignore the codes that govern average people" (Figures 3.1–3.3). Actually, as it turns out, men and women, in *Sanctuary*, obey the "codes" of social and sexual interaction only too strictly. The fourth printing, in 1961, features scenes from the film version of *Sanctuary* on the cover (Figure 3.4), and describes Temple Drake as "the sensation-seeking debutante who courts horror through her reckless passion" (Figure 3.5). Schwartz, in his study of Faulkner's critical repu-

Sanctuary and the Pornographic Nexus   89

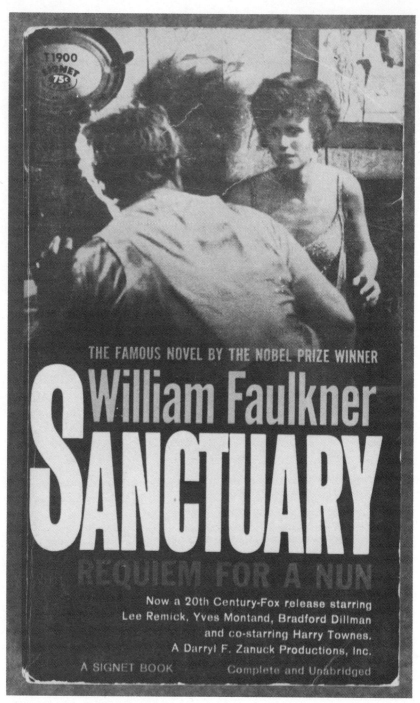

Figure 3.4

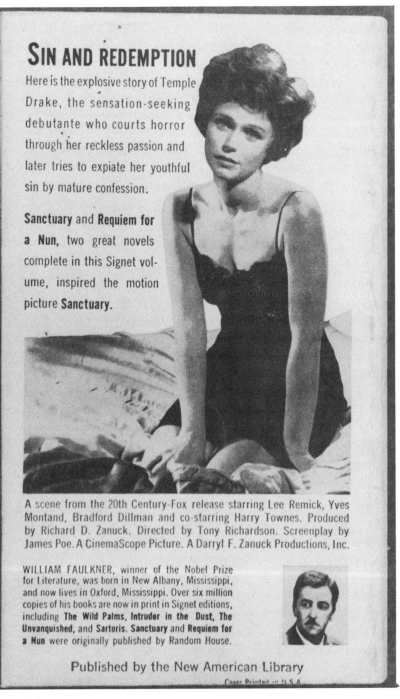

SIN AND REDEMPTION

Here is the explosive story of Temple Drake, the sensation-seeking debutante who courts horror through her reckless passion and later tries to expiate her youthful sin by mature confession.

Sanctuary and **Requiem for a Nun,** two great novels complete in this Signet volume, inspired the motion picture **Sanctuary.**

A scene from the 20th Century-Fox release starring Lee Remick, Yves Montand, Bradford Dillman and co-starring Harry Townes. Produced by Richard D. Zanuck. Directed by Tony Richardson. Screenplay by James Poe. A CinemaScope Picture. A Darryl F. Zanuck Productions, Inc.

WILLIAM FAULKNER, winner of the Nobel Prize for Literature, was born in New Albany, Mississippi, and now lives in Oxford, Mississippi. Over six million copies of his books are now in print in Signet editions, including **The Wild Palms, Intruder in the Dust, The Unvanquished,** and Sartoris. Sanctuary and **Requiem for a Nun** were originally published by Random House.

Published by the New American Library

Cover Printed in U.S.A.

Figure 3.5

tation, speculates that Faulkner was perhaps uncomfortable with the novel's notoriety, regretful that he would be known best for the sensationalism in *Sanctuary* rather than for its whole textual program (58).

The question remains, nonetheless, whether or to what extent *Sanctuary* is a pornographic work. There is no question of its sexual content, its sensationalism. It contains representations of voyeurism, sexual violence and aggression, fetishism, nymphomania, misogyny, and emasculation. The central female character in the novel is raped, becomes a nymphomaniac and later an avenger. The central male character has rape fantasies and uncontrollable physical desires for his step-daughter, and is psychically abused by his wife. Elizabeth Muhlenfeld's description of Temple Drake places the character squarely in a culturally pornographic mode of female consciousness. "Temple exists in a world which has offered her no opportunities to develop anything but her physical beauty," according to Muhlenfeld, "which has given her no glimpse of any concerns of her own, and which has, in short, effectively prevented her from growing up and discovering her own humanity" (46). Muhlenfeld argues persuasively that Temple's training thus leaves her incapable of coping with the events of the novel, with what happens to her. However, on a critical level, Temple discovers in *Sanctuary* that she has been prepared only too well for what happens to her. She has been trained and bred to participate, with self-effacing enthusiasm, in a pornographic system of sexuality. The disturbing quality of *Sanctuary* is not that its contents are pornographic—which they certainly are—but that it situates its pornographic content contextually within the dominant cultural system of sexual behavior, within the "codes that govern average people."

The characterization of Temple Drake by Faulkner illustrates the thematic core of the Feminist IX Conference, or "Pleasure and Danger." In her introduction to the published papers of the conference, Carole Vance states that "we admit that it is not safe to be a woman, and it never has been. Female attempts to claim pleasure are especially dangerous, attacked not only by men, but by women as well" (24). Faulkner's exploration of Temple Drake's sexuality places her squarely within the nexus of pleasure and danger. The novel repeatedly depicts her in danger, and her terrors are all related to her adolescent desire for pleasure and excitement. Female sexualization itself is marked by the initiation of the girl into the cultural nexus of pleasure and danger: The pleasures of sexuality are balanced with the dangers of pregnancy; the thrill of attraction is accompanied by the terror of rape. Male sexualization centers more on abstract ideas about responsibility and restraint: The pleasures of sexuality and the thrill of attraction are balanced by the "danger" of obligation and indebtedness—but not of actual physical harm. The issue of sexual power is made clear by the discrete means by which boys and girls are sexualized or made into culturally sexual beings.

Over the years, *Sanctuary* has been considered pornographic by those whose business it is to form such opinions. In the late 1940s, the New American Library paperback editions of *Sanctuary* attracted the attention of state antipornography interests. In 1948, *Sanctuary* was seized by an agent for Philadelphia's chief inspector of the vice squad, and booksellers were brought to court for selling obscene materials. In 1949, Judge Curtis Bok dismissed the indictments against the booksellers, ruling that *Sanctuary* was among those works that made "an obvious effort to show life as it was." Nonetheless, five years later the book was placed on the National Organization of Decent Literature's (NODL's) "disapproved list." It has since been banned on various occasions by local antismut groups (Haight, 77).

Sanctuary probably belongs on a list of culturally "disapproved" texts—but not for reasons shared by the NODL. While it is true that *Sanctuary* is indecent, its assault is not on the particular "decencies" of the moral order, but on the moral order itself. *Sanctuary* is a confrontation with pornographic images and pornographic conventions that ultimately undermines and defuses their legitimacy in the moral order. Narrative situations and events in *Sanctuary* bring to mind pornographic images and stories. However, each time a particular image is suggested, Faulkner uses it to confront rather than support pornographic ideology. The most obvious example of this strategy is in the character of Popeye, the impotent rapist. Identifying himself solely by a pornographic image of power and control, Popeye attempts to live out a pornographic fantasy with Temple Drake.

Popeye Vitelli, as Faulkner presents him, is wholly artificial, a cultural embodiment of male representational sexuality. The man rapes Temple with a corncob and carries her off to a pornographic wonderland filled with whores, jewelry, fancy clothes, fast cars, and even a stud. Faulkner, emphasizing Popeye's commodity status, describes him as lifeless: "His face had a queer, bloodless color" and "he had that vicious, depthless quality of stamped tin" (4). But Popeye is a self-made man who has successfully defied his nature, which was, originally, to remain presexual throughout his adult life. At five years old, Popeye's doctor predicted that "he will never be a man, properly speaking. With care, he will live some time longer. But he will never be any older than he is now" (323–24). However, by the use of cultural products and manufactured talismans—the guns, the tight black suits, the car, the Prohibition whiskey enterprise— Popeye becomes a man despite himself; at least, he becomes the societal image of manhood. Popeye Vitelli becomes a notorious Memphis gangster known in at least two states for his violence and criminality. His concern for his image obsesses him up until the last moments of his life, when he asks the hangman to fix his mussed hair before executing him. Faulkner's Popeye is not the study of a character; it is the examination of a commodified, artificial cultural image, a caricature of masculinity taken from detective magazines, pulp fiction, and other masculinity manuals.

When Popeye kidnaps Temple, he attempts to turn image into reality and live, with his flesh, the self-made caricature of manhood as if it were natural and alive. But it does not take Temple long to learn Popeye's "secret"—that he does not possess what culture calls sexual potency: "You couldn't fool me but once, could you?" she taunts (244). At once, Temple becomes a double-edged prize for Popeye. She is both symbolic of his masculine dominance—the capture of the Virgin—and symbolic of his ultimate fraudulence. Temple herself is no fraud, even if she is confused, but is a living, sexually adventurous and curious, feminine human being. As such, this woman must be "silenced," to borrow Griffin's idea of the silencing of eros by culture, and held in muted captive submission to the artificial powers of Popeye, that cultural creation. "Shut it," Popeye repeats to Temple after his assault on her and in response to her complaints about the bleeding and her discomfort. "Stop it now. You going to shut it?" (144).

Temple represents pure sexual potentiality in *Sanctuary*. Sally Page sees Temple's life as entirely "oriented toward sexual promiscuity" on the one hand, but on the other hand taught "to fear, above all else, rape by men outside her social group" (78). But Temple does not possess a definite sexual personality at any point in the novel.

Rather, she adapts, or attempts to fit herself into the demands and expectations of her environment—whether it is the collegiate social scene or Beale Street's perverse society of prostitution and whiskey. Only at Goodwin's farmhouse is she a confused and frantic actor, because there is no prescribed attitude or role for a seventeen-year-old girl among the "crimps and spungs and feebs" at Goodwin's. In fact, her presence throws everyone else's status into question and disrupts the entire precarious social alignment among the bootleggers. Temple knows at once the danger she is in at Goodwin's and does everything she knows how to do to get Gowan to take her away.

When she is terrorized, Temple thinks primarily of images she associates with order, civility, and authority. While hiding in the kitchen, Faulkner says she thinks "of the school, the lighted window, the slow couples strolling toward the sound of the supper bell, and of her father sitting on the porch at home, his feet on the rail, watching a Negro mow the lawn" (54). Similarly, Temple thinks about "the girls and men leaving the dormitories in their new spring clothes, strolling along the shaded streets toward the cool, unhurried sound of bells" as she awakes from her sleep in the barn crib (92). Back home, and at school, pornographic structures of sexuality are contextualized within a larger, inclusive cultural order where Negro men tend judges' lawns, and where "girls and men" alike stroll with a confident and secure sense of place. At Goodwin's the context of order and propriety is removed, and everyone goes "too far" in their prescribed roles, girls and men included. At Goodwin's, among the bootleggers, culturally defined sexuality is distilled to its pornographic essence, separated from its civil refinement. In the face of the disappearance of the rules and expectations of sexual interplay associated with polite society, Temple is reduced to a frightened, panic-stricken animal who no longer can trust in the rules mitigating the danger she is in as a woman. When she gets to Reba's whorehouse, she has an immediate affinity with Reba's two terrorized little dogs. "Oh," she says when she learns of their mistreatment. "No wonder they're scared" (162). Faulkner provides this image:

Beneath the bed the dogs made no sound. Temple moved slightly; the dry complaint of mattress and springs died into the terrific silence in which they crouched. She thought of them, woolly, shapeless; savage, petulant, spoiled, the flatulent monotony of their sheltered lives snatched up without warning by an incomprehensible moment of terror and fear of bodily annihilation at the very hands which symbolized by ordinary the licensed tranquillity of their lives. (163)

Through her emphatic appreciation of the two dogs, Temple becomes conscious of what is happening to herself, of the danger her cultural sexuality provides her. While "woolly" and "shapeless" might be read as vulgar references to female genitalia, "savage" is an image Faulkner uses repeatedly in describing Temple: "her eyes watchful and cold" (38); her countenance "cool, predatory, and discreet" (30); "her mouth painted into a savage and perfect bow" (299). Temple is certainly a "petulant" young woman, whether it is toward Popeye in the beginning of the novel ("What river did you fall in with that suit on?" [53]), or toward Popeye at the end of the book ("Call yourself a man, a bold bad man, and let a girl dance you off your feet" [248]). That Temple is a spoiled child of a prominent father is understood from the first of her many "My father's a judge" incantations. Finally, we know that Temple's life has been one of "flatulent monotony" and shelter by her repeated attempts to find excitement in slipping out nights with the town boys or with Gowan Stevens. What we know of Temple Drake's social life indicates that she has resisted the fear she is supposed to associate with her sexuality—and resists that fear successfully until she lands at Goodwin's farmhouse.

Victor Strandberg has pointed out that Faulkner often uses animal imagery to express "the biopsychology of sex" (29). The communication of Temple's tragic destiny through the medium of Reba's two little frantic dogs fits well into Faulkner's general depiction of Temple Drake. She does not move from place to place, for example, but "springs": "she sprang in, tucking her legs into her" (38); or, "she sprang to the door and pawed at the bolt" (243). At one point Reba calls Temple "a young mare" (273). When she gets angry at Gowan, he tells her, "Don't get your back up now" (39). Goodwin lifts her "from behind the box by the scruff of the neck, like a kitten" (55). And Popeye, finally, is always grabbing her "by the back of the neck" (145, 147, 148, 247). Indeed, the very name, "Drake," is also the name of a male duck, as well as the term for a May fly, used as fishing bait. By associating Temple Drake with such a variety of animal imagery Faulkner only further calls into question the "animal" or "natural" dimension of sexuality for the young woman. It is as if she (and the author) are searching for an appropriate metaphor from nature to describe what is happening to her body.

Sanctuary is about the snatching up "without warning by an incomprehensible moment of terror" of a seventeen-year-old girl by the symbols of her presumed security, adult males. Men, despite the traditional ideology that removes women from the masculine world and places them in a sanctified world of "licensed tranquillity," terrorize Temple by affecting her "fear of bodily annihilation" in *Sanctuary* and nearly destroy her. At seventeen, the "sexual animal" Temple Drake has not yet been fully "trained" (or culturally domesticated) and cannot yet distinguish those situations in which men are civil, and those in which they are not. In other words, she has not yet learned the complexities of the pornographic power relationship between males and females. She has, however, mastered the strategy of that power: the scant dress, delicate shoe, painted mouth. A novice in the culture of pornographic power struggle, Temple is the object of the sex-veteran Ruby's sympathy and scorn. "You poor little gutless fool," Ruby says. "Playing at it" (64). Temple has mastered the power of attraction, or "the ability to make someone look" at her (Holly 395). But she has yet to learn that the one who looks holds the ultimate power—and by attracting the gaze in her culture, she is offering to someone else the power to project what she desires. In a culture of objectified bodies, in other words, we all look through the lens of possession when we find something or someone attractive. To court notice is to make the self available for consumption.

At seventeen, Temple is "playing at" culturally defined standards of femininity, putting on the new spring fashions, comparing her body with the bodies of other females, experimenting with cultural modes of sexuality. When she arrives at Reba's whorehouse, she recognizes immediately where she is, and "even in her ignorance" knows herself to be "surrounded by a ghostly promiscuity of intimate garments" and of flesh "stale and oft-assailed" (151). The first time she is left alone in her room, she associates her new whorehouse environment with one particular aspect of her old one, when she and the other girls in her dormitory would dress for the Saturday night dance. Standing half-dressed in the lavatory, the girls look at one another, "comparing, talking whether you could do more damage if you could just walk out on the floor like you were now" (158–59). But then Temple remembers one of the girls claiming it was the clothing—the cultural images and masks—that makes sexuality into a power issue.

> The worst one of all said boys thought all girls were ugly except when they were dressed. She said the Snake had been seeing Eve for several days and never noticed her until Adam made her put on the fig leaf. How do you know, they said, and she said because the Snake was there before Adam, because he was the first one thrown out of heaven; he was there all the time. (159)

Sexuality as defined by culture—pornographic sexuality, defined by its structures of power—depends not upon "natural" physicality but upon sexuality as reconstructed by artificial, commodified images and systems of images. The sexualization program embodied in *Glamour* magazine will clarify this with precision. In this cultural system, women are trained not to love but to hate their bodies, to consider them ugly unless fitted into scant dresses, high-heeled shoes, or painted, shaven, and controlled. At the same time, this cultural system trains men to hold female bodies in contempt—to consider them as "temptations" away from productivity or as "dependents" inhibiting genuine freedom. This contempt is then turned on the masculine body itself for its "weakness" in succumbing to temptation and thus inviting dependency. Nonetheless, male status in the culture depends upon the degree of freedom and control achieved within the pornographic nexus of temptation and domination.

If culture teaches that sexuality—the Snake—is an evil that threatens the paradise of asexual existence, it also teaches that compensation for temptation may be found in domination. The same male body that may be tempted may also be the source of domination; the weakness may become the weapon. Faulkner's Popeye exemplifies this equation thoroughly. In a culture of representations and images, controlling the "fig leaf" is a signal for sexual prowess. Thus Popeye, the masculine pornographic creation, buys Temple clothes and furs and diamonds while she is at Reba's, and Temple, resists becoming Popeye's "whore," by pointedly assaulting these symbols of her captivity while trapped in her bedroom at the bordello. When she awakes on the last day of her stay at Reba's, the day on which she is to attempt her escape, she begins her morning by hurling Popeye's black suit into the corner, ripping her dresses off their hangers, and smashing the bottles of perfume and other "toilet things" that clutter her dressing table. That night, before she escapes from the house, she holds a pistol in her hand, "knowing that she would use it without any compunction whatever, with a kind of pleasure" (242).

Popeye's body and Temple's consciousness are the main symbols of the fraudulence of culturally determined sexuality in *Sanctuary*. It is not that the culture perverts "natural" sexuality in *Sanctuary*, for this would assume that such a phenomenon exists or is recoverable. Rather, in Faulkner's novel, the specific way in which this particular culture communicates sexuality is exposed as perverse and deadly. Studies of human sexuality in this century have universally concluded that sexual identification and sexual practices are social constructions and do not possess natural, inevitable forms. The recognition that sexuality is socially constructed indicates only that, as a construction, it is open to change (Silverman, 345). In *Sanctuary*, Faulkner presents the dual roles in any oppressive power relation: Popeye as its beneficiary, who can "rape" even though he is impotent, and Temple as its rebel, who can refuse, at any time, to be complicit in its system of justice.

Popeye's total alienation from a body that will not "perform" leads him to his assault on bodies that demand performance or that are capable of performance. He uses his pistol "without any compunction" on the sexually potent Red for the same reason that he uses the corncob on Temple: as a revenge against his exclusion from the pornographic myth of his own masculinity, as an effort to force his way into a culturally prescribed sexual identity. In the first paragraph of the novel, Popeye studies another man in apparent fascination. "From beyond the screen of bushes which surrounded the spring, Popeye watched the man drinking. A faint path led from the road to the spring. Popeye watched the man—" (3) We "watch" to learn how to be. Michel Gresset rightly points out that "with Faulkner watching is an explosive activity" (197) tied directly to power relations. The power struggle between Horace and Popeye in this opening scene is inconclusive. Popeye ends up watching Horace Benbow for two hours, and when they finally walk off together, he solicits Horace's protection from something in the woods. "Benbow felt Popeye's whole body spring against him," in reaction to a passing owl, "his hand clawing at his coat" (7). The animal imagery in this passage is identical to the language Faulkner later uses to describe Temple in her moments of terror—springing, clawing, cringing.

Popeye's fright, his instinctive appeal for protection, is rebuffed by Horace who taunts him for his irrational fear. When the two men arrive at Goodwin's, Popeye's reaction to his dependence is expressed in his verbal abuse of Ruby, and he reminds her of her sordid past (10–11). This pattern, in the first pages of the novel, is emblematic (and is repeated by various men, including Horace, Goodwin, and Tommy). The failure of Popeye's body—in fright, in sexual dysfunction—is the source and motivation of his will to domination. His affair with Temple is simply the final expression of his resistance to his body's cultural exclusion from the grammar of pornographic sexuality.

Popeye's body is finally destroyed in *Sanctuary*, and Temple survives. Temple's consciousness emerges, moreover, as the novel's strongest indictment of pornographic logic and assumptions, especially as that logic and its assumptions affect ideas about criminal justice and the social order. The dissenting nature of Temple's mind is exemplified in her triumphant "perjury" at the end of the novel, a perjury which is more truthful than the "facts" of what actually occurred at the farmhouse. Only a strictly literal reading of *Sanctuary* can hold Temple guilty of perjury, or one that believes Faulkner has created a naive or collaborative pornographic novel. At any rate, to overemphasize the perjury reveals a misunderstanding of Temple Drake, which Faulkner has given the reader good reason to avoid, but one which does attest to the power of those same cultural images and assumptions about sexuality and justice which nearly destroy the young woman herself.

Temple's sense of cause and effect, of reality, is not consistent with civil and legal definitions of truth—definitions that inform and reflect culture. She considers her night in Goodwin's spare bedroom as worse than the experience of her actual rape, which occurred the next morning. "Now and then Horace would attempt to get ahead to the crime itself," Faulkner narrates, "but she would elude him and return to herself sitting on the bed. . . ." All that Temple ever says about the actual physical assault is, "Yes; that. . . . It just happened. I dont know. I had been scared so long that I guess I had just gotten used to being" (226). The same consciousness that correctly perceived the images of sexuality to be her true captors—the dresses, the perfume bottles—also perceives not simple physical assault on the body but the fear and terror of imminent assault as the truly criminal. The rape is the legal, technical crime, the crime against society. It is the point at which societal structures fail because they encourage not pornographic fantasy but actual, physical assault. By raping, the man destroys the image and threatens the entire cultural system of sexual meanings and signals. But Temple, who has reached "a sanctuary, a rationality of perspective," earned by "passing through unbearable emotional states like furious rage" and "furious fear" (Faulkner, *The Town*, 27) sees a crime more fundamental and basic to heterosocial relations. It is the very images and the cultural system itself that are criminal; it is the working of human sexuality into a power structure that is unjust. The real crime against the person is the terror through which Temple was made to get "used to being" scared in her interactions with men. But this crime does not fall within the criminal code because it undermines the way in which society defines sexuality and "criminal" conduct.

In her interviews with adolescent women concerning their initial sexual encounters, Sharon Thompson found that "having sex—or at least beginning the sequence of romantic adventure, first fully desiring or being desired or desiring to be desired—is evidently perceived as equivalent to beginning to have a story worth telling" (378, n.5). The only extended discourse that Temple Drake has (or is allowed to have) in *Sanctuary* is the long story she tells Horace Benbow about her ordeal. "Horace realized that she was recounting the experience with actual pride," Faulkner relates, "a sort of naive and impersonal vanity, as though she were making it up" (226). What Temple has learned by this point is simply the ability to objectify herself: to see herself in the role provided her by the culture that erected Reba's whorehouse. "Dont think I'm afraid to tell," she proclaims to Horace. "I'll tell it anywhere. Dont think I'm afraid" (225). Temple's ultimate rebellion against her "story" is rooted in this refusal to be afraid, or to link defeat of her consciousness with the violation of her body. She goes on to provide Horace with a wide variety of impressions on her own sexuality and is proud of her ability to do so. The pleasure she discovers, however, is rooted not in her depravity but in the power of self-representation.

"Perhaps the most accurate test of whether a social group has political power is to ask whether that group enjoys the power of self-representation," according to Margaret Miles. "People who do not represent themselves live under conditions in which their subjective lives—their feelings, concerns, and struggles—are marginalized from public interest; they also live in constant danger of misrepresentation" (170). Temple's pleasure in having an audience for her story indicates her enjoyment of this new power of representation. She casts herself in a number of figures: as a boy, as a queen with a chastity belt, as a woman with the power to rape, as an old woman, as a man, and as a victim. With subject status, Temple has at her representational disposal any and all cultural images of self, which she can appropriate in order to communicate her sense of who she is and what threatens her. The story she tells to Horace alternates between images of her vulnerability and images of the power she desires in order to defend herself from attack. The story she tells Horace is not the one he wants to hear, just as the "truth" she tells in court is not the one many readers expect her to possess. This is, of course, the point. If those normally without the power to project (or to represent) reality suddenly come to possess that power, then the world will look quite different to all of us. Some of us may even become ill, or aroused—or both, as Horace does.

Through her heightened sense of perception at Goodwin's farmhouse, Temple comes to realize the centrality of rape, its invitation and its threat, to the presently dominant cultural system of sexuality and sexual interplay. When she gives Horace her account of the "crime," then, she dwells not upon the assault but upon the fear of the assault. To live in fear of rape is greater terror than one experiences when attacked unexpectedly or without provocation. Such an assault has, at the very least, a beginning and an end, and is without ideological content. But the terror of imminent sexual assault is neither temporally definitive nor meaningless once one understands how a pornographic culture reinforces and perpetuates it. As far as Temple is concerned, Goodwin is responsible for her rape because he terrorized her into the barn crib and even instructed Tommy on how to have sex with her (104). Temple feels as if she is pursued by every man at Goodwin's after being escorted into the terror by another man, Gowan Stevens. As such, no one is completely innocent of the crime against this woman.

Horace Benbow, who is technically Temple's attorney—or she is supposed to be his witness—actually loses his case because of her testimony. In a sense she condemns him as well, though not consciously perhaps, for his participation in this pornography. Horace originally left home because he could not cope with his desire for his stepdaughter, Little Belle (symbolized by the grape arbor, "hiding the hammock, the green-snared promise of unease" [14]), and because of his uxorious relationship to big Belle, his wife, before whom he is reduced to a "shrimp" [18]). This combination of desire and domination—each a contradiction of his expected, cultural role as stepfather and husband—drives Horace back to the familial security of his aunt and sister. He will not surrender entirely, however, and insists upon living alone in the old, abandoned house he and Narcissa own—the house in which he was raised. In an effort to regain his adult masculinity, Horace undertakes a legal defense of Goodwin, and, with even more vigor, a chivalric defense of Ruby. Hence his life parallels that of Popeye. Both men have been denied cultural masculinity and act to repossess it by "taking on" something they either cannot, or have no real desire, to accomplish.

Throughout the defense of Goodwin and protection of Ruby, Horace is under the libidinal spell of Little Belle. He left home partially because he learned that she was beginning to master and control images of herself in order to manipulate his responses. While she was crying and apologizing to Horace for calling him a "shrimp," Horace "could see her face" in a mirror behind her, "see her watching the back of my head with pure dissimilation." From this experience Horace concludes that "nature is 'she' and Progress is 'he'; nature made the grape arbor, but Progress invented the mirror" [16]. In other words, nature made the sexual desire, the desire he has for this young woman, stepdaughter or not, but Progress, or culture, invented the mirror—the system or thing by which images are created and controlled and nature overpowered or, rather, defined. Culture is "he," man-made and artificial; and nature is "she," controlled, monitored, and suppressed. The final straw, which led to Horace's flight from home, was his discovery of the rouge rag that Little Belle attempted to hide behind the mirror [16–17].

In chapter 19, Horace stares at Little Belle's photograph in "horror and despair," but when he reaches for it, he knocks it over. Now the face in the picture looks at him, with a mouth painted into a "rigid travesty" just like Temple's [175]. By the end of chapter 23, after Horace visits Temple and listens to the way she envisions what happened to her, his desire for Little Belle reaches it height. Temple's ordeal helps him realize what his feelings for Little Belle amount to; in a fantasy the images of Temple and his stepdaughter fuse.

The rape fantasy that Horace has when he returns home from his interview with Temple implicates him in the culture of pornography. The fantasy is, the narrative explains, the product of "all the nightmare shapes it had taken him forty-three years to invent" (233). He has found Temple's story as erotic as it is criminal. He has also discovered a culturally based potentiality within himself, which places him in collusion with a rapist. Any nausea Horace may feel in addition to arousal is due to the recognition that he is as much a victim and product of a cultural image system as are Temple and Popeye; specifically, he has been conditioned by his culture to equate sexuality with power and dominance. In this light it makes sense that Horace should begin to identify himself with the rape victim at the very end of his fantasy (235). In Popeye and Horace, Faulkner creates twin male pornographers. Popeye discovers rape as an artificial means of asserting sexual power; Horace discovers rape as the way he has been trained to envision his own sexuality. For both men, as Faulkner's novel develops their fate, the fantasy ends in destruction.

In the courtroom, Horace is speechless when placed face-to-face with Temple. Horace, "a man given to much talk and not much else" (14), is silent, self-condemned. He is probably looking once again into those eyes filled "with black antagonism," as Temple looked at him at Reba's, "with her black, belligerent stare" (225). He may well be afraid that Temple will name *him*, let alone Goodwin, his client, as culprit. Indeed, if Horace really wanted to help Temple, he could have taken her away from Reba's or informed her family of her whereabouts. After the trial, Horace is completely defeated. He gets into his sister's car "like an old man" and allows Narcissa to decide where home is, no longer demanding his separate residence (306). Horace and his youthful, quixotic attempts to change the world, or even to escape it, are finished. "Night is hard on old people," he explains to himself (314).

The trial has nearly destroyed Temple as well. She wholly lacks bodily will as she leaves the courtroom, surrounded by her protectors, her four brothers ("like soldiers") and her father the judge, escorting her out. She has, in effect, surrendered her body once again to masculine cultural definition: daughter and sister this time instead of whore and mistress. She cringes at the door when she leaves in a familiar pose of fear and terror. When she next appears in the novel, she is in Europe, where Horace said he would go after the trial ("When this is over I think I'll go to Europe . . . I need a change. Either I, or Mississippi, one" [140]). Sitting in the Luxembourg Gardens in the "season of rain and death" Temple sees herself in her compact as "sullen and discontented and sad"—a portrait, here, of profound ambivalence (333). She is so unable to feel anything now, having felt a range of emotions which has left her numb, that she must check her mirror not to primp but to discover her feelings. Similar to Popeye at the beginning of the novel, Temple is compelled now to *watch* her image in order to discover her identity.

In a sense Temple at the end of *Sanctuary* has entered the world of the mirror—of Progress, of nature commodified—and left forever behind the "sexual animal" that was the college girl at Ole Miss. She has much the same attitude about her as does Charlotte Rittenmeyer at the end of her ordeal in *The Wild Palms*, with "that complete immobile abstraction from which even pain and terror are absent, in which a living creature seems to listen to and even watch some one of its own flagging organs, the heart say, the secret irreparable seeping of blood" (5). This condition of sensual death seems to have fascinated Faulkner enough to return to it on occasion, as indicative of the limits of the human experience. "Because there is a sanctuary beyond despair for any beast which has dared all, which even its mortal enemy respects" ("Centaur in Brass" [1932], *Collected Stories*, 164). In *Sanctuary*, however, the limitations have more to do with the way in which cultural sexuality destroys pleasure by aligning it so inextricably with danger.

Sanctuary virtually reeks with sexual tensions, sexual energies, and sexual threats. The sense one gets from the novel is that there is something terribly wrong with the way in which the sexes interact, that the basic assumptions and definitions of masculinity and femininity are evil, malignly contrived, and sexually inhibiting. "Faulkner sees that sensuousness is not allowed free expression in our society," according to George Bedell, "but is suppressed by our puritanical distortions of human life, all of which results in the violence and terror of novels like *Sanctuary* and *Light in August*." Bedell claims that what T. S. Eliot has called the "dissolution of sensibility" has taken place in these novels, "and the demonic has rushed into the vacuum left when the sensuousness has been removed or suppressed" (36). But Faulkner himself did not intend or see Popeye, for example, as evil personified, but rather as evil culturally manufactured. Faulkner is quoted as discussing his character this way:

> Popeye is a contemporary Satan manufactured in carload lots for, let us say, Sears Roebuck. . . . Anything, like Popeye, that brings misery is bad, but there was no attempt to ascribe to Popeye qualities of evil like that in Milton's Satan because, to do so, is to assume that a trait is good or evil in its own right. (*William Faulkner of Oxford*, 131)

Faulkner's language here is wholly appropriate. Popeye represents the commodified sexuality of a pornographic cultural nexus. His evil qualities take on the attributes of commodities, and are available to him as they are to anyone in his culture. Popeye *made himself* a sexual force by picking and choosing from among the accouterments of sex and violence available to him in the cultural text at large—the "Sears, Roebuck" catalog of sexuality. His access to the catalog makes the idea of "good and evil in its own right" an anachronism, as anachronistic as a "natural" expression of sexuality.

Just as Popeye impersonates the "evil man," Temple impersonates the "evil woman" or whore. In the bathroom at the dance hall, after Popeye has struck her, Temple curses him with "a phrase, glibly obscene, with a detached parrotlike effect" (245). Parroting what she has been exposed to, Temple is still "playing at it." Even when she is coming on to Red in the private room, she is mimicking the pornographic: "murmuring to him in parrotlike underworld epithet" (243). Throughout *Sanctuary*, evil cannot be gauged by the mere appearance of things, but neither can it be detected beneath the surface of "reality," behind the mask. In *Sanctuary* there is no "behind" the mask. With cool irony, for example, Faulkner describes Temple and Popeye outside Dumfries' service station, when Temple is bleeding steadily at the beginning of her captivity, as a couple who "appeared as decorous as two acquaintances stopped to pass the time of day before entering church" (147). And comically, Faulkner most effectively displays this central idea in the Virgil and Fonzo episode of chapter 11, where the two apprentice barbers believe Reba's brothel is an innocent boarding house and the prostitutes just part of her large family. Virgil and Fonzo think the house is innocent; the reader knows the house is one of prostitution, where the pornographic logic of commodified sexuality is rehearsed over and over again. Horace speaks to this issue when he decides that his sister's "unflagging suspicion for all people's actions" is not what it appears to be, "mere affinity for evil but . . . practical wisdom" (210). Horace, of course, is wrong about his sister, as wrong as are Virgil and Fonzo about Reba's house, as wrong as is the impression of Popeye and Temple as a "decorous" couple—but Horace is not entirely mistaken. Narcissa's "practical wisdom" is her sense of the political necessity to maintain the "codes that govern average people" in order to uphold her own secure place in the culture of dominance and submission. The "joke" of the Virgil and Fonzo episode is their own compulsion to keep separate their whoring and their homelife when in fact, as the joke compels, the two are identical. And the impression of the decorous Temple and Popeye merely displays, once again, the centrality of rape to the "codes that govern" heterosexual relations in the pornographic nexus. The woman in the image is demure and supplicatory. The man is confident and in protective control. Together they form an image of the decorum and pious respectability of "average people."

In *Sanctuary* Faulkner invites his reader into a pornographic experience and demands that the reader see beyond the appearance of social misfits and sexual perversion to an indictment of cultural attitudes toward sexuality. Hyatt Waggoner has said that "the element of social criticism and moral judgment does not come to much" (96) in *Sanctuary*, which is correct if the novel is read merely as a set of images and reversals. In 1925, Faulkner wrote from Paris that sexuality in America "has become a national disease" and that Americans in Paris are catered to by "nasty" and "lewd" performances which the French shun (*Selected Letters* 24). When he wrote *Sanctuary* a few years later, he would get to the heart of the "national disease" in an attempt to define the system of images and artificialities by which sexuality is expressed in his culture. As a writer of fiction, Faulkner would explain years later, he made use of "the injustice of society, the inhumanity of people . . . with their aspirations and struggles and the bizarre, the comic, and the tragic conditions they get themselves into simply coping with themselves and one another and environment" (*Faulkner in the University*, 177). In *Sanctuary*, the major characters do not battle with each other so much as they struggle among the definitions of "male" and "female" made available to them by their culture. The extent to which they fail to produce an image of themselves, both expressive of their physical selves and accepted by society, is the extent to which culture has truly stifled the freedom to create alternative or unprecedented expressions of sexual life, placing culturally created systems of meaning in place of personally conjured sexuality.

Sanctuary exists as a problematic text for inquiry into the workings of pornography as a system of meaning—as a sexual ideology. John T. Matthews, in an otherwise precise and instructive study of *Sanctuary*, claims that "What preoccupies *Sanctuary* on all fronts is the status of culture's demarcation within nature" (253). Matthews's language reverses the issue. What preoccupies *Sanctuary* is *the status of nature within culture*—the ideological uses to which a pornographic culture puts ideas about nature. Reba Rivers, one of the sexual gatekeepers in *Sanctuary*, claims that Popeye's impotence and lack of sexual interest in her "girls" is "against nature." Everything about Popeye, in fact, is "against nature" as it is defined by his social order. The violence he generates in the novel is precisely that: a revenge against nature, against his submission to a natural dysfunction, a natural inferiority. In *Sanctuary*, however, it is not only Popeye who pits himself against nature. The entire culture, as Faulkner represents it, acts to subsume ideas about "the natural" under its ideological, or pornographic system of meaning—the "codes that govern average people"—to demarcate the natural within cultural categories and ideological divisions. No one in *Sanctuary* is naturally potent, naturally seductive, or naturally sensuous. These qualities are *produced*; they are constructed by Temple Drake's ubiquitous compact and painted face, Popeye's pistol and corncob, and the couple's fancy cars and expensive clothing.

There are no integral selves in *Sanctuary*, no sense of self that transcends the material, no inner qualities, no Miltonian inherent good or evil at the heart of the person. The freedom consequent to this idea of the self is itself a part of *Sanctuary*'s terror. The freedom to make oneself good or evil allows no sanctuary in the belief, or the faith, in natural depravity or inherent goodness. Beneath the facades of life there is really nothing; the facade itself, in all its mutability, is the reality. What *is*, ultimately, is the material fact of living and the material productions consequent to life. Among Temple's initial terrors at Reba's is "an agony for concealment" (151), an agony to be hidden or veiled behind some protective, inclusive cover. But throughout *Sanctuary* Temple is exposed: There is nothing to conceal, no secret self, no inner sanctum—and so the veil *is* the self, the exposure. If the "codes that govern" behavior exist to protect the self from intrusion, those codes are exhausted when that protected self is revealed as a fiction—another "code" with no material or transcendent justification. In other words, it is not the code of civility that has broken down in *Sanctuary.* Rather, the belief that gave rise to the code in the first place is exposed as a construct, an ideology. *Sanctuary* represents, then, the intersection of two ideologies of the self, an intersection where the integral or transcendent self is being displaced by the material or object self. Temple's terror, her "agony for concealment," reveals her nostalgia for a core sense of integrity into which she might withdraw for strength—or sanctuary. But her terror reveals that such a place does not exist. *Sanctuary* suggests that the self-as-represented, the constructed self, is no cover or protection but is, inherently, the meaning and limit of its own existence. Like any commodity, the way in which the self is represented will determine its ultimate worth and integrity. Pornography, under these conditions, is nothing more than a system of exchange.

The system of exchange deals in representations, in objects cast as human beings in photographs, on television screens, and over flesh and blood. This is why theories of sexuality increasingly center on ideas about representation and why the First Amendment, which seems to offer the power of representation to the largest pocket, becomes so problematic. Any effort to control representations created by human beings is censorship. However, if current ideas about humanity become predominant, if humanity cannot be separated from the ways in which it is represented, then "censorship" will become indistinguishable from laws governing civil behavior, once it is decided (by whom?) what people ought to look like and in what positions they can be cast. First Amendment issues divide feminists and others interested in the problem of pornography and amount to an impasse on discussions of sexual representation. Perhaps the lines of division are misleading.

Margaret Miles attempts to shift attention away from the politics of representation and onto the eye that beholds the representation. Miles advocates looking at representations of women, for example, "not with an appraising patriarchal eye, but with an eye that identifies with the person represented." Miles considers this "a necessary preliminary step toward noticing and understanding the visual clues that make that person's interior life accessible" (182). Reading early criticism of *Sanctuary*, for example, makes clear the failure of initial critics to see beyond Temple's pornographic, object status.* Miles's argument suggests that there is indeed an "interior life" to human beings but that the way in which we are taught to "look" at one another makes this interiority inaccessible. Miles is actually calling for a way in which to represent the invisible: the inner self of anarchic contradiction, which cannot be objectified. And like Ellison, Miles has recognized that the invisibility of that interiority is not a function of the object self but a function of subjective perception. We have not, in the wisdom of the postmodern era, discovered that there is no such thing as the inner "core" to the human subject. Rather, we have been trained away from an ability to recognize and represent it, and have come to believe that it does not exist because we can no longer see it. In order to untrain ourselves, we must first expose (or demystify) the system of representation by which we have incurred this blindness. Only then might we recognize the self not as object but as action.

* For a review of this criticism, see my essay, "Temple Drake's Truthful Perjury: Rethinking Faulkner's *Sanctuary*."

WORKS CITED

Bedell, George C. *Kierkegaard and Faulkner: Modalities of Existence.* Baton Rouge: Louisiana State University Press, 1972.

Brownmiller, Susan. *Against Our Will: Men, Women, and Rape.* New York: Simon & Schuster, 1975.

Buell, Lawrence. "American Pastoral Ideology Reappraised." *American Literary History* 1, No. 1 (Spring 1989): 1–29.

Dimen, Muriel. "Politically Correct? Politically Incorrect?" In *Pleasure and Danger: Exploring Female Sexuality* (see Vance, below) 138–148.

Dworkin, Andrea. *Pornography: Men Possessing Women.* New York: G. P. Putnam, 1981.

Faulkner, William. *Collected Stories.* 1950. New York: Vintage Books, 1977.

———. *Sanctuary.* 1932. New York: Vintage Books, 1987.

———. *Selected Letters.* New York: Vintage Books, 1977.

———. *The Town.* 1956. New York: Vintage Books, 1961.

———. *The Wild Palms.* 1939. New York: Vintage Books, 1966.

Gresset, Michel. *Fascination: Faulkner's Fiction, 1919–1936,* adapted from the French by Thomas West. Durham: Duke University Press, 1989.

Griffin, Susan. *Pornography and Representation: Culture's Revenge Against Nature*. New York: Harper & Row, 1983.

Gwynn, Frederick L., and Joseph Blotner, eds. *Faulkner in the University: Class Conferences at the University of Virginia, 1957–1958*. Charlottesville: University of Virginia Press, 1959; 2d ed., New York: Vintage Books, 1965.

Hollibough, Amber. "Desire for the Future: Radical Hope in Passion and Pleasure." In *Pleasure and Danger* (see Vance, below), 401–10.

Haight, Annelyn. *Banned Books, 389 B.C.–1978 A.D.* New York: R. R. Bowker, 1978.

Holly, Michael Ann. "Past Looking." *Critical Inquiry* 16, No. 2 (Winter 1990): 371–96.

Kappeler, Susanne. *The Pornography of Representation*. Minneapolis: University of Minnesota Press, 1986.

LaCapra, Dominic. *Rethinking Intellectual History: Texts, Contexts, Language*. Ithaca: Cornell University Press, 1983.

Lederer, Laura, ed. *Take Back the Night: Women on Pornography*. New York: William Morrow, 1980.

Miles, Margaret R. *Carnal Knowing: Female Nakedness and Religious Meaning in the Christian West*. Boston: Beacon Press, 1989.

Mink, Louis O. *Historical Understanding*, edited by Brian Fay, Eugene Golob, and Richard T. Vann. Ithaca: Cornell University Press, 1987.

Muhlenfeld, Elizabeth. "Bewildered Witness: Temple Drake in *Sanctuary*," *The Faulkner Journal* 1 (Spring 1986): 43–55.

Page, Sally. *Faulkner's Women: Characterization and Meaning*. Deland, Fla.: Everett/Edwards, 1972.

Rubin, Gayle. "Thinking Sex: Notes for a Radical Theory of the Politics of Sexuality." In *Pleasure and Danger* (see Vance, below), 267–319.

Schwartz, Lawrence H. *Creating Faulkner's Reputation: The Politics of Modern Literary Criticism*. Knoxville: University of Tennessee Press, 1988.

Silverman, Kaja. "Histoire d'O: The Construction of a Female Subject." In *Pleasure and Danger* (see Vance, below), 320–49.

Strandburg, Victor. *A Faulkner Overview: Six Perspectives*. Port Washington, N.Y.: Kennikat Press, 1981.

Thompson, Sharon. "Search for Tomorrow: On Feminism and the Reconstruction of Teen Romance." In *Pleasure and Danger* (see Vance, below), 350–84.

Tichi, Cecelia. *Shifting Gears: Technology, Literature, Culture in Modernist America*. Chapel Hill: University of North Carolina Press, 1987.

Urgo, Joseph R. "Temple Drake's Truthful Perjury: Rethinking Faulkner's *Sanctuary*." *American Literature* 55, No. 3 (October 1983): 435–44.

Vance, Carole S. "Concept Paper." *Pleasure and Danger* (see Vance, below), 443–46.

———. "Pleasure and Danger: Toward a Politics of Sexuality." *Pleasure and Danger*, edited by Carole S. Vance, 1–27. Boston: Routledge & Kegan Paul, 1984.

Waggoner, Hyatt. *William Faulkner: From Jefferson to the World*. New York: Noonday Press, 1964.

Webb, James W., and A. Wigfall Green. *William Faulkner of Oxford*. Baton Rouge: Louisiana State University Press, 1965.

CHAPTER 4

The Body as Popular Commodity

Glamour and Pornography

She opened the raincoat and produced a compact from somewhere and, watching her motions in a the tiny mirror, she spread and fluffed her hair with her fingers and powdered her face and replaced the compact and looked at the watch again. . . . Temple lay [with] her hands crossed on her breast and her legs straight and close and decorous, like an effigy in an ancient tomb.
—*William Faulkner,* Sanctuary

Today we have naming of parts. . . .
—*Henry Reed,* Naming of Parts

Looking Good

A parent whose young child is found looking at the photographs in a monthly adult magazine featuring sexually explicit images of women or men would probably react swiftly and confidently. Perhaps a talk would follow, the subject matter ranging from human sexuality and sexual representation to human bodies and self-respect—all the cultural antidotes that adults supposedly know already when they indulge in the same kind of looking. On the other hand, a parent whose child is found looking through *Glamour* magazine may take no action whatsoever, except perhaps to suggest a more intellectually rigorous choice of reading material or set of images to study. Sexually explicit material, it is commonly assumed, is potentially pornographic and must be monitored. *Glamour* magazine, and other magazines concerned with "health and beauty," it is commonly assumed, are not. These assumptions are, quite simply, wrongheaded. A magazine like *Playboy,* or *Playgirl,* where one's attention is drawn repeatedly to taboo images of exposed genitals, is far *less* pornographic in content and effect than a magazine like *Glamour* (or *Self, Mademoiselle,* or *GQ*), where one's attention is drawn repeatedly to mass-produced, repetitive images of incomplete, parceled, mutilated, and commodity-dependent human bodies.

The implausible perfection sought in the *Playboy* centerfold, or the naked man changing spark plugs in *Playgirl,* are innocuous images of purposeful degradation. Their social inappropriateness makes them offensive only to the literalist. In *Glamour,* however, the pornographic content is covert and far more insidious. *Playboy's* degradation of human bodies is explicit—it is exclusive, alienating, and forbidding to its audience; it mocks those who look but cannot possess or become its images, male or female. *Glamour's* degradation of human bodies is implicit—it is inclusive, invitational, and claims that its images are obtainable to its audience; it instructs its reader on how she may possess or become the images it represents. In *Playboy* and in other adult magazines, advertisements offer a kind of relief: If one cannot possess the centerfold, one can at least possess the car or the VCR. One effect of the advertising in *Playboy* or *Playgirl* is to make the marketplace world of commodities seem natural: perfect bodies, perfect things. If one cannot possess the commodities, of course, one can certainly afford the pictures. Possessing the centerfold, then, becomes an act of the imagination.

In *Glamour,* on the other hand, the advertisements and features are actually distinguishable only in form. Everything in *Glamour* is literally for sale; a shopping guide is appended to the back of every issue. Feature stories instruct readers on how best to read the advertisements; both ads and features initiate readers to a world in which everything from perfume to hair color to "body image," everything from product to human essence is considered an object or commodity. In this sense, *Glamour* is more closely allied to what is considered hard-core pornography—where advertisements and features are indistinguishable and where everything is made available for sexual adventurism. In hard-core pornography, the human body is the object of sadomasochistic fantasies of assault, rape, and dismemberment. In *Glamour,* the body is cut into pieces, assaulted with scientific objects and formulas, threatened with rape and disease, humiliated and destroyed, or "made over." In this sense, *Glamour* is much more at home in the universe of the kinds of pornography sold in adult bookstores than the varieties available behind the 7–11 Store counter.

In the span of a few successive pages of the October 1988 issue of *Glamour*, intimate apparel is featured ("Private Pleasures"), illustrated with photographs of women and men in sexy underwear, followed directly by an article informing readers that "Sterilization is the #1 Birth Control Choice," followed a few pages later by a condom ad, Trojan for Women: "It will show that you're thinking about his health, too." The underwear feature suggests a series of "carefree looks," including a "sexy weekend alternative" to mundane underclothes. The sterilization feature directly counters any idea of a "carefree" sexual existence, arguing that one way for a woman to take control of her body is to mutilate it in some way. And the condom ad, finally, reminds readers that "carefree" weekends may lead to far worse things than unwanted pregnancies. Within this series of thirty pages, the body invites sexual activity, and because it invites sex, it undergoes surgical alteration and is threatened with death. This is precisely the situation Carole Vance raises in the title of her collection of essays about female sexuality, *Pleasure and Danger*. But then again, the predicament fits precisely the *Glamour* program as well: If you want it, you pay for it.

Glamour is a woman's magazine. Unlike *Playboy*, which features naked women but advertises products primarily for men, or *Playgirl*, which features naked men but advertises products for women and men, *Glamour*'s features and advertisements almost exclusively reflect and represent women. There are similar magazines for men, such as *GQ*, where the features and advertisements are directed toward and represent males. These are fashion and beauty magazines, products of alliances between, on the one hand, the publishers and writers who produce the features, and on the other hand, the manufacturers and marketers who produce the picture advertisements that dominate the publications. *Glamour* magazine is a kind of cultural grammar for women: It instructs, it provides rules, guidelines, and boundaries by which women may achieve the goal of "glamour"—charm, romance, excitement, and allure. One looks at *Glamour* with the eye of a narcissistic consumer, the eye to possess information, products, and images, and to transform the self.

Looking, in fact, is what *Glamour* invites and depends upon. John

Berger, in *Ways of Seeing,* explains the cultural legacy of "the artform of the European nude." This classic form, consisting of painters, spectators, and owners, who were nearly all male, and nude objects, which were nearly always female, established a subject-object relationship which has subsequently become embedded in cultural attitudes about representation. As Berger explains, this relationship "still structures the consciousness of many women. They do to themselves what men do to them. They survey, like men, their own femininity" (63). *Glamour* is reflective of a culture in which it is assumed that a woman's body is looked at—surveyed, in Berger's terminology—by men and by other women. Therefore, as female, the reader of *Glamour* is taught that she must learn to do two things. First, she must learn to look good—to follow the instructions and advice, buy the products and services, consume what *Glamour* makes available to produce good looks. Second, she must learn to look well—to be able to identify weaknesses and errors in the way she looks, and in the way others look, and to internalize wholly the way others will look at her. In short, she must learn to see herself and to produce herself as object—a production born of commodities and mass media—and to maintain herself vigilantly as the commodity she has produced.

Margaret Miles uses the term "sexualization" to describe the way in which bodies are made to conform to the sexual patterns that exist in the culture at large: heterosexual as the norm; homosexual and bisexual as forms of dissent. "For women," according to Miles, "sexualization has taken the form of learning the arts of attraction, the delicate techniques of presenting themselves as simultaneously seductive and 'ladylike,' erotic and unapproachable" (188). *Glamour* is a primary text in this process. The women presented as models for female sexuality are "erotic and unapproachable"—which translates, in the language of the marketplace, as being desirable and unattainable. However, whereas Miles intends that this duplicity be aimed at men (who are taught to find in the female the erotic and the unapproachable), *Glamour* insists that women see the duplicity in themselves—or in the idea of female itself. The image of the *Glamour* woman is desired by the female reader, and yet its perfection is certainly beyond the reach of nearly all women who feel the need to buy the magazine. In this way *Glamour* teaches women to see themselves—that is, to see *actual* as opposed to representational females—in the same way that men are encouraged to see them: as imperfect approximations of a cultural ideal. It sounds positively medieval, this sense that women are, by definition (I mean just *look*), imperfect creations.

The striving for perfection is identical to the striving for objectification, meant to erase any vestige of the subjective (the idiosyncratic; the self-definitional) in the name of the achievement of a kind of sexual trademark: attractive, glamorous, desirable. But as Carol Munter points out, the attempt to be glamorous has less to do with sex and more to do with market exchange. "Our attempts to conform to a cultural ideal of the sexy or beautiful woman first appear to relate to sex, but in reality we change our bodies in the hope of being acceptable and being chosen" (228). While there may be nothing inherently evil in an attempt to attract a lover, something perverse occurs when those "attempts" are not left to the moods and desires of the body but are encouraged as daily habits. The image of *Sanctuary*'s Temple Drake at Goodwin's comes to mind here, trying to do her face, checking her self in her compact—while fearing imminent rape. With Temple Drake the arts of attraction no longer flowed directly from desire but were habitual activities, as "natural" to her as elimination of waste. "Pursued to its final degree," according to Munter, "this fantasy of the perfection of the body is a fantasy about the rejection of the self" (230) or a rejection of subjectivity in favor of the possession of an object called my body.

The pornographic content of *Glamour* magazine arises from this equation of the human body with consumer object. The pornography is embedded in this supreme domination of the physical self by the intellect or the cultural mind. Pornography, quite simply, is a system of representation in which human sexuality and the human form are re-created for mass consumption in order to make an ideological statement about human sexuality. An image of a man and a woman copulating, in any position, is not pornographic. The same image with the caption "all women secretly desire this" or "all real men do this" is pornographic. Pornography, of course, usually operates more subtly. In essence, however, all pornography, unlike simple, anarchic erotica, attaches some cultural meaning, boundary, or exclusion to an act or image which is essentially meaningless or only potentially meaningful. Pornography is a sexual display with an ideological subtext, such as the degradation of a specific gender, race, or historical group. Pornography is a system of *meaning*, not a system of sexual arousal or erotica, and it is aimed at human sexuality, which, as a natural phenomenon, is systematically without meaning or without exclusive significance. Culture exists to provide meaning and value to natural phenomena. Incest is valuable to a small society threatened with extinction; it is taboo to a large society in which that threat is absent. As possessors of a culture, human beings decide which natural phenomena to encourage and which to prohibit. It is natural to urinate when the bladder is full; it is culturally appropriate to fulfill this function only in certain ways. The culture provides an array of rules to govern bodily behavior—and physical functions. The earliest cultural prohibition the child learns is control over bladder and bowel. The quality of one's toilet training, of course, contains keys to subsequent attitudes toward authority, discipline, creativity, and independence—in short, the keys to cultural survival.

Pornography is no anomaly in this culture but rather a logical expression of it or a reaction to it. The ideas that pornography attaches to sexuality are the same ideas that the culture in general attaches to the human body and to its functions: control, discipline, power, and domination. Recent studies of pornography by Andrea Dworkin, Susan Kappeler, and Susan Griffin, discussed earlier, have each recognized that pornography is not the dirty secret of Western culture—this is to reverse the relationship. In fact, Western culture is the dirty secret of pornography. Griffin connects pornography to the "silencing of eros" by culture. Kappeler finds in the grammatical and observational structures of subject/object relations the prototype of pornographic representation and thought processes. Dworkin considers cultural sexuality as a kind of private terrorism—a power struggle emblematic of wider, pervasive patterns of political domination and control.

In its historic efforts to master and to control nature, Western culture has produced, as by-products to expansion, colonialism, and imperialism, a system of thought that can be recognized as ideologically pornographic. Literary critic Ann Kibbey has shown how linguistic patterns influenced genocidal and misogynist impulses among English Puritans in Massachusetts in the seventeenth century. Amy Schrager Lang, Annette Kolodny, Richard Slotkin, and others have done extensive work making connections between American literary and historical developments and pornographic culture. Lang's study of Anne Hutchinson places the antinomian challenge in a context of a general fear among Massachusetts Puritans of a breakdown in culturally prescribed gender roles. Annette Kolodny interprets American expansion as dependent upon elaborate metaphors of the landscape as conquerable female. And Richard Slotkin's massive reinterpretation of American culture points clearly to a national, cultural mind dependent upon strict delineations of race and gender. Without its pornographic content, Western culture would not exist. Nature, of course, is seldom as controllable or predictable as cultural prescriptions. In the natural world, races mix, genders transgress fixed roles, and few men or women exist without some "cross" or ambivalence of blood or psyche. In a culture that promotes control, however, social transgressions and other "crossings" are prohibited—or, at best, tolerated as weaknesses: Mulattoes become "tragic"; homosexuality exists as an "alternative." Pornography thrives within a cultural context of hostility toward anarchic physical phenomena, which resist being controlled, mastered, or somehow categorized and subsumed.

"Magazines reflect contemporary consciousness," according to Cecelia Tichi (26). To discover the logic of pornography in the popular mind, one needs to explore the magazine rack. Specifically, one needs to explore the seemingly innocuous magazines that purport to provide aide and guidance to the reader in his or her quest to be socially and sexually whole. "Magazines must help readers live as they want to, must address their perspectives," in Richard Ohmann's formulation. The world represented in popular magazines must "simplify, regularize, and smooth out the contradictions of social existence" (151). The way in which the culture of pornography translates into patterns of daily living, the way in which it informs "contemporary consciousness" in other words, is displayed in popular magazines for mass consumption. A critical examination of the October 1988 issue of *Glamour* reveals, in simplified, regularized, and smooth patterns, the logic of pornographic sexuality. The problematic object that compels *Glamour* is the human body, particularly the female body. The language of *Glamour* is consumerism, the language of commodity exchange. The function of *Glamour* is to "help readers live" and thrive in their culture. The magazine does not question the culture's right to hegemony, nor does it inquire into the reader's motives or her willingness to conform. Because of its simplicity and regularity, it provides a clear perspective on the pornographic nexus.

Consumerism is twentieth-century America's dominant mode of cultural communication. As commodities, all natural phenomena have potential manifestations as objects, and as objects, all natural phenomena are potentially controllable—as possessions. Sexuality, for example, becomes a collage of poses and objects to emulate. "What is Sexy?" asks the advertisement in *Glamour* for Jovan Musk cologne. The collage is composed of images appearing as if cut and pasted from other contexts: two human torsos interlocked with hands on each other's buttocks; a couple making love on a beach; a woman's upper body in a slip, placed between an alarm clock at 7:30 A.M. and a man's naked torso, suggesting competing desires; a formal-dress couple dancing; a peach with cream being poured over it; a man and a woman at a public restaurant kissing; and the picture of the literal product, the Musk, to make the point. Bodies, fruit, cologne—an equality of commodities. The point, of course, is to suggest a qualitative correspondence across a wide spectrum of images and representations. "Sexy" is sexual activity (kissing, dancing, embracing) and sexual images (the peach) *and* the product, the Jovan cologne. The advertisement suggests a correspondence not simply of ideas, which it claims, but also of commodities. "Sexy" is quite naturally human interaction—but it is not quite naturally captured in a piece of fruit or a bottle of cologne. However, this particular piece of fruit is photographed to resemble various parts of human anatomy; peaches and cream, of course, has its popular connotations and the term "peach" itself once served as a slang term for girl. The reader knows how to read "sexy" into the peach. And in case the reader happens to miss the point, an ad for Burlington Sheer Indulgence pantyhose explains the connection between "his favorite peach dessert" and the "delicious" feeling of a woman's legs. Through the associational qualities of clutched butts and stolen kisses, the viewer is being taught to read "sexy" into Jovan Musk cologne. More important, however, is the ultimate lesson in this grammar: that "sexy" can in fact be commodified. "What is sexy?" is answered by "What sexy is"—the caption below the Jovan Musk product, one bottle "for men," and one "for women."

The original inhabitants of the American continent were perplexed and outraged at the European idea that nature—the land—could be commodified and possessed. The idea, however, resulted in the historic expansion by which those who did not see it that way were dispossessed and effectively removed from history. The Jovan Musk

ad represents one example of the historic extension of this cultural commodity-fetish. What is a nation? A nation is land, images, and boundaries on a map. What is sexuality? "Sexy" is photographs, images and poses, commodities. American culture has always understood itself—its well-being and its progress—by what it possesses. Little psychic distance needs to be traveled before the body itself is included among national cultural possessions. In her study of "the decisive factor shaping the founding conceptions of 'America' and 'the American,'" Myra Jehlen finds that it is best understood as something "material rather than conceptual; rather than a set of abstract ideas, the physical fact of the continent" (3). In an insightful footnote, Jehlen speculates that "the modern emphasis on sexuality as the core of personal identity might be related to a desire to establish a material base for individualism" (240). The body may well be the final frontier of an expansionist culture. In this way the self, to borrow Jehlen's formulation, is best understood as something "material rather than conceptual." In the late twentieth century, when exterior, spatial frontiers have long since disappeared, the body itself becomes the final repository of ideas about control, possession, and cultural identity.

Naming of Parts

"You're a work of art," claims the advertisement in the October 1988 issue of *Glamour* magazine for Aziza Hypo-Allergenic eye makeup. The Aziza Color Series, called "eye art," comes in the form of "your very own palette" housing three shades of color. The woman in the photograph is holding an artist's paintbrush bearing the same shade of pink that adorns her eyes. The connection is clear: The woman is both work of art *and* artist, both product and creator—subject and object. The viewer of the ad is shown *what* and shown *how;* she is shown what to look like and how to look well. The caption over the photograph states plainly: "Eye for Color." The woman in the photograph looks good: She has masterfully applied the eye art to her face. Equally important, however, is that she looks well: Her countenance demonstrates discernment, the appraising and critical "eye for color" of the artist—but the work she labors over is her own face. She is studying something (a mirror?) toward which her artist's brush points, assessing whether she has succeeded in creating "the look," or the work of art, she has envisioned. She herself, however, is the "vision" provided for the consumer by the advertisement. Look-

ing at her presumably instructs the viewer to look well and to look good. The ad fetishizes the eye, furthermore, as the site of female beauty. In the upper right hand corner of the ad the eye is isolated for study. It is this same model's eye, removed from her face and closed, displaying the Pink Frost Color on her brush. This is the eye that the woman can never "see" unless she learns to view herself as a "work," or as an object she has created.

An ad for the Clairol Highlighting Collection makes the same point in regard to "hair painting." An empty frame is placed over the face of the model in the photograph, and the caption reads, "Highlights Suitable for Framing." The product comes with a brush—the artist's brush, again. "From the very first stroke," the text explains, "you're creating effects wherever you want, illuminating your self-image." The collection includes a number of shades, similar to the "palette" provided by Aziza. "So go ahead, paint yourself a masterpiece." The self is not expressed or conveyed but created, given light, by the product.

A specific work of art—masterpiece or hack work—does not exist prior to creation or production by the artist. As work of art, accord-

OCT.
$1.95

GLAMOUR

join our
makeover
MARATHON
a new you starts now

**how to live
RICH!
even if
you're not**

LOOK AGAIN
great clothes/
new ways
to wear them

15 WAYS
TO MAKE
LOVE STRONG

**FALL
BEAUTY
NEWS**
let's talk color!

ing to the logic employed by Aziza and Clairol, the woman (or the woman's self-image) is brought into existence by the beauty product, the eye art, or the highlighting of the hair. Artists, however, do not produce *themselves* when they create. They produce, rather, from within themselves a discrete object, an artwork, something separate from themselves. In *Glamour*, however, the metaphor of artistic production is applied to the creation of a self-image. And in a production like *Glamour*, which consists predominantly of images, self-image *is* self or potential self. However, the body is not understood as the raw material by which a self is constructed. The raw material is the commercial product—hair color, eye shadow, clothing, accessories. In this sense, Faulkner's Popeye is also an artist, creating himself from the "Sears, Roebuck catalog" of masculinity in the twentieth century. In *Glamour* the body is not the raw material, the natural resource, but is presented as the *canvas*, the blank space, which, until utilized or produced, is imageless, without "illumination." It is not a matter of art imitating or even enhancing life or life imitating or providing models for art. Rather, "art," here, *provides* life, provides life with the ingredient of recognition without which there would be no recognizable "I am" of existence. Like the colonist contemplating a "vacant" continent (imagining away indigenous inhabitants), the woman here is encouraged to contemplate a "vacant" self, a self awaiting the fulfillments of commodification. This is Temple Drake's world, where identities wait to be "parroted" or assumed. The physical self is understood as one's personal object of art. "Know thyself" is transformed into "produce thyself," and integrity—or self-reliance or even freedom—is replaced by productivity.

The October 1988 *Glamour* is rich with hostility for the natural body. "Join Our Make-Over Marathon" is the headline on the issue's cover: "A New You Starts Now." Self-loathing is one emotion the magazine must engender in order to maintain a need for itself in its readers, a need for the products, advice, and services it advertises and promotes. For example, *Glamour* claims to provide advice and instruction on Fashion, Health and Fitness, and Beauty. However, if one were to attain a satisfactory self-image, if one were to become confidently fashionable, healthy and fit, and beautiful, one would no longer need the magazine. Because of this central contradiction, *Glamour* must continually refine and qualify itself in order to maintain its audience. It must present its instructions and models for emulation as either economically unattainable (as in the case of the exorbitantly priced fashions, such as "casual outfits" for $500), or psychologically contradictory. The former is easily recognized as a market ploy: The same companies that produce the $200 sweaters also produce the $50 sweaters on the rack at Macy's; in any case, the point is not to buy any particular outfit but simply to keep buying clothing. The contradictory and anxiety-producing nature of the magazine as a whole, however, is far more insidious in its effect on the reader and far less apparent as a consumer ploy.

Glamour magazine contains advertisements that complement the articles and departmental features of the issue. There are advertisements for skin-care products, hair coloring and conditioning, perfumes, various makeup products (for eyes, lips, nails, etc.), underwear, pantyhose, whole outfits, shoes, and maternity clothing. The female body, in *Glamour*, is wholly colonized, parceled, and "deconstructed," a point not lost on contemporary feminists. The advertisements in late twentieth-century women's magazines compartmentalize the female body, according to Rosalind Coward, and depict, "a new definition of women's sexuality with *work*—a work with appliances and accessories" (Betterton, 55). A woman is thus instructed to colonize her own body, to divide it into plantations, so to speak, for exploitation and manipulation. If there is a whole body, a sense of wholeness, it is not distinguishable from the federation of its parts. The body's parts, in other words, are autonomous except for their relation to each other as possessions of the cultural self or the mind (the mother country?). This is clear from the very different modes of thought invoked for each "compartment" of the body. One does not think about skin with the same quality or mode of thinking that one applies to nails or hair or eyes. With naming of parts comes parceling of function.

Skin-care products compose the majority of the advertisements in the October 1988 *Glamour*. Perhaps the seasonal change and its effects on skin condition account for this. Nonetheless, the advertisements for skin-care products are particularly pornographic in their expressed hostility to such inevitable phenomena as the passage of time, aging, and physical change. Estée Lauder "Future Perfect" Micro-Targeted SkinGel promises to "*intercept* new visible signs of aging" and "to give your skin what *young skin* has at its best—luminosity." Again, the self is "given light" by the product, made recognizable and suitable for framing. Estée Lauder depends

highly, in this particular ad, on American myths of scientific progress. Its "Future Perfect" product is available through "Digitized Image Analysis (DIA)," a process "developed for the space program" and now in use by Estée Lauder beauty experts. A photograph of a woman, with flawless skin, wearing some kind of space outfit, accompanies the ad. This rather perverse reference to Christa McAuliffe certainly makes its point about the mutability of skin.

Other companies echo Estée Lauder's expressed hostility to time, age, and death, but none with such virtuosity as Nivea. A woman in a business suit is walking outside a city office building holding her briefcase in one hand and her young daughter's hand in the other. The woman looks good—and she is also looking *well* at herself in the building's reflective glass with a discerning, concerned countenance. The daughter, perhaps five years old, gazes admiringly at her successful mom—learning what to look at as she observes the object of her mother's attention. In fact, all eyes are on Mother: the woman's, the woman's image, and the child's. The caption asks, "Is your face paying the price of success?" The language could not be more precise. Don't pay the price of success, pay the price of Nivea. There are two drains on the woman's youth and beauty, the career and the

Is your face paying the price of success?

You work hard at work, you work hard at home. You're under a lot of pressure.

You skip a meal here and there. You're getting less sleep than maybe you should. Eventually, of course, it begins to show on your face: a little less resilience, a few more lines.

Now, from Europe's leading skin care experts, there's Nivea™ Visage.

Nivea Visage is a non-greasy, fast-absorbing moisturizer,

created especially for your face. Enriched with Aloe, Vitamin E, and a PABA-free sunscreen, Visage is specifically designed to fight the signs of premature aging and other effects of stress.

Nivea Visage helps replenish and nourish your skin by reducing moisture loss.

It also actually assists your skin's natural ability to renew itself. Keeping it looking and feeling firmer, smoother and younger, longer.

For over seventy-five years at Nivea, our concern has been the care of your skin. And it's still all we care about today.

Nivea Visage Facial Nourishing Lotion and Creme. Made to help you live with success.

AVAILABLE AT YOUR FAVORITE DRUG STORE.

From Nivea. Europe's Number One Moisturizer.

child, prefeminist and postfeminist markers of "success." The woman is "caught" between her own corporate image, reflected quite nicely in the office building mirrors, and the very image of youthfulness in her hand. Indeed, in one hand Mom holds her daughter's hand, her wrist wrapped by the tragic time-keeping watch, and in the other hand the Businesswoman holds her briefcase—a fine leather case that should last a lifetime. But it's a toss-up isn't it? Nivea products "fight the signs of premature aging" so that this mother's skin will continue "looking and feeling firmer, smoother and younger, longer." But how long before that daughter's "look" turns into a reproach?

Skin-care products in *Glamour* promise two things: beautiful "luminous" skin, and a return to a natural, youthful appearance. There is something perverse, of course, in the process of *adding* something to achieve naturalness. Sea Breeze Facial Cleansing Gel claims that "It leaves nothing on your skin but a beautiful feeling." To achieve "nothing" but a fine appearance and a welcome emotion, one must add the product in question to the skin. The product will then disappear, leaving nothing but the emotion and the appearance of cleanliness. Maybelline Soft Cheek Colors are applied to help one "to blush beautifully, glow naturally." The advertisement shows a grown woman and a young child, with identical blush coloring on their white faces. The ad identifies the particular color on display as "Innocent." Natural emotion, the ad suggests, disappears with virginity—but unlike virginity, blushing can be re-created, artistically produced, so that one may "glow naturally" again. The defiance of logic is emblematic here. Aging is reversed, the future is made perfect, youth is restored: What is natural is overcome and controlled by science, and the body is surrendered to the logic of commodification.

In advertising, of course, contradictions are essential. In the same way that contradiction signals authentic life for Ralph Ellison—in its ambiguity, ambivalence, and anxiety—it signals vitality for the advertiser who must re-create the living creature's sense of "necessities." The effectiveness of cigarette ads are actually improved by the inclusion of the Surgeon General's Warning: The contradiction between enjoying the cigarette and fearing the cancer or fetal harm participates in the pleasure and danger of pornographic culture. "You've come a long way baby": now you can place yourself in

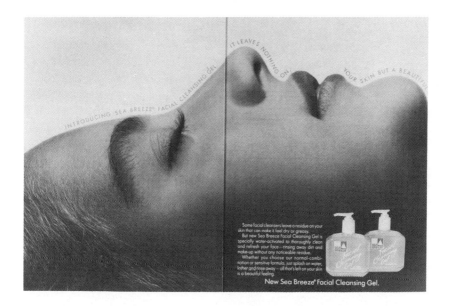

Some facial cleansers leave a residue on your skin that can make it feel dry or greasy. But new Sea Breeze Facial Cleansing Gel is specially water-activated to thoroughly clean and refresh your face—rinsing away dirt and make-up without any noticeable residue. Whether you choose our normal-combination or sensitive formula, just splash on water, lather and rinse away—all that's left on your skin is a beautiful feeling.

New Sea Breeze® Facial Cleansing Gel.

danger, just like the Marlboro Man. Contradiction signals vitality, curiosity, and vigor. If the message in the beauty product advertisement seems contradictory, the consumer is inclined to keep listening and to keep buying until she gets the point—and, of course, the product. Frank Lentricchia speaks to this consumerist logic, characterizing "commodity gratification" as "the instrument for structuring desire as intention not toward the commodity per se, but toward the capacity of the commodity to confer romance and wonder." Lentricchia sees the logic of consumerism as essentially conservative, "conserving and perpetuating consumer capitalism" (30). This is true: No matter how "subversive" the content of a consumer ad, its aim is to lead one to overspend, not overthrow. Consumerism acts to *insert* the self into the larger culture, the pornographic nexus. If pornography is an ideology, then consumerism is its myth-system, its language. Minna Stores answers any concerns about contradiction directly. "When logic and imagination meet" reads the incomplete sentence across the ad, which is completed pictorially: At first glance a woman, in some sort of Little Bo Peep evocation, is cut in two pieces. We can name the parts. The pinking shears, however, are not actually mutilating this woman but are creating her, creating

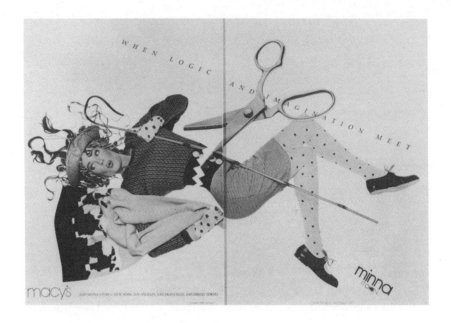

the jagged design on her waist. With logic and imagination, with mind, we can do whatever we want with this body—and if you've lost your sheep in the process, read *Glamour* to bring them home.

Hair products follow a mode of advertising consciousness similar to that of skin-care products, with the added notion of hair as frame, or emblem of value. A woman with hair flowing at a 45 degree angle from the left side of her head appears below the caption, "With Perma Soft they'll notice your hair. Not your perm." Hair is to be noticed (unlike skin, which is to be luminous, or, as Ellison would say, to be looked through). Hair is the body-commodity's first line of self-advertisement. It creates a desire on the part of the "they" who notice. If the body is a commodity, it is also a product: It needs to be advertised in order to be noticed, desired, and possessed. And like commercial advertising, there is no single way to sell or present one's product. Conair Fashion Plates II claims that "changing your look is as easy as changing your mind." The same model, in the Conair advertisement, appears in four very different self-images, her dark-rooted blond hair is presented perfectly straight, curly, frizzed, and in some combination, each with a discrete accompanying outfit. The "three interchangeable styling plates" teach the reader of *Glam-*

With Perma Soft they'll notice your hair. Not your perm.

That's the beauty of Perma Soft.®
The Shampoo, Conditioner,
Mousse and Hairspray are specially formulated for permed
hair. So your perm has plenty
of softness and curl. Looks
natural. And isn't that why you
got a perm in the first place?

Glamour and Pornography   135

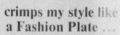

our a central lesson in postmodern existence. Changing your look, or changing your mind, are metaphors for changing your *self*. A commodity can be redesigned, a product line can be retooled and re-created; it can be made young or old, straight or wild. As "carload lots" of Temple Drake, the women of *Glamour* can be "made over" to fit the college scene, the debutante ball, or the whorehouse. The self is, like a work of art, essentially representational. This applies specifically to the sexual self.

The plasticity of the self provides the October 1988 issue of *Glamour* its primary editorial motif. The lead feature, the "Make-Over Marathon," displays over twenty self-selected photographs of *Glamour* readers, sent in to the magazine by the readers themselves. Underneath each woman's photograph is her name and what she "wants" for herself. Kris Marsh: "I want help for my damaged hair." Martha Meade: "I want an updated polished appearance." Lisa René Williams: "I want a healthy look." All of the women are average looking, but their amateurish snapshots, in the magazine's slick context, make them appear in dire need of *Glamour*'s advice. The essay instructs readers to "Get a New You Now," including "the motivation and the how-tos to make over your body, your hair, makeup, and fashion image." The essay contains a checklist of "bad habits" ("Eat at fast food outlets?" "Clean your plate?"); a chart to figure daily calorie needs, a diet plan, and exercise techniques. Subsequent issues will cover other areas for attention, but weight control is the October focus. The editors in this feature provide ample evidence that they are responding to reader interests. Margaret Caffrey wants to lose twenty pounds; Kim Garofolo wants to gain twenty pounds; Jennifer Wayne does aerobics but is still overweight and suspects she does not eat properly. Rachael Miller is given the final say and photograph: "After countless diets and resolutions, I'm counting on you, *Glamour*, to give me the incentive I need." Dissatisfaction with the self is *Glamour*'s reason for existing, as well as its primary suggestion to its readers. The magazine implies that physical self-perfection is entirely possible ("Future Perfect") and encourages women to look well at themselves and acquire "the motivation and how-tos" to achieve or attempt perfection. The physical contradiction of a perfected body is not addressed, but the contradiction empowers the magazine nonetheless. All of the women who submitted their photographs to *Glamour* express some kind of self-loathing, which translates into some specific need to change, or some specific product or service to consume.

In only one of the photographs depicting full-body does a woman wear street clothes—in all the others the women show themselves in bathing suits, leotards, or underwear. Although clothing affects bodily image, *make-overs* concern not clothing but *selves*. A commonplace notion once had it that the clothes made the man or the woman; a consumer notion has it that the woman makes the woman. Obviously one can buy a new dress, but can a new self be acquired? None of the featured women make claims to want to be healthy, live longer, or feel better. One woman does want to *look* healthy, however. Three flight attendants in matching leotards "want to look fresh all day." Another woman wants "to look 31," and a mother and daughter, in their bathrobes, "want to look our ages." Elizabeth Sachs wants "a professional, easy-care look." And the Rev. Sarah Wood Lee wants "to update my fashion image as a minister." The emphasis on looking is central to the *Glamour* pornography, from the body as work of art to the distinction, made meaningless, between being something and appearing as something. In *Glamour*, it means nothing "to be"— existence is simply the canvas on which the self is inscribed, painted, and constructed. The self is actually invisible—a darkness that re-

A NEW YOU NOW

Jump start your exercise

Without exercise, you won't lose weight and keep it off as effectively, or get rid of flab. If you're trying to gain weight, you need exercise to help tone and sculpt your body. If you're new to exercise, start slowly and build up gradually.

Fat-burning aerobics

Aerobic exercise, such as brisk (3.5-4 miles/hour) walking, jogging, dancing, cycling, that uses the large leg muscles continuously, speeds up your metabolism and burns fat. It also counteracts depression and reduces stress (often the cause of overeating or loss of appetite).

Are you getting the aerobic benefit?

Every little movement burns calories, but to burn the most fat, you must work out aerobically at a moderate but consistent level of intensity. Here are ways to tell if you are:

● Monitoring your heart rate: Measuring your pulse at the wrist or the carotid artery at the side of your neck tells you how many times a minute your heart is beating. That tells you how hard you are exercising. Take your pulse for 10 seconds when you are exercising and multiply by 6 to get the number of beats per minute, which should fall within your target heart range (THR). To find your THR, subtract your age from 220 (the answer is your predicted maximal heart rate or MHR), and multiply your MHR by 60 percent and by 75 percent (you burn more fat working out at a moderate intensity). A twenty-five-year-old woman trying to lose weight would find her THR this way: 220-25=195. 195 x .60 = 117. 195 x .75 = 146. THR=117-146.

● Perceived exertion: This is how hard you *feel* you're working out. For best fat-burning results, work out aerobically at a level that seems somewhere between "fairly light" and "hard" to you. As you become more conditioned, you will be able to exercise longer and harder without feeling you are doing more.

● Sweat test: Working out too intensely can sabotage fat-burning efforts and lead to injuries. A light sweat means you're getting a good workout; profuse sweating is a signal to slow down.

● Talk test: Can you talk comfortably to someone exercising beside you? If not, check your pulse; slow down if necessary.

Are you exercising long enough?

The longer you exercise, the more fat you burn. Start out exercising aerobically a minimum of 20 minutes at a time, 30 minutes if possible. Gradually work up to 45-60 minutes of aerobic exercise at a time; check your heart rate several times.

Body-sculpting

It's also important to strengthen your muscles—both to shape and sculpt your body and because muscle gives you added calorie-burning potential. You can strengthen muscles using rubber exercise bands or tubing; hand weights; weight machines; and exercises such as sit-ups, lunges and squats. Swimming also strengthens and tones muscles. Since muscle weighs more than fat, as you lose fat and strengthen muscles, you may gain a few pounds, but you'll lose inches.

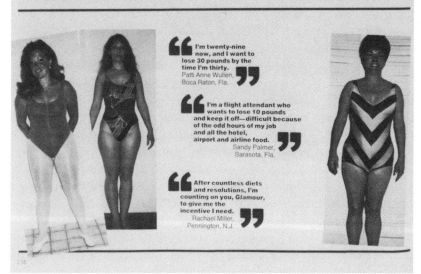

66 I'm twenty-nine now, and I want to lose 30 pounds by the time I'm thirty.
Patti Anne Wullen, Boca Raton, Fla. 99

66 I'm a flight attendant who wants to lose 10 pounds and keep it off—difficult because of the odd hours of my job and all the hotel, airport and airline food.
Sandy Palmer, Sarasota, Fla. 99

66 After countless diets and resolutions, I'm counting on you, *Glamour*, to give me the incentive I need.
Rachael Miller, Pennington, N.J. 99

Glamour and Pornography   139

quires illumination. However, where Ellison's conclusions about postmodern invisibility led to a liberation of the self from its racial and historical context, *Glamour's* implications lead back to enslavement. The pornographic content of *Glamour* is contained not so much in the message that there is no self apart from its representation, its object status, but in the message that, without the text (*Glamour*), the self would die.

The assumption that informs the grammar of *Glamour* places the magazine at the heart of pornographic representationalism. The observation that the self does not exist apart from its representations is what makes all art—including pornography—possible. *Glamour* assumes that since the self must be constructed, it must be constructed *in this approved way.* "The rise of sexual consumerism," in other words, indicates "the growing power of the mass media to enforce conformity to sexual norms" (Dubois, 43). The alternative to the *Glamour* assumption is to conclude that because the self is constructed, because it is not natural, there can be no single or correct way to mold it. However, this conclusion must be suppressed because it would turn *Glamour* into a consumer disaster. If there were no correct way to construct the self, in other words, *Glamour* could not "target" itself to its readers and would have no reason to exist. It would become an "underground" publication if it advocated anarchic sexuality—and Invisible Man would be among its subscribers. But who else would buy a magazine about "beauty" that claims that there are no set standards of beauty? Who would buy a magazine filled with invisible women? The assumption that sexuality is never natural but is always culturally coded means that use of the word "natural" as adjective is immediately suspect. Sexuality is anarchic: It cannot be argued that it is "natural" to do anything because you are told to do it. If you want sex, there is no natural way to get it, much less unnatural ways to get it. But "telling" is what *Glamour* does. Images do not reflect social arrangements; they *are* social arrangements. By representational means, magazines such as *Glamour* influence and produce ideas to define the sexual, the natural, the self. *Glamour,* as a text, instructs its readers on how best to imagine themselves, to *image-in* themselves to the dominant modes of looking good and looking well, and getting it. Hence the old question: "What do these women want?"

That so many women submitted photographs depicting themselves partially clothed, or in the semiprivate clothing of the wom-

THE HIDDEN SIDE OF THE
GIRL IN THE GRAY FLANNEL SUIT.

Vanity Fair

"Just because a woman wears sensible shoes and a single strand of pearls–it doesn't mean she's strictly 9 to 5–underneath her corporate uniform she may be very 5 to 9."

My Favorite Fantasy™ Bra. Secretly sumptuous. Quietly comfortable. A bra that can help turn a long, long day into a bit of a daydream. Now that's a reality you can live with.

Glamour and Pornography   141

an's gymnasium or bedroom, implies an agreement with Vanity Fair's claim that "The Hidden Side of the Girl in the Grey Flannel Suit" is the girl, or the woman, who appears beneath this headline in her bra and panties. Whereas the clothes, by the cliché, are said to make the man (a cliché that informs a magazine like *Gentleman's Quarterly*), the clothes are still understood to "hide" the woman. In the Vanity Fair advertisement, "underneath her corporate uniform" (suggesting conscription of some sort), the "9 to 5" woman is "very 5 to 9." The same idea is communicated by the logo, "Underneath It's Bali," which accompanies the Bali photograph of a woman in her underwear, partially draped in a satin sheet. Warner's advertisement shows a woman in her underwear reading the morning newspaper. The logic in these and similar ads for underclothing is consistent: The hidden side, or the essence of woman, is her "secret" self, represented by her nakedness. However, this "side" of a woman cannot be hidden to the woman herself.

Presumably, the Vanity Fair "girl" has seen herself naked and in her underwear. Similarly, the Warner's woman, fully made up, her hair done, wearing pearl earrings, is said not to mind "wearing a full figure bra . . . if it looks like this one." Looks like this one—to

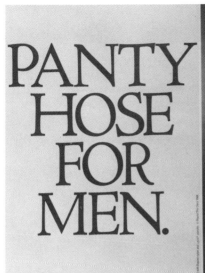

whom? Only to someone else, to a subject, are these hidden sides of women a secret, withheld from sight. Round The Clock Hosiery makes this point without subtlety. In a full two-page ad, the right hand page shows a woman's barely covered buttocks, long legs, and high-heeled shoes walking away from the camera. The caption, in large letters taking up the entire facing page, reads, "Panty Hose for Men." The observer here, as with the Vanity Fair and Warner's advertisements, is male: The camera, the "subject" for whom the women depicted are objects of observation, is an anonymous man. What is true here for Vanity Fair, Warner's, Bali, and similar ads is also true for *Glamour* as a whole: "Round the clock," in other words, a man is watching.

The male subject is made explicit again in the ad for L.A. Gear athletic footwear. A woman in leather displays her "athletic shoes" in a provocative pose (she is posing, not moving), which does not evoke competitive sports activities. Beside her head, as if meant to frame her thoughts, are the words, "It wasn't a fantasy. . . ." It is not clear why she would have this thought in her mind. In the background of the photograph, out of focus, is a man *holding a camera.* He is taking a close look at the blue-leather woman while walking

"It wasn't a fantasy..."

You've got the moves, we've got the shoes.

L.A. GEAR
FASHION ATHLETIC FOOTWEAR

Available at: **Lady Footlocker** · **Macy's** · **May Company**

4721 Redwood, Los Angeles, California 90066, 213-822-1995 • Information regarding L.A. Gear Socks please contact: 1-800-438-9127 • For Canadian distribution contact: Indeka Imports Ltd., Mississauga, Ontario, Canada L5L 1X7 416-826-6800 • ©1988 L.A. Gear

FOR STORES, SEE PAGE 297

toward her with his camera in hand. Obviously, then, the thought "It wasn't a fantasy" is the man's thought—the subject's thought, the opinion of the one who is looking. Of course, if the blue-leather woman has read *Glamour*, she may indeed have this thought herself. The placement of the words next to her head does suggest that they are her thoughts, that she has learned to look at herself with the same eye possessed by the man and the camera. How else did she learn to create out of herself his idea of fantasy?

Glamour defines the arts of looking good and looking well. The man is always watching, and the woman is always watching the woman being watched by the man. In a culture where selves are objectified, all selves are potential objects to be captured on film ("made famous," as Andy Warhol presaged) or made-over. *Glamour*, then, is an essential resource for the acquisition of power. In a culture of subjects and objects, watchers and watched, one needs to objectify one's self in order to achieve power and assert control over at least one image. If you cannot objectify someone else, at least you can objectify yourself. In *Glamour*, it is assumed that *looking* is a male prerogative. Women may look good, and they may also be taught to look well with a discerning eye, but this is only in preparation for the ultimate viewing, which will be done by the male. In other words, as John Berger has argued, when women look at themselves, they look at themselves with a male eye. And when women look with discernment, they assume a subjective, culturally male role with culturally prescribed male concerns for beauty, allure, and sexual invitation. Articles in *Glamour* such as "15 Ways to Make Love Strong," "How Much Should You Change for Him?" and "Your Pregnancy" all assume a male subject behind, beside, within, or in the future for the female object.

In an intriguing advertisement, Nordstrom men's wear for women ("softness is your strong suit, as men's wear takes on a fresh, new femininity") features a photograph of a woman in a "man's" blazer and pants, holding a camera. She has assumed the male subject and with it the power to objectify: to capture on film, to look and to make of her vision a commodity. Nordstrom should be read in conjunction with the one ad in *Glamour* specifically for a camera. An ad for Polaroid Cameras features ten photographs of men in various poses (three half naked, one in the shower) called "Ten 10's." The power to frame the object, which all *Glamour* readers understand, is available to women, according to Polaroid. "And we guarantee it,"

Softness is your strong suit, as men's wear takes on a fresh, new femininity.
From Sunny Leigh, blazer; 132.00. Shirt; 84.00. Pants; 78.00. In Point of View.
Washington·Oregon·California·Utah·Alaska·Virginia; opening in October at San Francisco Centre.

nordstrom

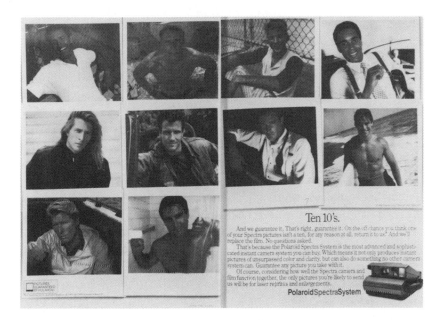

Ten 10's.

And we guarantee it. That's right, guarantee it. On the off chance you think one of your Spectra pictures isn't a ten, for any reason at all, return it to us. And we'll replace the film. No questions asked.

That's because the Polaroid Spectra System is the most advanced and sophisticated instant camera system you can buy. Which means it not only produces instant pictures of unsurpassed color and clarity, but can also do something no other camera system can. Guarantee any picture you take with it.

Of course, considering how well the Spectra camera and film function together, the only pictures you're likely to send us will be for laser reprints and enlargements.

PolaroidSpectraSystem

the ad copy reads. Clearly, looking—and "capturing" on film—denotes culturally recognized power.

The assumption that the self is an object to be looked at and possessed, and that this self is a commodity for production and display, enables the language of "make-over" to thrive in *Glamour*. If the self is a commodity, if self-image is something produced with the aid of various raw materials for sale in the marketplace, then the self, similar to any contemporary commodity, is also *disposable*. Commodities become obsolete—so do pornographic selves. Built-in obsolescence is absolutely necessary to the *Glamour* magazine production. If selves were "natural," or possessed integrity, souls, or spirits, how could a make-over be anything but an exercise in hypocrisy? *Glamour* does not advocate a simple, new look; rather, the magazine offers the possibility of "A New You." Only the absence of belief in an essential, unified self makes possible the particular kind of marketing used to promote the make-over. And only the belief that the presented self—the outerwear, the make-up, the hairstyle— is temporary and subject to revision makes possible the notion that the "real self" lies hidden. But hidden where? Once the Vanity Fair girl removes her underclothing, is that her real self?

Unlike Temple Drake, the modernist female with "an agony for concealment," the contemporary woman in *Glamour* seems to have "an agony for revelation"—but as there was nothing for Temple to conceal, there seems also to be nothing revelatory in *Glamour*, only the substitution of one image for another. Perhaps the real self must be *observed* to become real because, as Ellison intimated, invisibility itself is a function of sight, not the lack of projection. The actual "woman" in *Glamour* possesses the same kind of invisibility embraced by IM in Ellison's novel. She is "irresponsible" (shouldn't the Nivea woman be watching her child and not her face? Why aren't these woman ever doing anything?) We see her in various objectifications, we see her in parts, in poses, in fantasies—but do we ever see behind the face of things? Getting to a "real" self does seem to be the goal of many who wrote to the magazine for help. However, what if this real self, as so many readers insisted, was obscured by twenty to forty pounds of excess weight? In that case, "the hidden side of the girl" is hidden to all but her own memory of former, lesser poundage or vision of future loss. Perhaps time has destroyed or obscured the real self, making time an agent of evil, further estranging the self from its material existence. No wonder Estée Lauder placed its model in a space suit. In all, the cross messages in *Glamour* are beyond synthesis. Given the inherent confusions and the overwhelming difficulty of possessing the real self, what choice does the *Glamour* reader have but to grab next month's issue, hoping it will all become clear eventually? As Rachel Miller said so unequivocally, "I'm counting on you, *Glamour*, to give me the incentive I need."

Glamour gives and takes away simultaneously. In an issue devoted to make-over, the "Sexual Ethics" column by Carol Lynn Mithers asks, "How Much Should You Change for Him?" Amy and Roger are one focal couple in the essay. Amy uses the "f-word," and Roger does not like it, but Amy is put off by Roger's demands that she change her vocabulary habits. "She feels that Roger's request is more than a quibble over words. He is asking her to make a change in something as basic to her nature as the way she speaks. It seems intrusive," Mithers explains, "and it makes her wonder what's going to come next." Amy told Mithers, "I really love this guy . . . but how much am I supposed to change to please him? I certainly didn't go into this relationship looking for a make-over." Amy may not have fallen in love for a make-over, but readers of *Glamour* have certainly bought this issue "looking for a make-over" or looking for information about make-overs.

Mithers's critique is confusing, and contradicts the premise of the magazine about plastic selves. One's vocabulary is basic to one's nature, but one's hair color, hair type, eye color, body weight, and attitude toward existence itself are not. The magazine announces on its cover that a new self is *obtainable,* not discoverable. In any case, Mithers proves that *Glamour* has the answer after all. She informs the reader that there is "no rule which dictates how *much* one should change to please a lover." It seems "natural" that one will resist change. The question is not how much change, but how to go about persuading someone to change—how to get them to do it. It is the same as the task at hand for *Glamour.* Mithers's proscription for persuasion strikes at the soul of the magazine.

Roger's mistake was that he posed his make-over desires "not as requests but as *demands."* He failed to give Amy a sense of making her own choice. He, and other men like him, attempted "to remake their lovers in an image *they* had chosen." What Roger needs to learn is the language of cultural power: the ability to make Amy *internalize* his own eye (or ear, in this case). He needs to teach Amy to see herself as he sees her, to look at herself through his eyes. *Glamour* makes no demands on its readers; its advertisers make no threats against hesitant consumers. Advertising simply presents itself as a medium that makes options available. The consumer, according to this logic, is "free" to choose the product or to pass it up. No advertisement forces its product on the consumer. It's not "how much you change," Mithers concludes, "but *why* you're making the change." Changes made from self-choice, not from capitulation to demands, are good changes. The woman, then, will learn to love, and to recognize as a good man to love, the man who reasons with the logic of the advertiser, with the cultural mind represented by *Glamour* magazine. She will also, of course, learn to use this mind when she becomes the subject herself, when she looks well at her man (with her Polaroid eye for "10's") and attempts to change *his* habits. In either case, a happy object is the object who believes she (or he) is in fact the subject, the one in control. "The woman who makes an occasional change to please her lover while remaining true to herself is enlarged by the action." The question is begged, however, as to what this *self* is, or where it is, to which the woman remains true. "The woman who agrees to be remade in her lover's image is diminished," in Mithers's final sentence, "for she'll only gain approval at the price of losing herself." In a medium in which "A New You Starts Now," admonitions to be true to yourself—and the question of "How Much Should You Change for Him?"—can only produce anxiety. One cannot remain true to the self if the self does not exist. However, one can remain true to the *idea* that the self is a commodity—an object in need of consumer marketing and packaging, the guidance of experts—and this is the idea, the ideology, of *Glamour*.

Only a few pages before Mithers's "Sexual Ethics" column is the four-page photo feature, "Twin Cities Makeovers." Portrayed are four women who allowed *Glamour* experts to guide them through complete make-overs, from hairstyle to wardrobe. Civil engineer Terri Collins was given a more "confident style" to help her function in the masculine environment of construction companies. On the other hand, Anne Klein's clothes "have to fit a corporate culture"— and her new look includes "an updated haircut" so that her "image keeps up with her life." Newly divorced Suzanne Schurr wanted her "outward appearance to reflect the big changes in my life." And so, *Glamour* editors write, "We cut Suzanne's hair just enough to restore its natural wave and volume," shortening it from waist length to shoulder length, and changing her clothes from blue jeans to wool. Each make-over was dramatic but "proposed" or "suggested" (never commanded) by *Glamour,* and each was designed to fit better the life-style, occupation, or "change" in the woman's social situation. None of the women's profiles mention the loss or recovery of a *self*—only the alteration of an image—and all are portrayed as being pleased and satisfied with their new looks.

Glamour magazine reflects a world threatened by rapid natural changes—changes represented by various products, by aging and decay, and by the demands of others. Stability may be a goal in life, but stability is only purchased through the acceptance and control of change. Controlling natural changes is contradictory, of course, but, typical of *Glamour* contradictions, it simply compels further reading of *Glamour*. "Women embrace what's new," according to *Glamour*'s profile of the average Twin Cities woman, "but only if it promises longevity and is comfortable, functional." The Future, once again, Perfect. The first step toward achieving the *Glamour* image is to let go of any notion of a natural, enduring self and embrace the idea of a *produced* self, a commodified self. To *make over* requires a deconstructionist's view of the self—the self as text, perhaps. Is there a self in *Glamour* magazine? One of *Glamour*'s newer competitors provides a clearer expression of this pornographic issue in women's magazines. Is there a self in *Self* magazine? Or, perhaps "Self," as title, is the last gasp of the popular belief in an inner quality that transcends objectification, one that cannot be made over, one that contains a past that cannot be "forgiven" but must be corrected and compensated for.

The October 1988 issue of *Glamour* magazine contains a feature titled, "How To Live Rich Even If You're Not." The article is a rather ludicrous explanation of how to save money to buy goods and services beyond one's budget or class. The article claims, however, that "living rich is not always a matter of dollars and cents; it's an attitude—more about setting priorities, making the right choices, and *believing that you deserve to live well.*" The way to begin living rich is to think about the things that bring you "the most pleasure." The essay defines "living rich" as being able to be satisfied with what you can manage to afford and believing that you are rich. If living rich is an attitude, then *Glamour* provides the images and associations that are necessary ingredients—raw materials—to that frame of mind. Believing that the "true self" is poorly represented can go a long way toward convincing a homely or working-class woman that the "hidden girl" inside her is attractive and wealthy. If the subject, or viewer, determines the status of the object, or the "work of art," then one's attitude is wholly determinate of the image projected. The attitude of the viewer, of the woman who looks well, will determine how well she constructs her commodity. It is, after all, a narcissistic project, *Glamour*. As with Narcissus, in *Glamour* the images remain just out of reach.

The women who wrote and sent their photographs into the Makeover Marathon were primarily middle class and working class women, average looking to common, from a *Glamour* perspective. The fashions advertised in *Glamour*, however, would then be well beyond the budgets of these women. "2 Timers" features outfits that can be used in more than one social context—casual or formal—and this represents "the single, smartest move you can make" in the wardrobe. In the first example, a $500 formal outfit is transformed for use in a more casual setting by adding $260 in blue jeans and accessories. Part of a pants and sweater outfit ($460) is made useful for evening wear by adding $200 for skirt, shoes, and body suit.

Make-overs are not cheap. Another feature, "Private Pleasures," shows women in sexy underwear outfits ranging from $100 to $300. "Your private wardrobe may not be as extensive as your public one, but it reflects how you value your intimate moments." A very strong attitude would be necessary to close the gap between a working-class woman's income and a $283 "private pleasure" ensemble. "Pick a mood—chic, sweet, or sexy. Then pick the lingerie that suits it, suits you." The range of emotions open for perusal and choice are as varied as consumer commodities. As controlled self, one chooses emotions in the same way one chooses a chemise. Those who cannot afford to choose the chemise in the picture can *at least* choose the emotion—and those who cannot choose their emotion must be made over, so that their attitudes complement and accept their lifestyles.

The advertisements and features of *Glamour* magazine work together, mutually reinforcing each other, to present a singular and identifiable, but largely unattainable, image of the female self. The self is incomplete, transitory, and subject to periodic revision. The models in the magazine, however, are complete, enviable, and in control. The self must be made over, but must remain true to itself. The beauty product must be added, so that the natural self may be illuminated. *Glamour* proceeds by these contradictions, establishing a need for itself by the solutions it proffers. The underlying message to the consumer is unmistakable: *You will never get this right.* The only solution, then, is to keep buying the magazine in hopes that the contradictions will resolve. No one, after all, can be to blame. "The Past Forgiven," claims Estée Lauder. "The Present Improved. The Future Perfect."

Glamour magazine is a representational catalog in the ideology of a pornographic culture, an expression of the culture's consumerist language of commodification and plasticity. *Glamour* is a pornographic discourse. It is wholly good-humored, kind and gentle in its systematic endorsement of a culture of control, domination, and anxiety. It is equivalent, as a resource, to the Sears, Roebuck catalog out of which Faulkner claimed Popeye Vitelli was produced in carload lots. Temple Drake emerges from the pages of *Glamour* "cool, predatory and discreet," seeking pleasure and inviting danger, trying to fit into and be her "natural" self, looking for a make-over.

The effect of a close reading of *Glamour* approaches the final effect of *Sanctuary,* a sense of the effort resulting in "sullen and

Glamour and Pornography   153

discontented and sad" readers who can never quite get the magazine's message—because there is no message to get, as there is no self to reveal, conceal, or discover. There is no solution to the magazine's implicit, ritualistic problematics of allure, mystery, and beauty. The only question, ultimately, is whether the magazine will be purchased, and whether the reader will get her money's worth, until next month. Only in a pornographic, consumer nexus would someone pay for the privilege of learning what to buy next. But, hey, "For $1.00, Anything Goes."

WORKS CITED

Berger, John. *Ways of Seeing*. New York: Penguin, 1977.
Betterton, Rosemary, ed. *Looking On: Images of Femininity in the Visual Arts and Media*. New York: Pandora, 1987.
Dubois, Ellen Carol, and Linda Gordon. "Seeking Ecstasy on the Battlefield: Danger and Pleasure in 19th-century Feminist Thought." In *Pleasure and Danger: Exploring Female Sexuality*, edited by Carole S. Vance, 31–49. Boston: Routledge & Kegan Paul, 1984.
Jehlen, Myra. *American Incarnation: The Individual, the Nation, and the Continent*. Cambridge, Mass.: Harvard University Press, 1986.
Kibbey, Ann. *The Interpretation of Material Shapes in Puritanism: A Study of Rhetoric, Prejudice, and Violence*. New York: Cambridge University Press, 1986.
Lang, Amy Schrager. *Prophetic Woman: Anne Hutchinson and the Problem of Dissent in the Literature of New England*. Berkeley: University of California Press, 1987.
Kolodny, Annette. *The Lay of the Land: Metaphor as Experience and History in American Life and Letters*. Chapel Hill: University of North Carolina Press, 1975.
Lentricchia, Frank. *Criticism and Social Change*. Chicago: University of Chicago Press, 1983.
Miles, Margaret R. *Carnal Knowing: Female Nakedness and Religious Meaning in the Christian West*. Boston: Beacon Press, 1989.
Munter, Carol. "Fat and the Fantasy of Perfection." In *Pleasure and Danger* (see Dubois), 225–31.
Ohmann, Richard. *The Politics of Letters*. Middletown, Conn.: Wesleyan University Press, 1987.
Slotkin, Richard. *Regeneration Through Violence: The Mythology of the American Frontier, 1600–1860*. Middletown, Conn.: Wesleyan University Press, 1973.
Tichi, Cecelia. *Shifting Gears: Technology, Literature, Culture in Modernist America*. Chapel Hill: University of North Carolina Press, 1987.

III THE HISTORICAL SELF

CHAPTER 5 **Historical Movement**

What's Lost in

A Lost Lady

He can listen to the
herdsmen telling their
stories over and over, go
backward and forward
with their "dreamily
indifferent" habits
of thought. . . . His
brooding spirit wraps
the legend in a loftiness
and grandeur which
actual events can never, in
themselves, possess.
—*Willa Cather,* Not Under
Forty

He was eavesdropping on
the past . . . [and] his
reading made him wish to
be an architect.
—*Cather,* A Lost Lady

The Catherian Movement

Willa Cather is famous for her declaration that "the world broke in two in 1922 or thereabouts" (*Not Under Forty,* v). In Cather's eye, the world somehow fell apart during her lifetime and produced in her generation a profound sense of historical discontinuity. Her perception of that breakage influenced her writing in ways her critics have been discussing for decades. The rupture certainly led to her own close examination of the effects of history and of the past on her life and on the lives of her created figures. In *A Lost Lady,* written the year after the world fell perceptually into two pieces, narrative history is presented as an elusive and highly politicized field of intellectual struggle. Perhaps what "broke" in 1922 was what gave rise to this novel. *A Lost Lady* could not have been written by a mind secure in the idea that the past is something that can be "recovered" once it was lost or past. In Cather's thinking, history can be utilized, it may provide rationale and motivation, but it can never be objectively known. History is not subject matter in *A Lost Lady*, it is rhetoric.

American novelists have often concerned themselves with history. In particular, they have concerned themselves with the way in which the history of the United States land mass, as colony and as nation, produced a distinctive individual or self called the American. Many high school students are introduced to American literature by way of Nathaniel Hawthorne's *The Scarlet Letter*, a meditation on the way historical events construct character. All three writers examined in this study have written extensively on the effects of historical ideas on the present. Ellison's invisible man, when he descends into his underground bright white hole, "plunges" out of history. Although the characters in *Sanctuary* seem obsessed in a sensual present, Faulkner's characters in many of his other novels, particularly *Absalom, Absalom!*, are blocked from the sensual present by their obsession with the past. As strongly as race and sex, history possesses the power to turn the self into an object that must either be borne ("the burden of the past") or somehow resisted or abjured.

When one reads widely in American literature, one inevitably reads widely in American history. Even popular fiction, the airport terminal selection for example, is not lacking in novels set in such standard eras as the Civil War, the Old West, or the Family Farm. History, as an aspect contributing to a sense of character and self, is essential to the American equation. Of course, this leaves wide open the way that "history" might be defined. The reason we must read Willa Cather in order to contemplate the historical dimension of the self as object in America is not simply because she wrote historical novels—many have done that. Rather, we must read Cather because her novels are not only set *in* history but concern themselves with what exactly it means to possess—or project—a past.

Cather's historical novels raise important questions about history and about the construction of historical narrative. Historians hold a privileged position in American culture, and we tend to reward a good memory. The resort to the historical is often considered authoritative in its own right. One's history—the history of a person's family, region, or social class, for example—is understood as definitive. In the same way that race and sex transform the mind into the ghost within the *object* (the Black body, the Masculine gender), history transforms the mind into the product of the Past. The study of the past as a source of privileged or exclusive value, then, is the laying of the groundwork for another kind of potential oppression. The workings of this kind of oppressive limitation occupied Cather throughout her career. Even her last completed novel, *Sapphira and the Slave Girl* (1940), can be understood as Cather's own intellectual journey back to origins. But unlike many of her characters, especially her male narrators, the accident of Cather's origins—she was born in Virginia but left as a child—have not informed her consciousness without resistance. The novel makes a clear statement that this—the South and all that it means symbolically—is not what she is. Willa Cather may be from Virginia, but she is not of it. In the novel, although Henry Colbert does not believe in slavery, his "place" as Sapphira's husband commits him to perpetuating the institution. On the other hand, Sapphira, a proponent of slavery, must be defensive about the institution because she has moved to her husband's territory where slavery is not accepted. Husband and wife find themselves "misplaced" and therefore called upon to explain their historical selves. The novel, an odd one by the standards of most Cather readers, may be the author's own desire to explain her relation to her birthplace.

Does one need to "explain" one's past—and I do not mean biography here but the past of one's region, one's family, one's people, or one's nation—with the same kind of energy that one must account for, perform, or even resist the cultural code of one's gender or one's race? The racial self and the sexual self are objectifications of an intellectual phenomenon that cannot, in fact, be limited to one race or one gender. The same is true of the historical self, the self identified and objectified by its "heritage." The social and intellectual self that is produced by a cross section of racial influences and by the intersubjectivity of sexuality is also produced by the amalgamation which constitutes the historical dimension of consciousness. In other words, one assumes one's history with the same energy that one assumes a particular gender or race, and then struggles with the definition or finds solace in it. Willa Cather wrote extensively about immigrants. How else does an immigrant transform himself—*move* psychically as well as physically—but by suppressing one history and assuming another? In the same process by which a child in Ellison's Harlem is born African-American, or by which *Glamour* creates the feminine, the ideological function of the historical process demands affinity and association with events that occurred in the past of one's particular geographical setting. However, if by moving across space the immigrant can lose one history and assume another—or, conversely, can cling to the original history by an act of will—then what exactly is this historical dimension? The historical self, like the racial self and the sexual self, is an objectified fiction by which the self is taught to deny the radical discontinuities, or the multidimensionality, of its existence.

In *A Lost Lady* Cather raises central questions about the study of history, and in particular about the power of historical consciousness to objectify the past and to locate the "legacy" of that past on the present. In the late twentieth century we hear continuous calls to "historicize"—as if the act of historicism itself were some kind of cleansing act or exorcism, and, more importantly, as if the call to historicize indicated anything in particular. To historicize is to invoke historical context, but there is no limit to the potential contexts existing in history. To historicize truly would be to return to the limitations of any particular era and to embrace all of its confusions and contradictions without question. Captain Forrester is certainly being "historical" when he fails to explain much about the Indian encampment. After all, he didn't question his actions then: Is it ahistorical to question them now?

Indeed, what is called the new historicism simply masks a particular ideological program, just as new criticism masked its program behind formalism earlier in this century, just as social criticism did before that. Sande Cohen has called "historicity . . . an academic sign system, whose center is a narrative" and whose program is to "short circuit present critical knowledge . . . by manifesting the present as incapable of being known or transformed without history" (19). Certainly the study of history forces limitations on the present if the present is known *only* as a historical consequence. In *A Lost Lady*, Niel Herbert sees himself exclusively as the result of the past, so that he can barely function in the present without continuing to pay homage of one sort or another. Isaiah Berlin found that "the fuller our knowledge of facts and of their connections the more difficult [it is] to conceive alternatives" (74). The more history we unearth—and historical revision proceeds, formally, by the piling of the new monograph of facts upon the old—the more we need to know in order to understand history. However, the study of history proceeds as if human life did not proceed *a*historically. As Cohen implies, the historical dimension is only one of many that make the present, and historicism is only one of many critical means of interrogating that present. We deal here not in alternatives but in simultaneities. The present is historically produced, true; but it is also essentially ahistorical and mythic, also true. The self, no less, is as responsible to its history as it is independent of the past, at the same time moving across its dimensions.

Willa Cather's *A Lost Lady* is a deceptive work, which can be mistakenly read as a lament for a more glorious past, a kind of ode to the pioneer era in western American history. However, the novel itself does not represent a longing for a singular, objective past. Rather, it explores the process by which selective events are historicized, the ways in which an astute historical consciousness is able to transform a figure in the past into an object made useful to the present concerns of the historian. In Cather's novel, some understanding of the past is communicated, once competing interpretations of that past are settled into a single, dominant story or image. Once the past is turned into an identifiable, singular object, it can be possessed—digested intellectually—and then narrated. The problem lies in the fact that suppressed interpretations, or alternative explanations, cannot be silenced forever but have a tendency, in *A Lost Lady*, to resurface—and to insist to other eyes upon recognition. The past is represented in Cather's narrative in stories about the pioneer era told by her characters, in historical figures such as Captain and Mrs. Forrester, and in the unfolding fate of Marian Forrester. In all three categories of representation, various attempts at historical understanding, in the form of narratives, images, and tableaux about the past, compete to define exactly what happened in and around the Sweet Water region. Cather's title suggests this strategy perfectly. *A Lost Lady* shows that much of what actually occurred in the pioneer era has been lost in the context of self-serving and ideologically charged accounts generated by pioneers and their admirers. One admirer in particular, Niel Herbert, insists that Marian Forrester conform to his own preconception of what her life signifies in the West. He casts her as representative of a "lost" ideal. However, it is precisely this transformation of a historical figure into an ideological, or even a romantic, image that denies the multidimensionality of the subject by objectifying it.

Cather has been pursued as strongly by critics who want to categorize her as "woman" writer as have Ellison and Faulkner been pursued by "black" and "Southern" critical labels. In her lifetime, she reacted to this objectification with the same anxiety Ellison captures in his use of Louis Armstrong's blues, "What Did I Do To Be So Black and Blue?" For Cather, the song may have been "What Did I Do to Be So Woman and Other?" She resisted gender exclusiveness as strongly as she possibly could—as a young woman, she did so by dressing as a man and calling herself William Cather. This was no private matter. As a young woman she delivered her high school commencement address to parents, teachers, and community leaders dressed as a boy. In her first semesters at college, many of her classmates assumed she was male because of her dress and demeanor. More importantly, though, her discomfort with objectified gender roles is apparent throughout her fiction. A typical Cather male character, such as Carl in *O Pioneers*, is described as being "too sensitive for a boy's" body (10); and a Cather female, such as Alexandra in the same novel, is likely to assume a culturally male demeanor "not as if it were an affliction, but as if it were very comfortable and belonged to her" (6).

Sharon O'Brien, Cather's most recent biographer, avoids the trap of limiting the author to categorical literary description. O'Brien explains, for example, that Cather cannot be understood as being "rooted" to any particular place. Rather, the idea of "transplanting" and transmigration—of movement across spacial planes (and, of course, plains)—characterizes Cather's mind on a number of levels, including biographical, artistic, and ideological. Cather's childhood move from Virginia to Nebraska, "from one radically different landscape and community to another at a formative, impressionable age," according to O'Brien, "powerfully affected her writing" (59). Transformation seems to have taken hold of Cather's imagination and informed the way in which she contemplated and developed the ideas that dominate her fiction. The transformation of life experiences and memories into artful structures, the migration from one physical place to another or from one conclusion to another, and the transformation of present into past—in all these movements it was never the *place* (geographic or iconographic) that fascinated Cather but the way in which the person got from one place to another, one idea to the next, from conclusion to revision. As a writer, Cather had a profound distrust of the settled (and would often ridicule the sedentary—think of all the "ugly" houses in her fiction) and exercised a consistent disregard for set patterns and forms. Instead, her fiction is characterized by the same transmigrations that dominated her own life. This observation—and O'Brien's exposition of it does an invaluable service to Cather's work—implies that Cather's "movements," spatial and intellectual, might be considered now as a direct challenge to the objectifying habits of the American historical mind. At least, this challenge is made clear when Cather writes about, or in, history.

Movement, and resistance to movement, runs through Cather's fiction. In *The Professor's House* (1925), St. Peter's reluctance to move from "the dismantled house where he had lived ever since his marriage" (11) into a new house signals an impending crisis of spirit and intellect. The crisis is not overcome until he moves back, psychically, to "the realest of his lives," to "the person he was in the beginning" (264)—the person for whom movement, foundation, and creativity were natural functions. He does this, in part, by explaining his fascination for the dead pioneer archaeologist, Tom Outland. Recapturing and comprehending the story of Outland allows St. Peter to recapture his own younger self, and to narrate—and so to place in order—his own life, a life of intellectual transformations and productivity. However, St. Peter's vision of Outland is clearly influenced by his own anxieties about an encroaching materialism in the present. The context that St. Peter uses to "explain" Outland is one strongly influenced by the material ambitions displayed by his son-in-law. Consequently, in St. Peter's mind Outland becomes an object representative of the "good" idealistic past in the face of the "evil" present of monetary bickering and greed. But even St. Peter's hagiography cannot suppress Tom Outland's rather cruel treatment of his partner, Rodney Blake. Cather's idea of history in *The Professor's House*—of the study, contemplation, and production of narrative about the past—is one grounded in such "movement" back and forth between the objective past and the subjective present, where past and present exist in a kind of relentless symbiosis. However, in her novels it is clear that the present creates the past by transforming indeterminacy into fact or object.

The very form of *The Professor's House* is typical of the Cather novel for its structural shifts. The narrative moves from St. Peter's present to St. Peter's sense of Outland (the long midsection) and then back to St. Peter's present story. In *My Antonia* (1918), for example, Jim Burden's idea of Antonia's character is told in a number of movements, from one story to another as the narrative progresses, and not all the tales are about Antonia. *My Antonia* specifically concerns the writing of a historical narrative. Burden explains that "the idea of [Antonia] is a part of my mind," and that this idea influences his preferences and the very way he thinks, as well as directing the structure of the manuscript he has written (321). The way he tells Antonia's story, without, as he says "any form" but "simply . . . pretty much all that her name recalls to me" is the way, in Cather's imagination, any particular history moves in the mind. The narrator here begins with an objectified Antonia and sets out to unfold his object. But, as Cather makes clear, it is as much the workings of his own mind that are unfolded as it is the independent figure of Antonia. And Burden's mind is interesting indeed. His narrative is highly colored by his own feelings of inadequacy, compounded by his constant protectiveness of both his own ego and of Antonia (these two objects may, in fact, be indistinguishable). He is not eager to see change and alteration on any plane, because his mind is transfixed by indelible images. As he says, he "really dreaded" seeing the effects of twenty years on Antonia when he returns to her at the close of the novel. "In the course of twenty crowded years one parts with many illusions," he explains. "I did not wish to lose the early ones" (328). When he leaves, he departs not with a meditation on Antonia's tremendous transformation, her heroic adaptation to time and circumstances, and her ultimate survival, but with a series of tableaux, frozen in time: "Antonia kicking her bare legs against the sides of my pony . . . Antonia in her black shawl and fur cap . . . Antonia coming in with her work team," and, finally, Antonia as "a battered woman," with countless children and endless housework. Nonetheless, "she still had that something which fires the imagination" (353).

But what burns in this fire? If Antonia informs Burden's mind, and if the form that his mind takes from the idea of her is this series of images—then what is the past, what "form" does history take in the mind? Burden's mind is clearly ahistorical. In fact, it is actually mythical in its structure of thought rather than historical. Francis Cornford in 1907 used the phrase "winning over into the mythical" to characterize the "transformation that begins to steal over all events from the moment of their occurrence" (130) by the process of historical selection and the fact of conscious predisposition. Jim Burden's mind recalls not change over time but images in spite of time. His mode of consciousness is one that would recognize its

own change and alteration, which it would call intellectual development, but which would deny the same qualities to its surroundings.
As a consequence, his mind suppresses memories that contradict its
idea of reality. When Antonia's first marriage fails, Burden recalls, "I
tried to shut Antonia out of my mind. I was bitterly disappointed in
her" (313). He cannot shut out the very form of his consciousness, of
course, and his journey in *My Antonia* is, as it is for St. Peter in *The
Professor's House*, a journey back to the workings of his own intellect. His confrontation with Antonia at the end of the novel is not
with her but with his *idea* of what she is.

What Cather is approaching in these novels, and what she demonstrates most clearly in the masterful work, *A Lost Lady* (1923), is a
sense of frustration with the historical capabilities of the mind. She
will go further, too, and articulate in *A Lost Lady* a sense of the
ultimate *impossibility* of achieving objective historical understanding—or, rather, to cast a profound doubt over the possibility that
historical study can provide much of value or of use to the present.
The present informs the past, but the past can only provide rationale
to the present, nothing more. History—the movements of the
past—cannot be separated from the minds that objectify it in the
present. It may be that only once history is recognized as incomprehensible, or at least, only once it is recaptured in its multidimensionality, in its contradiction and obscurity, will history assume
a function in the present beyond the ideologically conservative.
Only then might history move beyond its function to *conserve* the
present as something inevitable, like the end of a good novel. More
often than not, though, Cather's characters are inhibited by history,
crippled by their knowledge of it as personal or communal memory,
as image and tableau, as object, and prevented by it from seeing
clearly and judging fairly the present. History is understood as the
linear stretch of time, running backward from the present to the
past, receding. But the mind, as Cather demonstrates repeatedly, is
incapable of this type of regression. Her historical novels seldom
proceed "historically," and none of her characters seems capable of
imagining history in a linear, *progressive* line of development. In
Shadows on the Rock (1931), for example, the settlers cling to the
past to the extent that the main character, Auclair, after years of
community development and personal drama, can agree with the
visiting bishop that "nothing changes" in the Canadian settlement.
"You have done well to remain here where nothing changes. Here

with you I find everything the same," the bishop says. He then looks for Auclair's daughter. "And the little daughter, whom I used to see running in and out?" where is she? Auclair responds, "She is married," has moved out of the house, leaving him alone in the land where "nothing changes" (277). Both men seemingly miss the irony here as they insist upon linear stability. The new world, in each man's imagination, is a refuge from historical change and personal crisis, and nothing can "happen" that will alter that intellectual frame of mind.

Shadows on the Rock documents a number of instances where human beings move from one place to another in body, but not in mind. The Ursulines and the Hôspitalières, for example, "were scarcely exiles" in Quebec. "They were still in their accustomed place in the world of the mind (which for each of us is the only world), and they had the same well-ordered universe about them. . . . [I]n this congenial universe, the drama of man went on at Quebec just as at home, and the Sisters played their accustomed part in it" (96–97). The nuns, like all adventurers, carry their gods with them and transform the found world into the world of "the mind and spirit" (98), which is, to Cather, the only world that matters or that has consequences. The same is true of Cather's informal historians—Jim Burden, Niel Herbert—who also carry with them into the past their view of the world, the predisposition of their own minds and spirits. This, however, is not progressive movement or even progressive understanding, but a retrogressive application of the present, or of a vision of the future, onto the past. The Ursulines, for example, have not come to a new world but have brought the old world to a new place.

Bishop Latour, in *Death Comes for the Archbishop* (1927), builds a European cathedral at Santa Fe in order to further impel the movement of Catholicism into the southwest territories. This novel is wholly antilinear and its historical drama unfolds by way of legends, anecdotes, episodes—as well as by continuous physical movement from place to place in the desert region. The novel opens at Rome, suitably enough, as it is the Roman Catholic imperial mind that controls the movement of this particular history, or at least, that sets in motion the drama and conflict of the narrative. The displacement of the Navajos, the nearly genocidal removal of them, is told as a consequence of a larger program of action and is clearly of no major concern. Latour, on his deathbed, predicts that "God will preserve" the Indians (297), seemingly oblivious to the fact that his entire career—the missions and the building of the cathedral—worked to accomplish their demise.

A good deal of Cather criticism argues that Willa Cather saw the present as a falling off from the past, a great decline from the heroic pioneer era when men and women settled, colonized, and personified historical foundation. *A Lost Lady* is read through this lens, and conclusions about the novel reinforce critical visions of Cather's romantic, historical nostalgia. Susan J. Rosowski concludes that the regrettable inability to maintain "a pioneer spirit of the land" gives *A Lost Lady* its tragic theme and that "hope for the future lies with the ability of men and women to translate this spirit into life ("Paradoxes of Change," 62). More recently, Rosowski has reinforced her view of the novel as tragedy, with Ivy Peters playing the role of villain, and the land itself acting as victim ("Fatality of Place," 91). Rosowski's reading is echoed frequently. Ann Douglas sees Marian Forrester as "an emblem of fading vision of a special order" in history (15). John J. Murphy, in an intertextual study, concurs, and he recognizes a pattern employed by Cather to "frame the story of a downfall of the heroine" (73).

Criticism of *A Lost Lady* centers largely on Cather's view of the past, her historical consciousness. The novel, however, poses difficulties in getting at Cather's view of a particular historical era, because it depicts the making of history, or the understanding of the past, as an ideological struggle among contending interests in the present. It does seem clear that those interests are, as Evelyn Helmick suggests, "both historical and figurative" and that Cather's characters in the novel "are not only themselves but representatives of something else" (181). There are certainly factions in *A Lost Lady*— road builders, handworkers, lawyers, investors—and these factions are contentious concerning what the objective world ought to be, or what it has been in the past. There is less concern in *A Lost Lady* with presenting a definitive portrait of the past than there is in depicting a present in which many minds compete for historic authority. Involved in this historicist struggle are complexities and alignments arising from social class, gender, age, and relative powers of imagination, articulation, and comprehension. One thing, though, is clear. In *A Lost Lady* the past is depicted as anything but definitive or static. The novel makes it reductively simplistic, and actually ahistorical, to state that "this happened this way and I understand it." Cather demonstrates with monumental subtlety the falsity of final judgment, the misleading quality of settled issues.

Interrogating the Past

A Lost Lady shows how context determines the color of fact: Historical contexts, narrative contexts, and textual contexts are employed to demonstrate that no fact or event exists prior to contextual interpretation, or predisposition. The various readings of Cather's novel all assume critical contexts, such as the lost pioneer era, the image of woman, and the intertextual, and emerge with readings largely determined by the critical frame employed. But the novel itself is about context and how contextualization, including historicism, aestheticism, and nostalgia, determines fact and, to a large extent, character. Missing in most Cather criticism is a rigorous examination of Willa Cather's ideological program. Readings that have considered *A Lost Lady* essentially nostalgic, or that have seen Cather as writing in awe of a "lost" era of pioneer foundation, have engaged in the same kind of historical representation that the novel depicts as naive. What has been missing, or "lost," in critical studies of *A Lost Lady* is a rigorous examination of what the novel depicts as the inextricable links between historical representation and ideological positioning. Missing is an explication of how, in *A Lost Lady*, the present *moves* into the past and in turn how the present is moved into the future by a particular view of history. The movements of history in Cather's fiction are precisely these: not the objective movement of events in the past but the subjective transformation of those events into narratives, the movements of minds.

Cather's references to Indians provide a good starting place for a discussion of historical movement in *A Lost Lady*. Any reader with a twentieth-century sensibility must condemn Ivy Peters for the way in which he acquires "splendid land from the Indians some way, [paying them] next to nothing," as Marian Forrester says, and must share in her disgust for "people who cheat Indians" (123–24). This does not stop Marian from letting Ivy invest her money, of course, but it does add to the general view of Ivy as "swindler" or "shyster," two terms applied to him frequently by Cather readers. In direct contrast to Ivy Peters stands Captain Daniel Forrester, a man of the previous generation, one of the heroic pioneers and road builders. Nonetheless, the captain's relations with Indians were not qualitatively different from Ivy Peters's: "Once, when [Captain Forrester] was driven out of the trail by a wash-out, he rode south on his horse to explore, and found an Indian encampment near the Sweet Water, on this very hill where his house now stood," Cather narrates. "He was, he said, 'greatly taken with the location,' and made up his mind that he would one day have a house there." And so he drove a willow stake "into the ground to mark the spot where he wished to build" (52–53). A number of questions are unanswered here concerning the captain's exploration and land claim in this passage. The novel does not indicate what sort of encampment he found—for example, whether it was the campground of a transient hunting party or the temporary encampment of a tribe of plains Indians. To understand and assess the captain's action fully, one would want to know more about this particular "spot," such as who owned it or whether there was a treaty in force regarding the area in general. Finally, the Indians themselves are curiously silent, or historically muted, in this account. Presumably, a white man on horseback galloped into their midst, cut down a tree, claimed ownership, and rode away. Cather's narrative fails to give the Indians a participatory role in this historical drama. Instead, the Indians remain passive observers, objects rather than subjects in Captain Forrester's act of discovery and foundation. Cather concludes the brief narrative of the captain's "heroic" action by saying only that "he went away and did not come back for many years; he was helping to lay the first railroad across the plains" (53). The point is that Captain Forrester is just too busy building the railroad and dispossessing the Indians to address questions about his right to do so. Cather's omission here, and the captain's selective presentation of his history, is epochal.

Cather offers enough clues, however, to let us know exactly *which* chapter of this American epoch we are concerned with here. "Captain Forrester was himself a railroad man, a contractor," according to Cather's introduction of him in the second paragraph of the novel, "who had built hundreds of miles of road for the Burlington,—over sage brush and cattle country, and on up into the Black Hills" (10). In any fiction, the imaginary components come to the reader without prejudice and must be judged solely by their fictional presentation and development. However, references to the world of shared, extratextual knowledge and experience come to the reader with exactly the resonance with which they exist in that world outside the text. Forrester may be a fictional character, and Sweet Water an imaginary place, but "the Black Hills" have a resonance in American history that signals quite a bit about the captain and his business. By the Treaty of 1868, the Black Hills (part of the "Great Sioux Reservation," encompassing much of what is now South Dakota) were provided to Northern Plains Indians in perpetuity by the United States government. In return for this land (along with additional "Unceded Hunting Lands" to the west) these tribes agreed to an end to hostilities. The peace ensured by the treaty led to a steady influx of white American settlers to the borders of the Indian territory. By 1870, however, "rumors of gold in the territory attracted speculators, prospectors, and railroad men to the idea of taking the Black Hills and Unceded Lands away from the Indians" (Slotkin, *Fatal Environment*, 326). Complicating this situation was the fact that the recently completed Union Pacific railroad needed business in order to make its line profitable, and a rush into the Black Hills would provide—and eventually did provide—a steady clientele. The retaking of the Black Hills included the famous Custer expedition and massacre in 1876, and the subsequent retaliatory extermination of the Sioux and Cheyenne by the American army. This then is the captain's epoch and the destination of his road-building enterprise.

Marian may not admire Ivy for cheating Indians, but she is married to a man who, either directly or as part of the general historical push West by the United States, made his living through such means. Nonetheless, Ivy is condemned by many observers, and Captain Forrester is granted an apotheosis, but his apotheosis is the result of the context in which his history is told. His heroic stature is the result of what is unsaid, lost, or left out of his history, and by what is selected as significant, worthy of narration, and expressed in language. The reader knows Ivy Peters is a swindler. All that is known of the captain, on the other hand, is that he built a railroad into the Black Hills and called it business—and drove a willow stake into the ground and called it home. Also made clear in the novel is that during the Panic of 1873 the captain paid off the bank's depositors out of his own pocket and that he did so out of old-fashioned "honour" (91). However, the novel is not clear on how the captain became a bank officer, just as it is not clear on how he became a military officer: Civil War? Indian Wars? Self-bestowed? Into these gaps the reader's imagination must enter, either in support of what the captain implies about himself or in interrogation of those implications.

The narrative does not explain, for example, the basis for Captain

Forrester's superior status in the town itself, the sort of behavior or accomplishments that resulted in his powerful position in Sweet Water. But again, clues are provided to indicate that his dominance may have come to him at some cost to the pockets of others before his own pocket was affected. Cather delineates "two distinct social strata" in Sweet Water at the outset of the novel. First, there are "homesteaders and hand-workers who were there to make a living," and second, "the bankers and gentleman ranchers who came from the Atlantic seaboard to invest money and to 'develop our great West,' as they used to tell us" (9–10). The irony of the last phrase is made clear by the general failure of the Sweet Water corporation, and the "us" of Cather's narrative places her sympathies with the other stratum, the "hand-workers." The outsiders are clearly those who have made a profit here, as opposed to those who have come simply to live. Captain Forrester may have paid his depositors out of his own pocket (a particularly paternalistic response to an economic crisis), but his pocket is not deep enough to replace the jobs and farms inevitably lost when banks fail. When the captain acts honorably, he saves little more than his own conscience. The banking incident, and other incidents in *A Lost Lady*, leaves much to the imagination as one attempts to understand Captain Forrester historically. One can only wonder, but one can never know, what else the captain has chosen not to relate.

Richard Slotkin has explained what happens "when historical narration is used for ideological purposes." According to Slotkin, "the account of the plot is always rendered in such a way that it justifies the political and social arrangements of the present, and predicts the fulfillment of the society's program for the future" ("Myth," 79). The captain tells nothing that would diminish or call into question "the political and social arrangements" that provide the context for dominance, wealth, and authority in the town of Sweet Water. But the facts selected as significant, the context created by the medium of communication, and the pattern in which both are arranged signal the ideological subtext of the narrative. When Marian Forrester tells the story of how she and the captain met, for example, she does not begin at what Niel knows is "the beginning of the story." Instead, she suppresses the scandal of her first engagement and begins the story with her injury and rescue by Forrester. Instead of beginning at the beginning—any beginning for that matter—Marian opens with "'Once upon a time'," a clear signal of the mythic nature of her narrative (164). In her story there is no philandering, murdered fiancé, no explanation of why she would go mountain climbing alone with "young Fred Harney," and good reason to "wonder" why she would marry her rescuer without hesitation. Her narrative does explain the political and social arrangement of her marriage and of her new status as widow and survivor, but it does so in the context with which she frames her story. The captain and Marian, patriarch and lady, did not come into being historically (as Ivy Peters is shown emerging), but, on Marian's terms, the Forresters come into being mythically, as if ordained by God or the Brothers Grimm: "The boys were genuinely moved," as boys would be, by her narrative (166).

Cather's novel as a whole shares in the ideological qualities of Marian's narrative of origins. A Lost Lady opens with a series of tableaux, frozen in unspecified time, "thirty or forty years" in the past. The Forresters' house is "ugly" but made pleasant by "the people who lived there" and by the railroad prosperity it represents. The captain is wealthy enough to afford the luxury of an uncultivated marsh "because it looked beautiful to him" and "he could afford to humour his fancies." Mrs. Forrester defines what is "ladylike" by whatever she does, which is to say her actions create their own context, and there is no imagining "her in any dress or situation in which she would not be charming" (9–13). What is missing in each of these images is a specific historical source, despite the fact that the narrative describes a point chronologically thirty or forty years "ago." Historically accountable information is not supplied in these opening pages. Someone had to have built the house, and some historical or social circumstances must account for the transformation of an ugly house, in a remote countryside, into a pleasant home. Furthermore, there are no doubt significant reasons why the house is so forbidding to the townspeople, reasons that would also account for the resentment expressed so vehemently when the captain has his second, and fatal, stroke. The novel does not tell of the sources of the captain's great wealth, nor does it make it clear what it means when it says that the captain "built" the railroad. Perhaps his methods of foundation and accumulation of wealth have something to do with the way the townspeople, the "hand-workers" who have also built things, look upon him, his house, and his corpse. To these people, at least, all this did not happen so long ago.

Cather's narrative raises the question, in these opening pages, of historical source and subject. By whose eye is the house hideous?

The captain, for one, thinks it is a "beautiful" place—so what does the house "really" look like? Marian's eternally "lady-like" appearance exists in *the captain's eye,* according to the narrative: "In his eyes . . . whatever Mrs. Forrester chose to do was 'lady-like' because she did it" (13). It is Niel's eye, of course, that controls much of the narrative, but other sources provide clues to Niel's subjectivity. The Blum brothers, for example, loyal underlings that they are, "realized more than their companions" that Marian's privileged status "was an axiomatic fact in the social order" (19). When Adolph Blum observes Marian and "the big stranger," Frank Ellinger, making love illicitly, the narrative asks how the scene would be portrayed had Thad Grimes or Ivy Peters, boys with class ambitions, witnessed Marian display the "soft shivers" of extraladylike activity. With Blum, though, whose "mind was feudal," there is no danger to Marian, "her secrets were safe" (68), just as the captain's secrets are safe with Niel. Blum will keep her secret because her look and manner are "among the pleasantest things he had to remember."

A "pleasant memory" is one that is useful in order to assuage something mundane, such as personal place, or to justify something political, such as the making of an empire. If the past is informed by the memory of a "spirit" that is absent today—pioneer spirit in this case—it is only because it is solicited, or conjured, by the act of narration and by the seemingly incontrovertible fact that something in the past can be said to exist. However, Cather's novel puts forth the position that the past *does not* exist until it is transfigured as an object and that events and images lack utility unless they are marshaled for some narrative purpose. Thus, in the novelist's eye, history is simply one among a number of ways to tell about and justify the present.

As an act of exclusion, however, historicizing rings false. The historical, in fact, is often employed as a corrective to perspectives that lack full explication. Events may exist mythically—Marian's rescue by Captain Forrester, the "pleasant" Forrester house, the Indian encampment—but this is not the same thing as providing these events and tableaux with subjective historical significance. When Marian tells of how she was rescued by the captain, she provides an ahistorical, romantic story line, moving formalistically from "once upon a time" to the salvational marriage proposal. Historically and biographically, however, the event of her rescue as recalled by her self-projecting eye must be contradicted, or given further dimension, by the addition of a context including a series of quasi- and direct sexual encounters. Placed in a biographical context that would include the gaudy millionaire, the captain, the young men of Colorado and California, Frank Ellinger, Ivy Peters, and Henry Collins, Marian's "rescue" is understood to be of a piece with her more general enjoyment of, and, perhaps, reliance upon, males. In the company of women, by contrast, Marian is truly "lost," or perhaps besieged, as when the townswomen overrun her home when the captain is dying. Only by countering the romantic mountainside rescue with another eye on Marian's biography, and with her social and economic condition, does one not have to "wonder" why she marries the captain without thinking twice. It is not that Marian's romantic vision of herself is erroneous—for it certainly is an interpretation she evokes. Rather, this romantic vision is simply not true, historically, until it is contradicted. A single dimension is an incomplete picture, lacking the holistic perspective provided by contradiction and ambiguity. Only through contradiction does truth assume the multidimensional form necessary to save the self, as Cather implies, from being lost.

Niel Herbert is the chief consciousness of the novel, and largely through his eyes the narrative proceeds. He has however, a rather strong, identifiable, and singular predisposition toward the events he witnesses. By intervening in his material, he emerges from the pages of *A Lost Lady* as representative of the ideological function of narrative history—history in the service of the present. "Curiously enough," Cather remarks with characteristic understatement, "it was as Captain Forrester's wife that [Marian] most interested Niel, and it was in her relation to her husband that he most admired her." The curiosity increases when the narrative explains that above all it was "her loyalty" to Captain Forrester that "stamped her more than anything else" in Niel's mind (78). Niel must suppress a lot of detail about Marian's life to achieve this stamp. In the next pages, Cather explains how Niel does this.

Niel has been reading a lot (Byron, Montaigne, Ovid), and keeps returning to favorite authors who "seemed to him to know their business." As he reads, he begins to see himself "eavesdropping upon the past." His readings into history "gave him a long perspective, influenced his conception of the people about him, made him know just what he wished his own relations with these people to be." The conclusion he reaches is as astounding as it is revealing.

The narrative explains that Niel comes to know just what "his own relations with these people" was to be: "For some reason, his reading made him wish to become an architect" (81–82). Reading history, as well as poetry, essays, epics, and mythology, has provided Niel the motivation to *design* and to construct. The chief, formalistic activities of the historical consciousness as Cather envisions it are not discovery and revelation but projection and design. The scene which follows Niel's meditations has him bringing roses to Marian's bedroom window in "an impulse of affection and guardianship"—the natural feeling of an architect toward his creation. When he hears Ellinger inside, he leaves with "his eyes blind with anger" (86). Clearly, this is not a scene that Niel can "see" as historical witness, because it is not something he has projected as architect. The scene cannot be transformed by Niel into history; in fact, it is useless to him as a way to know Marian, because it contradicts what he is looking for when he views her. "It was not a moral scruple she had outraged," Cather comments, "but an aesthetic ideal" (87). In the eyes of the architect, the aesthetic ideal precedes the final product, directing and guiding its creation. In order to complete this structure, the architect will have to overcome this obstacle—or, in the language of the historian, he will have to suppress it, ignore it, or find it without significance. The chapter ends with Niel wondering about "beautiful women. . . . What was their secret?" The reader may also wonder whose secrets are the secrets of history—are they the secrets of the historian or of the historical record?

All writing is interrogation. The historian inquires into the past when he constructs a narrative, the fiction writer interrogates the real when she writes a novel. In *A Lost Lady*, Cather interrogates the capacity of the mind to know and to produce history, interrogating at once the past itself and human attempts to use that past. As the novel's main consciousness, Niel Herbert demonstrates that history can be quite useful, but that like any useful tool, it lies meaningless until put to use. The specific use to which Niel puts Marian is to prove the greatness of the captain, and to confirm his ideals about romantic loyalty, for example. This project requires him to keep secret a number of details—or at least to neglect to pursue a number of questions that arise concerning the past. When he wonders what the "secret" is that guides the behavior of "beautiful women" he raises Marian to a categorically "unknowable" object in his romantic project. More precisely, though, Niel makes it clear that he isn't going to ask and doesn't want to know exactly what moves Marian. The same is true of the captain. Cather remarks, early in the novel, that Niel and his uncle, Judge Pommeroy, consider Captain Forrester's repose to be "like that of a mountain," a man who possessed "a conscience that had never been juggled with" (48). When this mountain speaks, moreover, the way he spoke, "the way he uttered his unornamented phrases gave them the impressiveness of inscriptions cut in stone" (54). No one is going to question or interrogate this Western Moses, especially not Niel Herbert, and no one in the novel will ask what actually moves this mountain. Even when the old man says something as ludicrous as "We dreamed the railroads across the mountains, just as I dreamed my place on the Sweet Water" (55), his listeners sit in respectful awe, "with such sympathy," according to the narrative. What Daniel Forrester actually did is kept secret by the captain, a secret enforced by Niel and left, by the narrative, to the reader's interrogative imagination.

These secrets are not safe, however, with Ivy Peters. The second half of the novel is largely concerned with the struggle between Ivy and Niel for "control" of Marian—and Ivy clearly wins out. What he wins is interpretive authority. Niel's vigil at the Forrester house—he takes time off from his studies at MIT to fulfill this protective obligation to the Forresters—is contrasted to Ivy's ambitions outside the house. The captain finds Ivy offensive ("he ain't overly polite," the captain says, in Wild West cadence) but is powerless to do much about it. Nonetheless, as Ivy works outside, the captain and Niel have "a long talk about the building of the Black Hills branch of the Burlington" (120). This comment reminds us, of course, that the captain was not "overly polite" in his own dealings when he was Ivy's age. After the captain's death, Ivy assumes his place in Marian's financial doings. Like the captain, Ivy is at the forefront of his generation's search for wealth. In fact, at the time of the captain's actual death, Ivy is in Wyoming, "called away by a telegram which announced that oil had been discovered near his land-holdings." After the captain's death, Ivy is seen sitting on Marian's porch "as if he owned the place" and sitting in the captain's place at the card table. Cather suggests that Ivy is the new "captain" of the economy. "He had not made his fortune yet, but he was on the way to it" (153). In the past, Marian was greatly moved by men like the captain— "mountains" who acted but did not explain or apologize for their business. Ivy acts squarely in this tradition.

Niel would like to become an architect, a visionary mover, but in the novel he is consigned the role of observer and narrator. He would like to rescue Marian himself, for example, but he has no idea where to take her: "If only he could rescue her and carry her off like this,—off the earth of sad, inevitable periods, away from age, weariness, adverse fortune!" (110). In other words, he would like to carry her out of history. The men who do rescue Marian all carry her into history, to the next transformation, the next "inevitable period" of her life. Captain Forrester takes her to her role as mistress of the railroader's big house; Frank Ellinger reconfirms her sexuality; Ivy Peters secures her financial solvency; and Henry Collins, at the end of the novel, provides her renewed wealth based upon postfrontier colonialism. But Niel wants her to remain the same; she is his "aesthetic ideal" (87), his "most finished artifice" (110), a frozen image that recalls the tableaux of her in seductive dishabille at the beginning of the novel. Despite the fact that Marian tells Niel she has "such a power to live" and that she feels "held back" in Sweet Water (125), and despite the fact that Niel knows and "rather liked the stories, even the spiteful ones, about the gay life she led in Colorado, and the young men she kept dangling about her every winter" (78–79), Niel never quite comprehends the successive contexts in which Marian engages and expresses her character. Niel has a one-dimensional sense of historical time, a sense of historical—or in the personal case of Marian, biographical—context that does not allow for transfiguration. Nearly everything Cather wrote about history was informed by an opposition to this sort of fixation.

Niel knows that the people and the country are changing, but he considers this phenomenon of change to be an aberration in the order of things. In Niel's mind, it is clear that

> he had seen the end of an era, the sunset of the pioneer. He had come upon it when already its glory was nearly spent. So in the buffalo times a traveller used to come upon the embers of a hunter's fire on the prairie, after the hunter was up and gone; the coals would be trampled out, but the ground was warm, and the flattened grass where he had slept and where his pony had grazed, told the story. (168)

It is not self-evident what "story" is being told here. The coals, the warm ground, and "the flattened grass" are evidence of a human being having camped on the spot, but this is not a story. The story would involve the person's place of origin and destination, his back-ers or supplies and their interests, his prospective customers—if he was a hunter—his thoughts and ideals, his intentions, his values: The "story" would involve a great deal more than the picture of flattened grass and dying embers. But, as Cather's image makes clear, it is by such emblems that Niel knows "the era" he mourns; only by such romantic set pieces does he understand the era of "the road-making West." It is a history and a reality that Niel will not interrogate and so, in the logic of the novel, it is one from which he will never be liberated. Cather's language intensifies as this passage continues. The pioneers are all getting old and dying off, as far as Niel can see. It is, for Niel, as if

> it was already gone, that age; nothing could ever bring it back. The taste and smell and song of it, the visions those men had seen in the air and followed,—these he had caught in a kind of afterglow in their own faces,—and this would always be his. (169)

"And this would always be his": the frozen image, the tableau of the pioneer spirit as if it existed or could be represented in a photograph, out of context, without origins or historical consequences, as if a century of imperialism, genocide, and warfare, of homesteading, mining, and road building, could be reified into something Niel could possess like a memory. This is not historical consciousness but a crippling intellectual inertia.

It is worse than inertia, however, because Niel would like to act, or transform the world, in accordance with his historical blindness. Niel, like Ivy Peters, is of the new generation. And where Ivy acts historically, carrying on the pioneer tradition of land acquisition and, for better or worse, exploitation, Niel is carrying on the pioneer tradition of transposing history into myth. These young men of power and influence will continue the path forged by the men who flattened the grass. Again, Niel's treatment of Marian demonstrates this point. The source of his "contempt" for Mrs. Forrester is "that she was not willing to immolate herself, like the widow of all these great men, and die with the pioneer period to which she belonged" (169). If Niel were a supreme architect, he would put Marian out of her misery, just as he attempted to put the blind woodpecker out of its misery. (Just as the U.S. Army put the plains Indians out of theirs, perhaps.) This time, however, Niel has broken something less easily mended then a young boy's arm. Through her depiction of Niel Herbert, Cather demonstrates the real potential for cruelty—a cruelty far worse, and with far greater consequence, than Ivy Peters' childish act against the woodpecker—inherent in Niel's objectifying historical consciousness. His seeming refusal to consider the evidence around him concerning the historical context and consequences of the "pioneer spirit," and his view of historical change as contemptible, lead to his imaginative preference of death for Marian Forrester. If she were dead, he could honor her memory. Alive, she poses problems to his vision of a static, glorious past. It is not only Captain Forrester whose memories and voice resemble "the lonely, defiant note that is so often heard in the voices of old Indians" (55). In Niel's eyes, the only "good" Marian Forrester is a dead Marian Forrester. In fact, "eventually, after she had drifted out of his ken, when he did not know if Daniel Forrester's widow was living or dead, Daniel Forrester's wife returned to him, a bright, impersonal memory" (171). Although Marian would not immolate herself in order to protect his ideological priorities, Niel succeeds in immolating her in order to privilege Daniel Forrester's historical significance.

Niel has had numerous stories told to him, and has witnessed enough events, to have come to a clearer understanding of Marian long before he finds her in Ivy's arms at the end of the novel. Similarly, the townspeople of Sweet Water, and the "us" of Cather's narrative, have heard enough stories and know enough history to question the validity of Captain Forrester's historical narrative and of the portrait of the heroic pioneer in general. The captain's "philosophy" of life and history, that you will get what you want in life "unless you are one of the people who get nothing in this world" (54), is exemplary of the "ideological purposes" Richard Slotkin says inform historical narrative. The captain and Niel Herbert assume a kind of historical necessity in which the "losers" in history—the Indians, "Black Tom" (Judge Pommeroy's servant), and finally Marian—are "immolated" with their era and are edited out of the historical narrative. According to this logic, the nature of the Indian encampment is irrelevant; Niel can cut the phone cord and "save" Marian from further speech; and Black Tom can be "borrowed" by Mrs. Forrester when a more "formal" servant than the Forresters' own is called for (36, 50). Not even his own father's financial ruin can awaken Niel Herbert to history, to the social and economic complexity of the pioneer era. His father "was one of the first failures to be crowded to the wall" as a result of speculative practices of the investors who,

What's Lost in *A Lost Lady*   179

like Daniel Forrester, came to "develop our Great West." When Mr. Herbert leaves Sweet Water, Niel stays behind to read law and to continue his resolution "to remain a bachelor" (32–33). Historical evidence, community knowledge, and even personal experience are not enough to change Niel's predisposition to honor the captain's memory and disparage, or suppress, Marian's. In the logic of the novel, his vow to remain a bachelor is a vow to remain outside the dynamics of history. When his father leaves town, Niel goes on to live alone, "with monastic cleanliness and severity," safe from the unclean world of history, and safe from the disorderly world where lost ladies continue to find their way.

Niel equates a "kind of cowardice" with "the fear of losing a pleasant memory, . . . a dread of something that would throw a disenchanting light upon the past" as he contemplates Mr. Ogden's decision to abandon Marian (152). The definition serves the novel as a whole. A "kind of cowardice" manifests itself in a refusal to seek out a contradictory past, to refuse to recognize the historical context in which images, tableaux, or myths of the past are produced in order to suppress the complexities and ambiguities of human life. It is much more "pleasant" to imagine heroic hunters and pioneers, trampled coals and flattened grass, abandoned or vacated Indian encampments, and lost ladies, than it is to imagine violent contests for land and natural resources, dispossessed Indians, and men and women who do not "immolate" themselves in the name of anyone's ideology but go on demanding that "things turn out well for them," to paraphrase Marian Forrester Collins's last message to Niel (179). Pleasant memories are nourished at the cost of continued historical oppression, as minds like Niel Herbert's emerge as powerful interpreters of past events. Kathleen L. Nichols finds Niel's status as center of consciousness "suspect" in the novel because of such intellectual failures (187). True, he cannot be relied upon—in fact, his vision must be interrogated and unmasked. As interpreter and narrator, Niel becomes the "architect" of his youthful ambitions—the architect of historical understanding, defining values and identifying heroes who will come to inform and personify historical tradition. Niel is relieved to find that Marian "was well cared for, to the very end" but not that her story might supersede the captain's narrative as authoritative history. Such a view would recognize Marian's resurfacing in "Buenos Ayres" as the survival of the American "pioneer spirit" in South America, internationalized now and still having "everything." Marian's marriage to Henry Collins is the lost lady's San Juan Hill: The American pioneer spirit has moved off the continent and into international politics, wed to "a rich, cranky old" English imperialism (173). This sort of contextual recognition, of course, is impossible for Niel. In his mind, Marian's survival is an image more akin to that of a twentieth-century Indian reservation, a curious relic of an era considered long ended, for people who refuse to immolate (or assimilate) themselves "and die with the pioneer period." It is a curious and dangerous sense of history which Cather locates in Niel Herbert. To Cather, it is a form of intellectual cowardice that consigns to death and historical obscurity visions and events in the past that counter or challenge the particular arrangements accepted as the inevitable present.

The Unmasking of History

The twentieth century has played host to the rise of historical study as an academic force in the United States. John Higham's institutional history of the profession makes clear its ideological role, as each generation casts its own concerns and obsessions onto its study of the past. Patrician historians in the late nineteenth century located "the forging of national unity" (and of their class) in the same past that progressives would subsequently see as "full of real and vital conflicts between contending groups" (151, 173). "History," as Hayden White has concluded, "is never only history *of*, it is always also history *for*. And it is not only history *for* in the sense of being written with some ideological aim in view, but also history *for* in the sense of being written for a specific social group or public" (*Tropics*, 104). White has been at the forefront of postmodern attacks on the privileged status of historical knowledge. Once the past is narrated, according to White's most provocative thesis, it ceases to be something found and is transformed into something created.

"What is 'imaginary' about any narrative representation is the illusion of a centered consciousness capable of looking out on the world, apprehending its structure and processes, and representing them to itself as having all the formal coherence of narrativity itself," according to White's most recent formulation. "But this is to mistake a 'meaning' (which is always constituted rather than found) for 'reality' (which is always found rather than constituted)" (*Content* 36). The historian may claim objectivity, or even, by the lights of this age of irony and relativism, explain the biases and interests that guide his endeavor. But nothing in the past demands to be made a part of the present, or insists that it be recalled or written about. The historian's eye is ideological: It creates when it claims to discover; it plants when it claims to unearth.

The distinction here is crucial to an understanding of the devastating effects historical objectification has had on the twentieth century. A typical method of historical inquiry begins with the identification of some concern in the present, some current dilemma. Perhaps the problem is racism, sexism, urban crime—it really does not matter. What the historian might do is research the past to a point where the problem did not exist and then to scroll up, as it were, to the first instance, or evidence, of the contemporary issue. Winthrop Jordan, for example, went back to Elizabethan England to discover the roots of racism; American historians are always looking at the Revolutionary era to discover the roots of almost anything; and social scientists with historical leanings could get nowhere without Tocqueville. With Jordan's study, racism is understood as, arguably, "caused" by certain historically perpetuated conceptions of the meaning of physical pigmentation. In order to erase these preconceptions, the reader must "go back" to a point in history where such preconceptions did not yet exist. What this means—and what all historical inquiry means—is that the solution or the key to the solution of the present predicament is in the past.

By placing the solution to contemporary evils in the past, historical culture precludes the possibility of remedies lying somewhere more accessible—namely the present or the future. If evils such as racism or sexism are the product of the generational transmission of wrongheaded, ignorant, or misinformed ideas about human nature, then the *historical* study of the roots of these ideas does nothing less than perpetuate them—even if the overt purpose of the study is to vilify that perpetuation. Image makers in this age of sound bytes and media hustle know that exposure, regardless of content, is valuable to the communication of an idea imagistically. W. J. T. Mitchell has argued that ideology proceeds not by argument and exposition but by the image, "in the notion of mental entities or 'ideas' that provide the materials of thought." These ideas exist in the mind as images "projected on the medium of consciousness" (164). The particular purpose of unearthing images of past abuses, then, does nothing less than perpetuate the *idea* that such abuse is historically legitimate—as the historians say, it becomes the "burden" of the past on the present. Historical inquiry is inevitably a reactionary process if it pursues objectivity. The study of history as the source of privileged insight into human possibility acts as a constraint on the freedom of the minds to whom the study is addressed.

The ideological function of the predominance of historical inquiry in the twentieth century is clear. History places the solution to any present state of injustice in the past, in a purely intellectual realm where nothing can be done. The "weight of history" is invoked as if it possessed an autonomous existence, self-evoked. "History cannot be rewritten," as the historian-pedant says; "we are the products of the past." Howard Zinn has confronted the oppressive nature of historical study. Zinn reminds us that events in the past have the look of being inevitable because historians stress historical decisions rather than decision processes, events of closure rather than contingencies—hence the single-dimensionality of history, the sense of inevitability that gives to the study of the past its implicitly anticreative weight. Anyone who has taken an undergraduate history class knows the opprobrium reserved for what is called "if" history, for any imaginative assaults on the record. "The necessariness of the past tends to carry over into our thinking about the future, and weigh down our disposition to action," according to Zinn. "Man, wounded by his history already, then tends to be transfixed by it" (281). It is those who study the past who are, in fact, condemned to repeat it—simply by virtue of the stifling effect the historical has on alternatives that seem to have no basis or precedent.

The reliance of historical communication on narrative, an essentially literary artifice, results as well in the muting of past alternatives for the sake of coherence. Narrative is an artifice of selection, and the underside of selectivity is suppression. A "good" history is one that provides cohesion to events that need to be sorted out and put into comprehensible order—events not yet fully understood or explained. Hindsight, as historical common sense has it, makes things clear. What this means is that time allows the confusions and contradictions that characterize human experience to give way to the form and artifice that characterize narrativity. But what happens to "events and processes attested by the documentary record that [do] not lend themselves to representation in a story?" (White, *Content*, 28). Sande Cohen has argued that "historical thought is located, intellectually considered, near its suppression of the nonnarrated—because the kinds of historical narratives" that

Cohen has studied "do not allow the nonnarrated (theory, definitions, forms of voice and mood, argument) an independent status"
(69). What happens to the undramatic, the contradictory, or the forgotten is that these qualities are "lost," to borrow Cather's term
from *A Lost Lady*, lost to the momentum of the good story. Fernand
Braudel has defined narrative history as "not an objective method"
but "a philosophy of history," which assumes that the past is "dominated by dramatic accidents, by the actions of those exceptional
beings who occasionally emerge and who often are the masters of
their own fate and even more of ours." Braudel concludes that this
"philosophy" is "a delusive fallacy," which could not be farther from
actual human experience (4, 11–12). One consequence of this fallacy
is the diminution of actual, lived human experience into the trivial
or the sordid. Only the value of history could convince Niel Herbert
that Captain Forrester was heroic but that Peters was dishonest.

Narrative history as well has the tendency to make the present
seem exceptional for its disorder and aimlessness. The neatly told
story of the past quickly disintegrates as the present era comes into
focus by the historian. As a result, the past grows in its attrac-
tiveness because it is a source of order and comprehension. Not only
are the solutions to the dilemmas of the current era located in the
past, but the past is also depicted as a time in which decisions were
made and problems confronted, where "exceptional beings"
emerged to take control and provide the drama its indispensable
heroism. As a result, the present field of action seems crammed with
evil figures standing in the way of progress, threatening to "reverse"
the historical process or narrative. Again, historical culture thereby
encourages a reverential attitude toward the past at the expense of
the present. No one wants to ruin a good story by disrupting his
place in the narrative order. What is lost here, of course, is the fact
that the past, as narrative, was produced by the present out of its
absolute freedom to create the past as it wished. And so what is lost
(as was nearly "lost" to Marian Forrester) is the continuation of that
original freedom, to move and to create the conditions of the self.

The most oppressive kind of narrative history is the chronological
or the linear. Linear history provides the past with a coherence clearly lacking in the present; it recounts over and over the "rise" of
problems and their inevitable solutions—a process largely absent in
any particular present. Linear history also privileges its ending as its
climax (and asks continually, How did we get here?) and values

origins only insofar as they shed light on outcomes. But the out-come, as we in the present know, is unintelligible from the perspec-tive of historical inquiry. The study of linear history can do nothing for the present but inhibit it and diminish its ambitions. The study of history cannot yield insight into contemporary problems nor can it yield predictions of the future. The very utterance of a prediction makes it a part of the past against which the present and future react. In other words, only the silent, muted prediction—the "lost" voice in historical terms—has any power of foresight (this is no doubt why we romantically revere the lone voice and secretly identi-fy our idiosyncrasies with it). Once voiced, the prediction becomes the source of its own negation. It is no wonder, then, that the con-temporary anarchist group that calls itself the Yippies relies so heav-ily on conspiracy theories and the idea of a "secret" history. If nar-rative history is pure artifice, and if linearity is the result of the historian's rage for (law and) order, then what really moves history must be what is lost to the record, what is secret or unheeded. This is certainly the case regarding Marian Forrester as far as Niel Herbert can tell.

Perhaps a history that is more true to actual human experience would be *horizontal* rather that vertical—that is, would proceed by association rather than chronological order. Louis Mink finds that in the contemporary world it is "for the first time possible to entertain a picture of the past as discontinuous with our own institutions, interests, and modes of understanding" (101). Discontinuity would lead to the abandoning of chronology as anything more than source material—as valuable to history as the dictionary is to imaginative literature. As Braudel insists, "we must renounce the linear. We must not believe that a civilization, because it is original, is a closed and independent world" (200). In her fiction, Willa Cather did much toward this renunciation. In her novels the route to the "past" is not a linear journey but one informed by the associative qualities of human memory. What actually informs the past, what moves it and what shapes it in the human mind, is (as Jim Burden states at the end of *My Antonia*) "incommunicable"—or lost. What explains, however—what is "communicable"—is form, narrative method, the ideological component of historical inquiry. "History," according to Walter Benjamin, "is the subject of a structure, whose site is not homogenous, empty time, but time filled with the presence of the now" (261). The secret of historical study is that present concerns inform all historical inquiry, despite the professional claims of historians regarding the control of bias. It is a secret so closely guarded that many in our historical culture will deny it with complete integrity, believing the denial. Thus "presentism" is denigrated among historians as the unpardonable sin. Once held in the light of day, however, the secret reveals the essentially ideological nature of historical narrative. History enforces the inevitability of the present, its methods of linearity and chronology serve conservative interests, even those of "liberal" or reformist leanings. History, finally, is the authoritarian soul of the present order of reality, and as such will inevitably be interrogated by anarchist forces in the name of the liberation of the self from object status.

The linear past is summoned to explain the present, to account for a particular situation or (as often) to call a halt to some dangerous tendency among outgroups or contending forces. Missing or suppressed in that linearity are details that might call into question or obfuscate its narrative cast or mold—or perhaps make itself redundant. In *A Lost Lady*, the narrative explains, through literary depiction, that what is lost to a historical narrative is indeed what provides its very movement. Cather made such absence into an artistic method, calling it, in a literary essay, "the inexplicable presence of the thing not named," the thing "that gives high quality to the novel or the drama, as well as to poetry itself" (*Not Under Forty*, 50). The "thing" here cannot be named because it cannot be objectified, it exists in an anarchic dimension of pure absence and shifting coherence. As an artistic declaration it provides insight into Cather's own ideological concerns, concerns that remove her from the position of a nostalgic writer of historical romance. Nostalgia and romanticism fill the mind with an overwhelming presence, and this is certainly true of Cather's depiction of past realities. Nonetheless, if what brings these things to mind, if what forms them is "the thing not named," or the thing lost, then the critical eye must turn away from the image itself that "fills" the mind to what it is that *moves* or provides form. There certainly is a nostalgic content to Cather's writing, but it is informed and transferred to the page by something far more volatile than self-comforting memory. What is lost, what disappears as soon as it puts history (and all narrative) into motion, is the anarchic self: the self which will not stay put but will continue to migrate among its dimensionalities and to resist the object classifications of history.

Benjamin, Walter. *Illuminations*, Edited by Hannah Arendt. Translated by Harry Zohn. New York: Schocken Books, 1969.

Berlin, Isaiah. *The Hedgehog and the Fox: An Essay on Tolstoy's View of History.* New York: Simon & Schuster, 1966.

Braudel, Fernand. *On History* (1969). Translated by Sarah Matthews. Chicago: University of Chicago Press, 1980.

Cather, Willa. *A Lost Lady* (1923). New York: Vintage, 1972.

_____. *Death Comes for the Archbishop* (1927). New York: Vintage, 1971.

_____. *My Antonia* (1918). Boston: Houghton Mifflin, 1977.

_____. *Not Under Forty* (1936). Lincoln: University of Nebraska Press, 1988.

_____. *O Pioneers!* (1914). Boston: Houghton Mifflin, n.d.

_____. *The Professor's House* (1925). New York: Vintage, 1973.

_____. *Sapphira and the Slave Girl* (1940). New York: Vintage, 1975.

_____. *Shadows on the Rock* (1931). New York: Vintage, 1971.

Cohen, Sande. *Historical Culture: On the Recoding of an Academic Discipline.* Berkeley: University of California Press, 1986.

Cornford, Francis M. *Thucydides Mythistoricus.* London: Edward Arnold, 1907.

Douglas, Ann. "Willa Cather: A Problematic Ideal." In *Women, the Arts, and the 1920s in Paris and New York,* edited by Kenneth W. Wheeler and Virginia Lee Lussier, 14–19. New Brunswick: Transaction Books, 1982.

Helmick, Evelyn Thomas. "The Broken World: Medievalism in *A Lost Lady.*" In *Critical Essays on Willa Cather,* edited by John J. Murphy, 179–86. Boston: G. K. Hall, 1984.

Higham, John. *History: Professional Scholarship in America.* Johns Hopkins University Press, 1983.

Mink, Louis O. *Historical Understanding.* Edited by Brian Fay, Eugene O. Golob, and Richard T. Vann. Ithaca: Cornell University Press, 1987.

Mitchell, W. J. T. *Iconology: Image, Text, Ideology.* Chicago: University of Chicago Press, 1986.

Murphy, John J. "Euripides' *Hippolytus* and Cather's *A Lost Lady.*" *American Literature* 53 (1981): 72–86.

Nichols, Kathleen L. "The Celibate Male in *A Lost Lady.*" In *Critical Essays on Willa Cather,* edited by John J. Murphy, 186–97.

O'Brien, Sharon. *Willa Cather: The Emerging Voice.* New York: Fawcett Columbia, 1987.

Rosowski, Susan J. *The Voyage Perilous: Willa Cather's Romanticism.* Lincoln: University of Nebraska Press, 1986.

_____. "Willa Cather's *A Lost Lady:* The Paradoxes of Change." *Novel* 11 (1977): 51–62.

_____. "Willa Cather and the Fatality of Place: *O Pioneers!, My Antonia,* and *A Lost Lady.*" In *Geography and Literature: A Meeting of the Disciplines,* edited by William E. Mallory and Paul Simpson-Housley, 81–94. Syracuse: Syracuse University Press, 1987.

Slotkin, Richard. "Myth and the Production of History." In *Ideology and Classic American Literature*, edited by Sacvan Bercovitch and Myra Jehlen, 70–90. Cambridge: Cambridge University Press, 1986.

_____. *The Fatal Environment: The Myth of the Frontier in the Age of Industrialization, 1800–1890*. New York: Atheneum, 1985.

Urgo, Joseph R. "How Context Determines Fact: Historicism in Willa Cather's *A Lost Lady*." *Studies in American Fiction* 17:2 (Autumn 1989): 183–192.

White, Hayden. *The Content of the Form: Discourse and Historical Representation*. Baltimore: Johns Hopkins University Press, 1987.

_____. *Tropics of Discourse: Essays in Cultural Criticism*. Baltimore: Johns Hopkins University Press, 1978.

Zinn, Howard. *The Politics of History*. Boston: Beacon Press, 1970.

CHAPTER 6

The Yippies' *Overthrow*

What Everybody Knows

in America

"The world broke in two in 1922 or thereabouts. . . ."
—*Willa Cather,* Not Under Forty *(1936)*

Everybody knows the boat is leaking, Everybody knows the Captain lied. Everybody's got this broken feeling Like their father or their dog just died. Everybody's talking to their pockets, Everybody wants a box of chocolates Or a long-stemmed rose: Everybody knows . . . Everybody knows it's coming apart: Take one last look at this sacred heart Before it blows: Everybody knows.
—*Leonard Cohen,* "Everybody Knows."

Yippie!: From Chicago '68 to 1984
"Yippie is the expression of a fundamental social rupture," according to Yippie editors Dana Beal and Steve Conliff in the Introduction to *Blacklisted News, Secret Histories: From Chicago '68 to 1984.* Yippie is the expression of "the ever-recurring self-aware revolutionary moment of rejection of straight society as a whole," and of the ways in which "society manipulates the straights for the corporate rulers" (XV). In this statement is the essence of the Yippie political project in the 1980s and 1990s. The contemporary anarchist group is devoted to maintaining a channel for the recurring "moment of rejection of straight society" experienced by what it calls its national constituency of "nobodies." Above all, the group aligns itself against corporate encroachments on individual autonomy and on critical

Jazz Police are paid by J. Paul Getty, Jazz is paid by J. Paul Getty too.

—Leonard Cohen, "Jazz Police"

I'm Your Man *(CBS Records, 1988)*

thought—and on the production of historical narrative. *Blacklisted News* and the Yippie quarterly newspaper *Overthrow* are attempts to reclaim history through the emphasis on the "fundamental rupture" between those who accept the "corporate" accounts of history and those who reject them.

The Yippies' declaration of historical rupture echoes Willa Cather's sense of a world broken into pieces in 1922. In the same way that Cather's perception led to a prolonged meditation on the sense of a historical self, the Yippies' sense of cultural fragmentation has led the group to a concentrated assault on all attempts to provide linear order to what they see as the chaos and conspiracy of American history. The Yippies were created in political upheaval, during the tumultuous period that often goes by the misnomer of "the 60s" or "the youth movement." Both names are misleading because they turn what was a massive cultural upheaval into a rite of passage. Nonetheless, in the midst of that chaotic era of public revolt and antiauthoritarian expressions of personal liberty, the Yippies emerged as a coherent (which is to say recognizable) emblem of the anarchic self.

The Yippies first came into existence in late 1967, following the March on the Pentagon that October. The group was created by Abbie Hoffman and Jerry Rubin (who would become its initial leaders), Dana Beal (who would clarify Yippie ideas in the 1970s), Paul Krassner (of Liberation News Service, an underground network), and others. Of all, only Beal remains active in the group and has assumed a visible role in the group's activities. The political "movement" known by the name "Yippie" and even the term itself were conscious creations, made for the mass media. The purpose of the original Yippies was to attract participation, through publicity about the group itself, in mass demonstrations planned for the Chicago Democratic National Convention in August 1968. According to Todd Gitlin, Hoffman and Rubin "used media to invent an 'organization'" and "formulated a theory of organization *through* media" (*Whole World*, 156). In fact, Yippies may be the first "made for TV" political movement in history. According to Hoffman's version, "the task of getting huge numbers of people to come to Chicago," including "performers, artists, and theatre groups" posed budgetary problems for his small group of antiwar organizers. And so, Hoffman explains, "we created a myth. What is a Yippie? A hippie who is going to Chicago." The term "Yippie" was "the name of the myth that created free advertising for our Chicago confrontation. We never had to pay for ads" (*Soon to Be*, 145).*

The original Yippies were successful in getting the media attention needed to publicize antiwar activities planned by Hoffman and Rubin. Thousands attended the Yippies' Festival of Life in Lincoln Park, Chicago, in 1968. The group was also effective in its efforts to spread the general anarchic and antiauthoritarian spirit of that era by claiming it as the guiding principle of Yippies. The Chicago Seven trial, which prosecuted the "conspiracy" behind the Chicago demonstrations, is marked in particular by the disruptive activities of the Yippie component in the defense. The often bizarre tactics of Hoffman and Rubin resulted in an overwhelming amount of press coverage for Yippies during the trial in the winter of 1969–1970. The rioting for which the defendants were indicted was re-created in their courtroom demeanor, and the trial itself emerged as a replay of the politics of Yippie-style symbolic, media-directed protest.

The Yippies of the late 1960s explained in visual and highly dramatic terms why so many young people at the time were flouting authority in the substance and style of their lives. The Yippies set themselves up as a counterforce to mainstream culture, representing the politicized "hippie" of that era. Yippies countered the popular, majority viewpoint concerning the war in Vietnam, a viewpoint that refused to consider the possibility that the government might have been mistaken or that "official" activities or versions of events might ever be in error. The original Yippies challenged the legitimacy of all authority (Judge, History, Parent, Pig) and raised questions about the assumptions that govern civil behavior in America. Throughout their short life in the media spotlight, the Yippies held as their purpose the explication of societal constraints. By breaking as many rules of behavior as possible, Yippies showed just how many rules there were—evidenced by the numerous citations for contempt of court gathered in the Chicago Seven trial, and by Abbie Hoffman's long term "underground" in America before his emergence—and death—in 1989.

* For a more complete account of the origins of Yippies, see my essay "Comedic Impulses and Societal Propriety: The Yippie! Carnival."

The Yippies faded from the national media spotlight after 1970, but did not cease to exist as an anarchist organization. The fates of the two most prominent founders, Rubin and Hoffman, are legendary still, with Rubin going to Wall Street as a successful corporate networker and Hoffman continuing to serve radical causes. Their exclusive biographies remain emblematic of so many rebels of that era who wanted both revolution and social influence, who wanted to destroy the state and simultaneously—in their terms—to love everybody. The period's most popular team of songwriters, John Lennon and Paul McCartney, exemplify the contradiction again. Lennon goes on to radical politics and violent death, McCartney becomes a major holder of musical rights and continues to produce, in his own words, silly love songs. The "split" made emblematic by these two famous duos is played out more often in the very souls of those who lived through or have found inspiration in the era of revolt. The contradiction, in other words, has produced the political ambivalence that characterizes the historical generation that witnessed "the fundamental social rupture" when the world broke into pieces—in Chicago '68, in Vietnam, in Watts, and around the dinner tables of an affluent, suburban America that could not eat in peace.

In November 1972, Abbie Hoffman and Jerry Rubin were ousted from the Yippies because of their endorsement of George McGovern for president. After the removal of Hoffman and Rubin, the Yippies did not set up substitute leaders. According to their own account, the group moved away from "household names" leadership to "face to face grassroots networking" (*Blacklisted,* 534). In 1983 the Yippie Book Collective published a 733-page "pamphlet" explaining its activities and political philosophy. *Blacklisted News, Secret Histories . . . From Chicago '68 to 1984* contains four sections: "The Secret History of the 1970s" explains the political alliances that control American society and is itself an attack on that incorporation; "The Dreaded Yippie Curse" outlines the activities of Yippies in that history, such as protesting at national party conventions, "pieing" public figures, organizing the Rock Against Racism (RAR) concerts, and hosting the marijuana "smoke-ins" every July 4 in Washington, D.C.; "New Yippie Manifestos" covers National YIP Conventions through 1979 and explains the "new nation" of Yippies in America; and "The How To Revolt Handbook" contains tips on Yippie survival, from cheating on schoolwork to gate-crashing, free food, birth control, disruption of public events, self-defense, and how to organize a local Yippie chapter. As a whole, the volume describes an extremely active and articulate anarchistic group dedicated to the disruption of what everybody knows, and the awakening of Nobody to political involvement.

The Yippies are not so much an organization (they've never been "organized" in any identifiable way) as they are representative of a popular state of mind, a permanent disloyal opposition. They are themselves, in anarchist fashion, ruled by Nobody; they are obsessed with conspiracy theories and rely on a similar obsession for their support; they are pragmatic in their alliances and in their ideology—contradictions do not upset them, in fact, they seem to thrive on contradiction—and finally, they are hedonistic in principle, claiming comfort ("getting high") as their primary private enterprise, and resorting to violence only when provoked or when they wish to provoke. There is no identifiable Yippie "program" in the leftist, political sense, no consistent ideology outside the patently American one of hedonism, consumerism, and property. Conliff and Grace Nichols claim, in "A Few Modest Proposals on National Yip" (the concluding segment of *Blacklisted News*), that "YIP is more like a traditional American party, complete with funny hats and puking on the carpet, than most radical parties." Most radical parties "are patterned after European political parties, ideological in nature and hence outside the mainstream of American culture. Ideas count for very little in America. Power, money, sex, turf, and drugs are what's important here" (726).

As a mode of consciousness, Yippie taps into the "social rupture" that occurred in 1968–1970 when the full force of the state was exposed in its efforts to control dissent in America. Out of this rupture came a sense that a lie had been foisted on Americans—and Yippies have been exploiting that suspicion ever since. What *Blacklisted News* attempts to do is to establish the fact that "reality" and "history" are products of a conspiracy—of conscious and unconscious complicities in status-quo corporate-power relations. The project does this by dwelling on historical conspiracy theories, government by assassination, links between corporate maneuvers and state policies, and unanswered "coincidences" in the historical record. The effect of reading through Yippie manifestos and historical narratives is to share in a popular view that social reality is never what it purports to be, that what is really going on is somehow hidden from the eye of the average citizen.

On Yippie terms, reality, whether in the form of the interpretation and manipulation of contemporary events or in the form of historical narration, is, increasingly, coming under the control of corporate interests in America. Cather's Captain Forrester represents a pioneer in this field—able to convince himself and his awestruck listeners that what he accomplished in the Western territories was purely benevolent. Only Ivy Peters was, in Yippie parlance, "hip" to what the captain was all about and not willing to romanticize his exploitative career. "Someone is truly hip when he always looks for the factors behind the facts," according to Yippie writer George Matefsky (*Blacklisted*, 508), echoing Ellison's *Invisible Man*. *Blacklisted News* is filled with examples, leads, and insights into this "hip" mode of consciousness, a mode that simply does not believe in historical "events." To be hip is to be like Ellison's IM: suspicious, irresponsible, and overwhelmingly tempted by an invisibility encouraged by the corporate environment that really does not want to hear this "buggy jiving." But this jive is a prevalent mode of popular consciousness in America, similar to what Braudel has called "a social unconscious." History at its worst, Braudel argues, is "under the illusion that it could derive everything from events. . . . Unconscious history proceeds beyond the reach of these illuminations and their brief flashes" (39).

Unconscious history is what "everybody knows" to exist just beneath the official rhetoric of state and corporate history, or the reverence for visible (and often staged) events. Braudel was "hip" to what, in Yippie terms, moves events into historical narratives—they certainly do not move of their own volition. Louis Mink prefers to reverse the association between events and narratives by placing the *event* in service to the narrative. "We need a different way of thinking about narrative," Mink argues. "'Events' (or more precisely, descriptions of events) are not the raw material out of which narratives are constructed; rather, an event is an abstraction from a narrative" (147). Sharing this insight, Yippie historians look not to events but to what produces or stages the event. The Yippie assumption is that nothing occurs accidentally, no event "emerges" naturally from the political landscape. Rather, events are driven by the dominant narrative structure of the era—the corporate power relations that characterize contemporary American culture. This is what it means to look underneath history or to seek the "factors behind the facts." This is also what accounts for the irresponsibility of Yippie activities and the atmosphere of suspicion characteristic of Yippie writing, the obsession with conspiracy and secret deals, the paranoia.

For Willa Cather the world broke in two in 1922, cutting her generation adrift from its confident past. In 1968, according to the New Yippie Book Collective, that same world began to shatter into a number of pieces. The Chicago police, along with United States militia called into Chicago to restore order and suppress demonstrations, broke into a number of fragments the world in which young people represented the future, and the streets belonged to the public. The world before 1968 was one in which the young could protest the perceived madness of their elders without fear of military confrontations and without fear of police records that would follow them in their future. We have televised records of police and militia beating protestors with billy clubs, shattering that old world into pieces, imbedding graphic images of pain and physical abuse into our memories of what happens to people who stand in the way of "events" staged and paid for by the state. Out of "Chicago '68" (the term itself a synecdoche for fragmentation) emerges a clear image of the price extracted for political involvement and for attempts to change history. "The whole world is watching" went the chants of the protestors there—but what the whole world saw was the force and power of the American state.

Since Chicago '68, however, Yippies have maintained efforts to explain what happened when the world broke into pieces and to resist state and corporate attempts to piece it back together through various narrative strategies. The consumer apparatus in America, for one, would turn the radicalism of that era into a personal style, or a form of adolescent passage—now out of style, now passé. The state itself would present the Watergate purges as its own version of radicalism, implying that through Watergate the state, the system itself, cleaned house. The Yippie Book Collective and the Yippie publishers of *Overthrow* resist both these narratives—on the one hand, by continuing radical activities despite the corporate media blackout, and on the other, by presenting Watergate as a state-sponsored sideshow, to deflect attention away from the solidification of state power that followed '68.

Yippies claim that a silent coup occurred in America after Chicago '68, resulting in an overt corporate-state-paramilitary alliance. The alliance removed the last of the political individualists from the presidency, Richard Nixon—the last president to attempt to win an election by his own resources. Since Nixon, the presidency has been filled by men selected by the postcoup alliance for either their ineffectiveness (Ford, Carter) or for their willingness to be wholly controlled by corporate and military interests (Reagan, Bush). Yippies challenge the legitimacy of this new state alliance by participating in the general commitment of the underground press to undermining traditional authority (Watson, 95) and traditional modes of narrating recent American history. "An alternative culture," according to Ian Angus, "provides a *context of interpretation* which is a public pedagogy, and can provide the external conditions for the reception of an alternative content" (14). This captures the Yippie program in the 1980s and 1990s with precision: It is an effort to provide a context of interpretation—a mode of consciousness with which to consider what has happened in the United States since Chicago '68.

To give the Yippies' postcoup American state an appropriate, postmodern name, we might call it postfascism. "Modernism tore up unity and postmodernism has been enjoying the shreds," in Todd Gitlin's words ("Postmodernism" 351). One result is seen in the spirit of the present age, a spirit that requires an I've-seen-it-all attitude of "weightless indifference" (352), the attitude captured in Leonard Cohen's song "Everybody knows." Yippies are concerned that those shreds Gitlin speaks of are increasingly being located under the control of corporate power. In the postfascist age, Yippie writers see a gradual encroachment on public space by corporate interests, where a cultural style of personal arrogance only serves state purposes in cultivating a passive, deluded population of blasé citizens. Under these conditions, the corporation easily replaces the polity as the average American's source of identity and object of loyalty.

Academic critics have responded to this postfascist age in a number of ways. Gerald Graff attacks "the sophisticated skepticism of the literary culture," a skepticism which "is mirrored in the popular desire to be told that our knowledge and perceptions cannot be trusted, that we—as opposed to the technocratic controllers to whom we surrender objective knowledge and power—are lovably mixed-up people who therefore cannot be blamed for the horrors of modern history" (26). University teachers who claim that contemporary students do not know anything and don't want to know anything are correct, perhaps, in the indictment—but they miss the important correlative point. Contemporary students do not believe it is *necessary* to know what is on Hirsch's list or Bloom's curriculum because their "technocratic rulers" know it and will use it for what it is good for. Frank Lentricchia sees the same abdication of intellectual power in the academy where American humanists feel "vaguely out of it, desiring change but crushed, stifled, and enervated by the fear that the robust, active will may not succeed" (51). Academics, through their actual or televisual memories, and students, in the atmosphere created by their parents and by the news media, have suffered the psychic blows delivered in Chicago '68, "crushed, stifled, and enervated" by the riot gear, the subsequent trials, and the political harassment afforded those "robust, active" citizens of the recent past. Fredric Jameson has argued (with great influence) that as a result of these cultural changes the political dimension of contemporary life for most citizens has been "relentlessly driven underground." The political is "no longer visible" in cultural productions and "has at last become a genuine Unconscious" (280), which must be managed by the state. To awaken the contemporary mind to the political, then, is to break the control over consciousness and perception held by "technocratic rulers" of mass media and historical narrative.

According to the Yippie Book Collective, the alliance of state, corporation, and military works to control public space, define personal identity, and—of particular significance here—to assign meaning to historical events by either controlling those events or by controlling the interpretation of events. This alliance is something "everybody knows" about, to borrow Leonard Cohen's mock homage to it. Its strength, according to Yippie writers, is that despite what "everybody knows," Nobody cares—and what Nobody decides becomes law in America. These Nobodies are Lentricchia's populace of "crushed, stifled, and enervated" men and women, Graff's "lovably mixed-up people," and Jameson's politically Unconscious. However, where the academic critic despairs, the Yippie delights. In their celebration of Nobody—also defined as an objectless mass of fragmented, corporate-loyal workers without interest in the political—Yippies capture the transformation of *citizens* into *corporatists*. The anonymity that Americans crave makes them a plurality of Nobodies, a status bolstered by a corporate history that defines the politically active as the ultimate losers. This was proved in Chicago in 1968, at Kent State in 1970, and on all those police records of men and women who sought to change the world in 1968–1975 but now find it hard to get a job.

Yippies do not despair in the face of this evidence, but delight in its implications and seek to thrive within its boundaries. According to Yippie writer Steve Conliff, Nobody has controlled the American government for decades. In 1980, Conliff points out, 49 percent of all those eligible in America voted for Nobody, while Ronald Reagan received 26 percent of those votes and Jimmy Carter 21 percent. "Nobody," Conliff declares, "wins by a landslide" (*Blacklisted*, 205). In 1976, Yippie activist Wavy Gravy nominated Nobody for president at the Yippie presidential convention outside the Republican National Party Convention in Kansas City. "Who cares?" went Gravy's slogan: "Nobody cares." According to Gravy's nomination speech, "Nobody has been in office for quite some time. In fact if you look at the record you would discover that Nobody lowered taxes last year, Nobody balanced the budget, Nobody stopped the war, Nobody is feeding the hungry and the destitute, and Nobody loves you when you're down and out" (321). History is rhetoric. The retreat to private space—called (at home) togetherness in the 1950s, called (out of home) careerism in the 1980s—is a flight from politics, sponsored by corporate America's need for stability and enforced by its reprisals against both those who prove unstable and those who do not prove loyal to the corporation.

The Yippie Book Collective presents the late twentieth century in the United States as an era of postfascism. Steve Conliff, for example, claims that contemporary fascism (or postfascism) is built not on polarization but on fragmentation. Postfascism differs from its original form in Germany and Italy in the 1930s and 1940s. Today it is no longer necessary, according to Conliff, for everyone to hate Jews or communists or blacks—it is not even desirable for this to occur. "If people can agree about anything, in ten years they might all agree to hate the government." "Fascism," Conliff claims, "is not men with guns at your door in the middle of the night. Fascism is the *fear* of men with guns at your door in the middle of the night" (344). The corporate state encourages the spread of this fear in order to increase dependence on its police forces. "Are you starting to feel frightened? . . . Of course you are. Why do you think the government lets it happen?" (225). The postfascist age is one in which every conceivable fear—of other races, of drugs, drug users, drug pushers, of drunk drivers, of violence, fascism, communism, of punks, parents, teachers, of sex, AIDs, you name it, becomes the rationale for increasing the size and capabilities of internal public and private police forces, allied and backed by the military. Under postfascism, the self is eager to surrender its multidimensional autonomy to the protective custody of the state, the corporation, or the army.

Yippies attempt to present an alternative to fear through popularized historical explanation (the spread of "hip" insights into what is "really" happening) and carnivalesque antistate and anticorporate activism. Yippie investigative reporting has covered, for example, the John F. Kennedy assassination conspiracy (identifying future Watergate alumni E. Howard Hunt and Frank Sturgis on the grassy knoll in Dallas); the government-phone company wiretap alliance; the military's experiments in weather-warfare ("greenhouse effect" is a cover for military experimentation in climate control); the heroin conspiracy (heroin traffic is government-fostered to provide the rationale for reinforcing internal police forces). "The How to Revolt Handbook" consists of various ways to take things back from corporations. The logic is similar to the logic of the nineteenth-century American slave's rationale for "taking" from the master: If the slave master "owns" the slave, then it is impossible for the slave to steal from the master. What the master calls stealing is simply the movement of his property from one place to another. The logic applies equally to citizens who recognize that their lives—their history, their fate, and their fortune—belong to corporations. Accordingly, the Yippie does not "steal" from a corporation (although the state, in its alliance, will claim so) when he or she learns "phone freaking," "making it underground," or getting free food and products from major businesses. This is not corporate theft but the rearrangement of corporate holdings from one pocket to another.

One might call it the consumer theory of value. If a product or service is offered to the consumer through advertising or other means of corporate speech, then the consumer "owns" it prior to and distinct from any purchase. Advertisers rarely indicate the inaccessibility of a product and in fact go far to suggest the availability of any product to anyone. Prices are seldom mentioned. The Yippie would embrace this consumer atmosphere as the natural habitat of the late-twentieth-century American. Being offered a product, hearing a "message," consuming an image—by these means does the Yippie come to own a piece of the corporation. In other words, if corporations are ubiquitous in influence and presence, if they are in fact the environment, then "stealing" from them is as meaningless as stealing an apple from a tree. This is the Yippie position, illegal, illicit, but not entirely ill-thought. Americans, as any hotel owner will tell, are notorious thieves.

Blacklisted News symbolizes the enormous relevance of the Yippie mode of consciousness to contemporary America. This way of thinking resists the burial of the anarchic self beneath the weight of state and corporate versions of reality, including individual identity. Dana Beal devotes much of his Yippie actions to organizing "alternative culture actions" to those sponsored by the state or by private corporations (17). Beal's writing has consistently centered on the "permanent government (military, bureaucracy, CIA) existing behind the scenes, which can dispense with elected officials [such as Richard Nixon] when they prove embarrassing" (70). Beal controls the layout and pagination of the Yippie newspaper *Overthrow,* which is itself devoted to continual exposition of this mode of thought.

The main component of postfascism is corporate takeover—not of other corporations (although this is a vital, continuing strategy) but the completion of what Alan Trachtenberg has called the "incorporation of America," which began in the late nineteenth century. America solidified nationally in that era, according to Trachtenberg, who uses "incorporation" as the most appropriate metaphor for that solidification. Now, at the end of the twentieth century, America, Inc., is being taken over by private corporations. This historical movement has been documented in great detail in a recent book by Herbert Schiller, *Culture, Inc.* Schiller centers his attention at one point on the legal issue of corporate speech:

> As the cultural industries increasingly occupy pivotal positions of social, political, and even economic power in the latest period of capitalist development, their symbolic outputs, however entertaining, diverting, esthetic, or informative, are essentially elements of corporate expression. Corporate speech, therefore, has become an integral part of cultural production in general. Most imagery and messages, products and services are now corporately fashioned from their origin to their manufacture and dissemination. (44)

According to Schiller, "the corporate 'voice' now constitutes the national symbolic environment." In this environment it becomes increasingly difficult to differentiate between individual and corporate speech—because individual speech is saturated with this "corporate voice." Schiller calls it "the corporate colonization of consciousness" (110) and urges a return to public control over corporations. What Schiller endorses by legitimate politicking Yippies encourage through guerrilla tactics.

Schiller provides an array of examples to support his thesis concerning the corporate environment. He points out that a massive redistribution of the tax burden has occurred in America since 1952. In that year, 42.2 percent of the government's tax source was from individual income and 32.1 percent was from corporate income. The remaining tax revenues were gathered from social insurance programs, excise taxes, and estate and gift taxes. Thirty years later, in 1983, 47.2 percent of tax revenues came from individuals and 6.6 percent came from corporations, with most of the remaining taxes collected from social insurance programs and excise taxes. Everybody knows this, of course, because tax sources are public knowledge. Only a "remarkable public relations achievement" could induce Americans to accept this redistribution as just and keep them from staging a tax revolt. "This 'achievement,'" says Schiller, "may be regarded as one of the tangible outcomes of the corporate envelopment of public expression" (29). The corporate-state alliance has convinced Americans that the redistribution of the tax burden is inevitable and beyond politics. After all, no media corporation (CBS? NBC? *New York Times?*) can be expected to sponsor a move to raise its taxes. As long as corporations control the media of public debate, the message, to echo Marshall McLuhan, will be influenced greatly by the media's own profit margin.

Corporations control more than information; they have actually "colonized" nearly every public space in America. Mark Tushnet suggests that "corporations dominate the media through which we interpret the world beyond our personal experience" (253)—but the arena of "personal experience" is growing smaller. Libraries rely on private vendors for data bases, thus connecting corporate resources to "free" information; museums rely on corporate sponsors for funding, thus connecting the creative arts to corporate beneficence; the shopping mall transforms the public marketplace—historically associated with public actions and potential disruption—into an exclusively private domain. These movements are all accompanied by the aura of corporate benevolence. In order to get "commercial-free television" on cable TV, for example, the consumer has the privilege of paying a corporation *directly* instead of having the programming broken by commercials. Even city plazas, public forums that these have been throughout history, are becoming the sites of corporate colonization. Schiller points out (102) that at AT&T Plaza in New York City there is a plaque which reads:

PUBLIC SPACE
Owned and Maintained
by A. T. & T.
550 Madison Ave., N.Y.C.

Information and "news," the public agenda, the arts, the marketplace, and the city plaza—each attests to the steady encroachment of the corporation over the human environment.

Especially pertinent to a discussion of the Yippie alternative, though, is what Schiller calls "the corporate sponsored, mass media history machine" (7). Professional historians are always decrying the lack of historical consciousness among Americans, or the pervasiveness of historical myths at large in the culture. Despite revisionist historians, who have produced "an outpouring of thoughtful and provocative works" on race relations, gender issues, warfare, technology, and other vital and often subversive topics, the media-saturated public remains ignorant. In fact, radical historians are themselves becoming an "underground" as almost none of their work receives media attention (excluding that in professional journals). This is because "the corporate history machine has at its disposal the means by which it becomes the national narrator of record. Television, which takes its screening orders from corporate marketing, furnishes the history (such as it is) that is seen by millions." What emerges from these historical narratives—the news, the "specials," the dramatizations—are versions of historical events suitable to "the taste of the Established Order" (7–8). Cather's Captain Forrester is the prototype: the Mountain speaks, everyone else consumes or listens.

The corporate history machine was responsible, for example, for perpetuating the perspective on history called the Cold War, based on the highly unlikely possibility of a Soviet assault. Anticommunism became a dominant perspective, informing television programs, spy novels, feature films, actual political events in America and abroad, and becoming part of American folklore. In the 1990s, with the political changes in the Soviet Union and throughout Eastern Europe, this perspective must be altered. We may expect the corporate history industry to retool itself in order to make Eastern Europe and the Soviet Union acceptable trade partners. Nonetheless, Schiller's point is clear. The dominant perspective on historical events in America comes from "the tiniest stratum of the propertied class," which controls the media-informational companies (40). Revisionist historians make up an underground of academic resistance to corporate versions of history—an underground funded by corporations, of course. It is unlikely, though, that Mellon or even the National Endowment for the Humanities would fund a Marxist television series with the same benevolent approval given to a Marxist monograph. Nonetheless, the underground revisionist industry is a secure one. In 1987 Daniel J. Boorstin, no radical historian, published a book entitled *Hidden History*, advertised on its book jacket as containing material "that has eluded the historian's spotlight." Here "secret history" itself becomes a marketable commodity, endorsed by the corporation and dedicated, by Boorstin, "To the Library of Congress."

The corporation is the environment. Very few spaces are left, physical or psychic, which exist beyond corporate influence and control. Those that do exist—city streets, for example—are associated with crime, and calls for increased police protection and corporate involvement are actually public cries for a postfascist presence. When it is not surrounded by corporate protection, the individual feels threatened, the self endangered. Its very safety—its future and its ability to create a history—depends upon corporate beneficence: the lighted courtyard, the shuttle service, the fellowship. What is true of the streets is true of the academy. "Commodity" theory and "production" theory are beginning to dominate academic thinking about culture. Richard Slotkin has written about the corporate environment that contextualized contemporary events in the nineteenth century. Slotkin describes the currency of a set of narrative frames or "myths" employed by newspapers and the state to explain such unexpected events as Custer's massacre (*The Fatal Environment*). A number of contemporary critics not only write about but subscribe to the language of the corporate environment. Gerald Graff has argued that ideas in a consumer society take on the attributes of commodities—easily bought and discarded—where subversion might be "in" in one season and out in another. Commodity-theory is the academic term for the fundamentally conservative

program of corporatism. Frank Lentricchia suggests that "the perpetual production of the 'new' commodity ensures . . . that desire is
unappeasable, which is what consumer capitalism is all about: turning the potentially revolutionary force of desire produced on capitalist terrain toward the work of conserving and perpetuating consumer capitalism" (30). Graff and Lentricchia share a sense of
futility with academic posturing and with "radicalism" among critics in general. The corporate-state alliance actually becomes stronger with each academic attack on it because the attacks are funded by
the targets themselves. It is only through the benevolence of various
forms of state and corporate funding that the best critics of state and
corporation can support themselves and do their research. In this
environment ideas take on the values of Lentricchia's perpetually
"new" commodities and the corporate environment emerges as the
most current tarbaby for Brer Critic to assault.

This is what corporate history is all about as well: creating an
intellectual environment in which academic historians will be
funded to continually overturn their colleagues' findings. In this
intellectual ecosystem, the average reader is left at the mercy of the
only reliably consistent perspective in town—the multimedia corporate version of reality. In any case, as academics assume the language of the corporation (production, commodity), they serve corporate interests acting to colonize speech and place in America. One
cannot separate speech from thought. If ideas are commodities (and
academic publishing would certainly attest to this), then the cherished differentiation between mind and matter, idea and form, is put
aside in the corporate environment—and the ivory tower, by its own
terms, deconstructs. The collapse of mind and matter could well be
the last laugh of romanticism—it is more likely the first words of
totalitarianism, of the Yippies' professed journey from *Chicago '68
to 1984*. "These ideas are my stock in trade": The University might
as well place this slogan beneath its teaching and publishing enterprise: "Over One Million Sold." But of course the numbers would be
inflated.

As long as historians participate in linear recordings of history,
they will serve corporate interests—no matter how revisionist, subversive, or radical their histories might be. Linear history always
serves corporate interests, because it places the present dominance
of the social order by corporations as the *outcome of history*. Unearthing a long-lost radical movement or telling the "untold" story

of some historical figure (read: historical loser) will not undo a sense of historical progression simply because that progression is revealed as unfair or insensitive to the aspirations of some minority group, economic class, or religious community. Linear accounts of history inevitably contribute to successful corporate efforts to "box in" or safely enclose American citizens in depoliticized spaces: in shopping malls, in front of television screens, and in the mode of thought that places the present at one end of historical progression. The only way to resist the corporate voice ("His Master's Voice," as RCA Victor once put it before coming to its senses) is to resist the corporate style of accounting for its presence. This is easier said, of course, than done. The entire weight of common sense and historical scholarship—not to mention the legal structure of the state itself—rests squarely on the presupposition that the past precedes the present, that precedents have objective significance, and that any postulation made by the historian must be accompanied by the footnoted gesture to one's priors.

For its part the United States Supreme Court has decided, in the face of corporate movements over public spaces, that judicial precedent leads to the conclusion that corporations are not simply collections of market interests but are persons themselves. Originally, eighteenth- and early nineteenth-century corporations were publicly authorized, state-sanctioned combinations of interests in capitalist society. In 1886, the Supreme Court decided that the Fourteenth Amendment's due process clause applied to corporations as well as to people—in effect, suggesting that, for legal purposes, corporations were persons (Tushnet, 260). This, of course, was during the era of the likes of Cather's Captain Forrester, men who needed the mythology of corporate individualism to clear the way for their profit-making ventures west. Since a corporation was a person, its right to build a railroad was measured against an Indian tribe's right to resist—and we know how that went. In the late twentieth century, a different landscape stretches before the corporate horizon.

In 1978, the Supreme Court decided (*Bank of Boston* v. *Bellotti*) that because corporations are legal persons, they are entitled to the same First Amendment protection granted to actual American citizens. As such, "the right of a corporation to engage in the political process, and, by extension, in cultural affairs in general was affirmed" (Schiller, 54). The implications of the decision are profound, as they enable corporations to use their vast resources to, in

Schiller's words, "assert hegemonic authority over the informational landscape." As we stand together before the Court, in other words, McDonalds' right to speak out on an issue is "equal" to my own—there is no differentiation between a billion dollar corporation and an individual citizen in the eyes of the Court. It seems clear who will have the louder voice.

The Supreme Court's logic follows what is called the development of capitalism in America. As space, ideas, and persons become commodities, it seems inevitable that speech as well would become commodified. We are dealing with an information *industry* after all. "The corporate speech cases" that culminated in *Bellotti*, according to Tushnet, "do no more and no less that treat speech as a commodity like any other" (234). If the local diner's right to make hamburgers is equal to the local McDonalds' right to make hamburgers, then it follows that each business's right to participate in the political process is also equal. But the more interesting question is this: If corporations are persons for legal and judicial purposes, then what does this in turn imply about persons? If "person" provides an acceptable metaphor for a corporation's existence, does the reverse hold true? Are persons corporations (and not simply for tax purposes)?: Collections of interests guided by the profit margin, interested in politics only to clear the way for corporate (self-) advancement? The characterization may not suit everybody; it may suit Nobody.

Actually, the corporate speech cases provide a definition of actual persons not as speakers or participants in the political and cultural process but as recipients or consumers. Edwin P. Rome summarizes the guiding principle behind the Court's expansion of corporate speech rights in the 1970s and 1980s. The courts, according to Rome, have emphasized the rights of the *consumers* of corporate messages: "Potential recipients, as citizens in a democratic government who must make intelligent choices of their political leaders and knowing and intelligent choices concerning alternative public policies, must have full access to all sources of information, opinion, and viewpoint" (56). This is the legal equivalent of literary reader-response theory, a critical method contemporary with the commercial speech decisions of the 1970s and 1980s, emphasizing the function (or the rights) of recipients while disregarding the intentions and sources of "information, opinion, and viewpoint." As early as 1964, the Supreme Court upheld "the right of the public to suitable access to social, political, esthetic, moral, and other ideas and experiences." In 1969, the Court emphasized "the right of the viewers and listeners" as it granted increased powers to corporate control over and use of the media (Rome 37). Today, tobacco companies defend their right to billboard advertising on First Amendment grounds, and freedom of speech grants corporations the right to make "public service announcements" of various kinds. Missing in the Court's logic, though, is the fact that corporations have a great deal of "say" over what is and is not made available to those privileged recipients.

The issue of corporate speech dominates Yippie concerns in *Blacklisted News* and in *Overthrow.* "The Secret History of the 70s" (*Blacklisted News*, 1–2, 111–113) opens with a series of reports on the financial bailout of *Rolling Stone* magazine made by Xerox in 1968. In an article taken from the June 1976 issue of *Yipster Times* (the forerunner to *Overthrow*), Mark Chance explains *"Rolling Stone* magazine was paid $100,000 in the spring of 1968 by the Xerox Corporation in return for a pledge not to support leftist demonstrations at the Chicago National Presidential Conventions that summer. The loan prevented the collapse of *Rolling Stone. Rolling Stone,* for its part of the arrangement, published several editorials decrying the 'Festival of Life' and urging demonstrators to stay away from the convention. After the convention the editorials blamed the demonstrators for causing the trouble." Chance's source of information is one of the founders of the magazine, Susan Lydon, who quit *Rolling Stone* over the issue of Xerox's editorial influence.

In May 1968, while the newly created Yippies were hyping their Chicago plans, *Rolling Stone* editor Jann Wenner made his famous statement (famous in rock 'n' roll circles, that is) that "rock music and confrontation politics don't mix." After Chicago, the magazine continued its attacks on the New Left while attracting enough recording industry advertising to make *Rolling Stone* the most successful magazine of the decade. David Armstrong substantiates this Yippie accusation in his book on the alternative media, although he places the actual injection of corporate funds a bit later, in 1970 (176). Armstrong points out that Wenner "assailed the very notion that politics could be a solution for young people" and seems, by his own experience, to stand for the idea that "solutions" come from corporations, not public action (124).

Rock music, of course, makes its way as an industry by commodifying rebellion and dissent. When Wenner, backed by Xerox, denounced politics in favor of "'the vague spirit of rock and roll' as youths' only hope to create something new" (Armstrong, 124), he was standing up for Nobody's sense that only losers emerge from politicking. The *Blacklisted* editors consider the revelations of Wenner's deal with Xerox to be "the most important" detail to come to light after Chicago. It signifies the removal of history's mask, for an instant, which led to the conviction that the world nearly fell to pieces in 1968. The Xerox–Warner Brothers–Max Palevsky (the man whom Yippies, and Armstrong, claim engineered the deal) connection is part of what Yippies call the "key nexus of liberal control— the advance guard of cultural reaction" at the core of the corporate takeover of public space. Schiller points out that when the American media quotes from *Pravda*, it often prefaces the quoted material by saying the information comes from a "state controlled" press. "Would it not be equally appropriate to preface domestic reporting with the indisputable point that it customarily comes from privately-owned billion-dollar companies (the networks, the Times, etc.)?" (167)

The inspiration behind the creation of the original Yippies was the 1967 insight, that the news media made—rather than reported— news. Armed with this credo, Yippies allowed—and insisted—that the media create them. The credo led as well to their demise, since the corporate media, dealing in commodities, went on to something else once it became clear that Yippies were no longer hot. The inspiration behind the continued existence (and persistence) of Yippies in the 1980s and 1990s is the insight that history itself is made, not reported. It is made, moreover, in a very particular way, informed by a progressive sense of inevitability that imprisons the present with each successive year, decade, and era. The group fits David DeLeon's criteria for American indigenous radicalism—"a resistance to institutional authority" and a participation in "the historical continuity of an ahistorical, untraditional anti-institutionalism" (153). However, the Yippies' "ahistorical" tendency manifests itself more as a questioning of the historical dimension itself as a source of identity. "The Secret History of the 1970s," for example, is presented as a series of news clippings, narratives, photographs, drawings, and cartoon characterizations presented *not* in chronological order but in a narrative order employed to make its argument about secrecy and historical movement. Any particular story "is positioned for the sake of the narrative," according to the editors, so that the narrative proceeds by *association*, not by chronology. *Blacklisted News/Secret Histories* is a horizontal account of an era, from when the world fell apart in *Chicago '68* to its gradual reconstitution as a corporate enclosure somewhere "in" *1984*. Since "1984" it has been the express purpose of the Yippie publication *Overthrow* to counter this enclosure with its persistent voice of opposition.

Overthrow: Any Better Offer?

Throughout the 1980s Yippies in New York City published a newspaper called *Overthrow*. The newspaper is part of the North American Greens Network, signaling the move, in the 1980s, of Yippies to the Greens' political umbrella. The underground press, according to Yippie writer George Matefsky, is responsible for "the slow education of a mass constituency, and the organization of a few others to keep on working no matter what happens to the 'leaders'" (*Blacklisted*, 512). The move into the Greens' network and the work to produce four issues of *Overthrow* each year signals a move away from media-spotlight confrontation politics. According to an article in the April/May 1986 issue of *Overthrow*, the North American Greens are devoted to long-term projects under four "pillars" of activity: ecology, social responsibility, peace and nonviolence, and base democracy. Ecology encompasses various holistic health projects, antinuclear activities, and animal rights; social responsibility means civil and human rights activism around the world; peace and nonviolence refers to universal state disarmament and the formation of local militia; and base democracy signals movements for local control of corporate utilities and the mass media as well as community-based political structures. *Overthrow* is largely concerned with promoting these causes and continuing the Yippies' mode of perception on the political scene at large.

Overthrow's Spring 1988 issue has the headline (Figure 6.1) "Any Better Offer?" below a drawing of a human fetus imposed on a backdrop of missiles and industrial pollution. This is the cover page, not page 1. The illustration makes its ideological pitch for the Yippie alternative in the face of the perceived imminence of global apocalypse. On the back cover (Figure 6.2) is an advertisement for the paper, mocking the sobriety-craze of the present era with "Just Say Yo," an invitation to subscribe and partake in the Yippie's alter-

native version of reality: $10 "for one year's worth of your paganistic, synergistic, harmonic convergent publication." The two covers, front and back, are visual embodiments of what is for sale here for $1.00: information leading to the awakening of Nobody.

Page 1 contains three stories and captures the range of interests in the newspaper as a whole. "Spy Satellites Back!" raises the issue of government surveillance in America; "The Contragate Conspiracy and Coup d'Etat in the USA" continues the *Secret Histories'* narrative of postfascist control; and "Close Marion and Lexington Control Unit Prisons!" is the first of a number of Greens-based stories on human rights. The page contains no photographs but does include drawings to illustrate the stories: a satellite; a man chained to a wall; two hands gripping (fascist) barbed wire.

The spy satellites story centers on "Room 4C-956" at the Pentagon: "the National Reconnaissance Office (NRO)," which is responsible for maintaining surveillance of "the entire planet's surface." The concern over government surveillance is consistent with the Yippies' efforts to expose what Aryeh Neier calls "the principle American way of political repression" (17). Political activities are monitored in the United States by the FBI, the CIA, the National

Security Agency, the IRS, the Secret Service, and other government agencies (Morgan, 7) to which *Overthrow* adds this obscure military agency, the NRO. All of this spy capability is the state's form of "looking" in a culture where "modes of looking . . . have been linked to surveillance and control over those perceived as inferior" or threatening (Betterton, 12). Surveillance, to Yippie writers, is the state's way of maintaining a position of secret dominance, of keeping control over the camera eye. With its camera eye, the state (and the corporation, with its ever-present in-store video camera) expresses contempt for the objects of its gaze, a citizenry of closely monitored consumers.

The "Contragate Conspiracy" story concerns another obscure government office, the Federal Emergency Management Agency (FEMA), responsible for maintaining plans "to declare martial law, suspend the U.S. Constitution and round up protesters and Central American refugees in detainment camps in the event of widespread internal opposition to the invasion of Nicaragua." FEMA is part of the "shadow government" of the United States, which grew out of the post-'68 coup. According to the article, FEMA was founded by President Carter as part of the nuclear defense system, but the agency maintains various contingency plans for evacuations, detainment camps, and martial law—operations that will not necessarily depend on nuclear war for implementation.

The Spring 1988 issue of *Overthrow* contains a number of human rights and environment stories: prison conditions in America, dissident crackdowns in Malaysia, U.S. government harassment of Navajos, political repression in Denmark and in Guatemala, postwar ecological disasters in Vietnam, the destruction to the American great plains caused by livestock grazing, a follow-up on a previous story about SDI, news from the nuclear resistance movement, revelations of Immigration Service internment camps planned for Louisiana, a series of articles on rain forests and world farming conditions, genetic restructuring of animals, and the ongoing McDonald's boycott. Lists of Alternative Media and Greens Network contacts are provided, as well as an events calendar, some advertisements for other underground newspapers, and letters to the editor. There is no exploitative advertising, no "sex ads" or "personals," and the paper maintains a consistent, well-edited, visually appealing format characteristic of alternative media.

All of the articles in *Overthrow* eschew the mass media's pose of objectivity and invite reader involvement. Many of the Greens Network articles conclude with a "What You Can Do" section providing addresses and organizations for political activism. Others attach brief bibliographies or additional reading lists. The "Events" list, the full-page list of "Contacts" around the country, and the full-page list of "Alternative Media" all contribute to a sense of a vast, active underground of political involvement. The format of the paper invites and prescribes direct action, and resists the mass-media definition of the reader as a consumer in favor of defining the reader as a participant in political activities.

John Downing's definition would place *Overthrow* in the context of "the slow maturation of a specifically North American alternative consciousness" rooted in "'68" and continuing into the 1990s. Downing cites the popularity of the *Utne Reader* and *The Left Index* as "more evidence of this growth pattern"—serving a readership that tends to be politically inactive but is largely dissatisfied with the state of the nation (153). This readership is far from a revolutionary constituency, of course, but is a part of the literate, educated, and battered population of Nobodies currently under attack by social critics and educators.

These Nobodies, looking for "Any Better Offer?" are catered to by more powerful interests than *Overthrow,* however, or than the *Utne Reader.* Philip Lawler has described the corporate sponsorship of various "alternative" media sources, which span the conventional political spectrum in America. The Fund for Investigative Journalism, for example, makes grants of $500 to $1,000 to support freelance investigations. Its board, which includes such prominent media figures as Roger Mudd and Barbara Cohen, administers the grants on a $75,000 annual budget (9). Newspapers can subscribe to the Pacific News Service, a "syndication service" that sends out daily "news analysis" pieces (10). The Center for Investigative Reporting, funded by the Stern Fund, sends similar materials to television stations. The magazine *Mother Jones,* funded by the Foundation for National Progress, a nonprofit organization, is known for its contemporary "muckraking" activities. All of these organizations are liberal or reformist in orientation—and all of them are funded at least in part by one multinational corporation, the Institute for Policy Studies, based in Washington, D.C. Each organization is left-leaning, suspicious of American corporations, suspicious of the military and intelligence agencies—and each is part of "a powerful opinion-molding influence" (86), which makes anticorporationism and antistatism a profitable enterprise in America.

Equally successful, however, are efforts to counter the "liberal bias" in the American news media. Each of the organizations funded by the Institute for Policy Studies has its conservative counterpart, according to Lawler. The Fund for Objective News Reporting makes grants to writers and acts as a "very unusual literary agent" (23) by placing the finished products with magazines and newspapers. The Sabre Foundation exists to "counteract the liberal bias in the print media" (24) by commissioning articles at $1,000 apiece. *Reason* is published by the conservative and libertarian Reason Foundation, although it is not as successful as *Mother Jones*. In all, Lawler describes an environment in which corporations—public and private—compete to provide news sources and news outlets. What disappears in this environment is credibility: Any bit of "news" can be countered by a corporation whose express purpose is to counter, to provide the "other" side. The situation is not unlike the current way of doing business in American research institutions. The only clear victors in this situation are the news corporations and the benevolent foundations that thrive on the debates they underwrite.

As a result of the situation Lawler describes, an anarchist newspaper like *Overthrow* voices suspicion of the entire political spectrum, reserving its strongest denunciation for the liberal reformist. The longest article in the Spring 1988 issue, for example, is "Death and Destruction on the Open Range," which denounces liberal alternatives to "factory farming." Grazing, according to Lynn Jacobs, "causes more death and destruction than any other business in the western U.S." (6). Instead of abusing cows in forced-lot feeding systems, the beef industry has turned to destroying the ecosystem of the Great Plains. Jacobs's article provides a brief history of the "cowboy" beef industry and a detailed account of the effects of that enterprise on the western United States—and then lists ways the reader can become involved in the issue.

Overthrow and the Yippie Book Collective are manifestations of what George Lipsitz has described as "the desire to connect to history, the impulse to connect present problems in historical terms," which pervades popular culture in the face of corporate efforts to control or mystify the historical (36). Advertisers manipulate historical images for commercial ends, corporations "fund" news stories for profit or to enforce an atmosphere conducive to their own interests—in this environment the citizen is likely to find comfort in being the Nobody. This "media abundance," as Downing calls it, acts not to inform but to numb, to "suppress all independent thinking or action" (1). According to Schiller, corporate control of the media and the evolution of corporate speech protection signals "the erosion of democratic principle and practice in the informational-cultural sphere" (162–63). When history itself becomes a commodity, subject to packaging and marketing (or "funding"), the path to "the corporate enclosure of cultural space" extends to the polity's sense of its own past. If this program is successful, then Cather's Captain Forrester will have returned, the person no longer a "mountain" but a corporate interest.

The Yippie Offer

Ralph Ellison has referred to "the underground of our unwritten history," which percolates below the surface of the sense of an "official" American past (GT, 126). Ellison's statement is mirrored by a strong current in popular (or is it anarchist?) culture. Other critics of the way in which history is composed have shared this sentiment, arguing that the conventional historical pantheon is limited to the victors in the past—to the effectual—leaving the contemporary self with perceptions of personal failure or historical inconsequence. Attacks on history come from all quarters in the late twentieth century. These challenges are not made to the legitimacy of the historical dimension of existence, but rather to conventional methods of narrating and creating that dimension. Dominick LaCapra refers to the historical truism that implies "the only things worth studying are those that had a social impact or effect in their own time, thereby depriving historiography of the need to recover significant aspects of the past that may have 'lost out' " (34–35). To write a history of historical loss would be a monumental undertaking in historiography. Such an enterprise would explain what, in any given age, was "immolated," to use Cather's phrase, and to what historical purpose each immolation was employed. I suspect that Cather, again, would provide an accurate guide here. There is no such thing as lost history (or "lost ladies"), only a loss of perspective.

James Baldwin implies that the attempt to "overhaul a history" is merely revisionist—and revisionist history is the stock-in-trade of the corporate history machine. Ideas, as commodities, are cheap. They are readily thought and easily overturned, and each successively "new" idea serves to build obsolescence into all ideas. Revisionist history, the term itself, implies that an authoritative version can be found—eventually, once errors are corrected and clear (re)vision is accomplished. But this is nonsense. The air of futility that surrounds current historicism (and literary criticism as well) will not clear until rational notions of the authoritative are abandoned. Here again we can take our cue from the novelist. Instead of revisionism, Baldwin calls for new efforts to "excavate a history." He explains: "To be forced to excavate a history is . . . to repudiate the concept of history, and the vocabulary in which it is written; for the written history is, and must be, merely the vocabulary of power, and power is history's most seductively attired false witness" (*Just Above*, 480). What Baldwin sees as the power-laden vocabulary of history has been questioned by critics using literary modes of analysis on historical narratives. The attacks on historical narrative might be seen as attacks on the authority of history or on the exclusive right of history to determine what is understood as inevitable or fixed in the present.

The Yippies represent a distillation, in popular form, of the kind of antihistory (in favor of the idea of histori*es*) developed by critics such as White, LaCapra, Slotkin, and others. The Yippie Book Collective repudiates History while working hard to create histories: highly politicized pieces of historical insights and evidence, serving to enforce the hip idea that nothing is what it appears to be. In this atmosphere of hidden agendas and secret movements, *good reading* is perhaps more vital to a sense of multidimensionality than ever before. As object-history masks profound discontinuities in the past, the self as object provides a shield for the indeterminate, invisible essence of individuality. We do not need to read in order to memorize information, but we do need to possess the critical perspective necessary to discern why certain information is presented to us as authoritative or as indispensable—why certain objects come to possess meaning and why others are lost. Objectivity, in this mode of thought, is simply a mask worn by those in power. George Lipsitz has argued that there exists in popular culture a strong and persistent historical sense, but it is not the sense developed by mainstream American politicians or by the corporate history machine. "Collective popular memory," according to Lipsitz, the memory embedded in such popular forms as television shows, rock music, and contemporary film, often sees "the manipulative use of tradition" by corporations and advertisers "as a conscious strategy, as an attempt to create artifacts that conflict with actual memory and experience" (72). Lipsitz argues persuasively that in various popular cultural forms we can see a real resistance to efforts at this kind of bogus tradition building. The Yippies are squarely behind (one hesitates to evoke a "vanguard" among anarchists) this popular mode of consciousness.

The repudiation of corporate history (or state history or, in Cather's vision, history provided by the victorious and powerful) has its roots in texts written by this century's literary artists. Willa Cather, William Faulkner, Robert Penn Warren, Ralph Ellison, John Barth, Alice Walker—actually, the list of writers raising historical questions in this century is quite extensive. In the present era, the entire postmodern mood mitigates against the linear-historical, while opponents of the anarchic leanings of postmodernism insist on a return to history or to what is called historicism. David DeLeon has pointed out that "anarchy and authority" form a continual dialectic in American culture (7). In the present era the voices of authority insist upon historicism and contextual studies while the voices of anarchy call for deconstruction and reader rights. The Yippies, however, seem to have embraced both poles: obsessed with the secrets of history and determined to make of those secrets what they will.

The title of the Yippie Book Collective's project is *Blacklisted News/Secret Histories*—indicating the strong sense of the ideological subtext beneath any society's national history. Rather than seek an authoritative history, the book project finds anarchy in the historical record. The past, as presented by the Collective, does not compensate for the disorder of the present, but *accounts* for it fully. Hence, the Yippie is comfortable in the present and not alienated from the past, secure in the awareness that sensual experience and historical narrative are distinct phenomena. Experience is provided by corporate interests—the environment is a corporate one in America, and one eats, breathes, and makes love (safely now) to the rhythms of the transnational marketplace. Historical reality is revealed only once the marketplace can bear such revelations. In fact, such revelations are good business, as the revisionists know.

It is misleading to speak of a "history" when any breathing, conscious self experiences and is aware that the past contains histor*ies*.

The self alone has a history of its own body and of its gender, its race(s), its family, its nation, its local community, its profession, and its workplace. The self extended contains the past of what it knows but does not necessarily experience: the past of its parents, of its ethnic or racial origin(s), of the other sex, of the world—the dimensions are limitless and the components contradictory. The history of one's own body may contradict the history of one's gender or one's race, and the self may be an exception to any specific historical tendencies. But the self, nonetheless, contains these contradictions and can only flatten them, or harmonize them, at a severe psychic cost. Nonetheless, American culture (Inc.) would assign to the self a singular history with the same insistence that it would assign to it a singular race or gender. Thus, the self is objectified through history, by denying its psychic connection to the histories of every present phenomenon. Just as no American can be "white" or "black" exclusively, or "male" or "female" exclusively, no American can identify with any singular historical progression to the exclusion of the multitude of histories narrated and awaiting narration.

The emphasis on historical victors induces in the populace a reverence for its own oppressors—to identify with the winners in history leads one to identify, or to see as inevitable, the "winners" in the contemporary era. Nonetheless, Yippies stand opposed to victor history by abjuring categories of winning and losing. After all, their history project, their newspaper, and their office in New York (always a target for government searches) appear to be monuments to futile effort. Every history essay, every news story, every disruptive act, every marijuana smoke-in is, if winning is considered possible, completely futile. At best, a news story might eventually be picked up by the mass media (in the normal funnel between the alternative media and the national press), occasionally elevating as well some alternative news reporter into high-salaried legitimacy. But as the Leonard Cohen song indicates, "everybody knows the fight is fixed," and Yippies are not looking for victories in the historical sense of that term. In fact, a sense of futility is as foreign to them as is the expectation of victory.

Even if the struggle cannot be won because the fight is fixed, individual and collective alternatives to defeat can be salvaged by personal choices. The Yippie project demonstrates and asserts that the definition of political activism must be wrenched away from the state (and from the corporation) with its petitions, gunfights, and high-priced justice system. The "How to Revolt Handbook" in *Blacklisted News*, for example, spends far more time instructing readers how to get "free stuff" (or how to steal back) from corporate America—everything from rebate scams to abortifacients—than it does explaining how to build bombs or get guns. The theory is that in America there is truly enough for everyone and that most things are in stock. Again, corporate theft is considered ideological not criminal. At stake throughout Yippie writing (as was at stake in Cather's historical novels) is not reality but reality's definition, not the facts but the narrative.

Blacklisted News and Secret Histories concludes with "A Few Modest Proposals on National Yip" (724–26), which explains the nonorganization's "procedures and structure." For example, the manifesto notes that the "structure and process" of the Yippies "is likely to change as the nature of Yip changes as a function of political developments." Yippies recognize themselves, in their tradition of self-consciousness, as a "function" of the American state that changes as the state changes. The group might best be described, if labels are necessary, as *anarchoreactionary:* reacting to political and historical developments that are understood to have become increasingly exclusive and secretive, but which proceed without a clearly stated direction—in fact, *which proceed in defiance of clearly stated directions.* And so, there is no Yippie party program, no identifiable ideology outside the patently American one of "Power, money, sex, turf, and drugs."

In an era when "everybody knows" that the fight is fixed, the boat is leaking, and the captain lied, in an era when Nobody controls the state, the "hip" stance, or the Yipster position, is to embrace modern cynicism and transform it into the postmodern pleasure of knowing what is *really* going on in the world. It is the pleasure that Ivy Peters feels, in *A Lost Lady*, when he asserts control over Marian Forrester in body and in finance, and when he reveals Captain Forrester's methods as less than heroic. Ivy Peters and "everybody" reading and looking know that, from the Yipster's eye, you just do not believe what you see, or hear, from the captain. Historical narration is the most suspect of all the arts of persuasion.

According to the Yippie Book Collective, social reality, and the corporate history that undergirds it, is the ultimate conspiracy theory in America. The conspiracy called "American history" that is taught in secondary schools is one example; the conspiracy called the electoral process is another. What the *Secret Histories* attempts to do is to show that notions of "reality" are products of conspiracies—of conscious and unconscious complicities in status quo power relations. The same can be said of the dominant literary canon in any era. In either case, the reality (or canon) is unmasked by dwelling on conspiracy theories, assassinations (of bodies or of texts), and unanswered "coincidences" in the historical record. The effect of reading through Yippie materials (or of following literary debates) is to share a popular (and academic) view that social reality is never grounded in what it calls the inevitable.

Blacklisted News and the continued publication of *Overthrow* represent the enormous relevance of the Yippie mode of consciousness, or the Yippie alternative, in contemporary America. It resists corporate encroachments on self-creation and identification, and it resists the single-dimensionality of the historical self. As a group the Yippies have survived and objected to the Reagan/Bush politics of the 1980s and 1990s, the general post-60s culture of indulgence and professionalism, the new sobriety, the self-congratulatory post-Watergate era. The group has survived all this without a structure, without an identifiable leadership, without an official plan of action. It has done so because it represents what is endemic to American culture, as endemic as the natural, narcissistic resistance of the self to objectification. Yippies claim as their constituency the Nobodies of the "Outlaw Nation" within America. This, they claim, "consists of everyone who will hide a political refugee from the pigs, because they've already had to hide something about themselves from the pigs." Yippie constituency in the postfascist age consists of those who find themselves in situations of "permanent confrontation and simultaneous interchange with straights," the mass of Nobodies parading as somebody else: anyone who has driven above the legal limit for alcohol; anyone who has smoked marijuana; anyone who has hidden something from the IRS; anyone who has ever considered his or her singular circumstances an "exception" to the rule of law at any time; anyone who hides something about his or her personal life or sense of self for the sake of a job or a reputation. Their constituency, Yippies claim, may be vastly greater in potential than it is in actuality. Nonetheless, it is a potentially revolutionary class of Nobodies, and everybody knows it.

Angus, Ian H., and Sut Jhally. "Introduction." In *Cultural Politics in Contemporary America,* edited by Ian H. Angus and Sut Jhally, 1–16. New York: Routledge, 1989.

Armstrong, David. *Trumpet to Arms: Alternative Media in America.* Los Angeles: J. P. Tarcher, Inc., 1981.

Baldwin, James. *Just Above My Head.* New York: Dell, 1979.

Bercovitch, Sacvan, and Myra Jehlen, eds. *Ideology and Classic American Literature.* New York: Cambridge University Press, 1986.

Betterton, Rosemary. *Looking On: Images of Femininity in the Visual Arts and Media.* New York: Pandora, 1987.

Boorstin, Daniel J. *Hidden History.* New York: Harper & Row, 1987.

Braudel, Fernand. *On History.* Translated by Sarah Matthews. Chicago: University of Chicago Press, 1980 [1969].

DeLeon, David. *The American Anarchist: Reflections on Indigenous Radicalism.* Baltimore: Johns Hopkins University Press, 1978.

Downing, John. *Radical Media: The Political Experience of Alternative Communication.* No city: South End Press, 1984.

Ellison, Ralph. *Going to the Territory.* New York: Vintage, 1987.

Gitlin, Todd. "Postmodernism: Roots and Politics." In *Cultural Politics in Contemporary America* (see Angus), 347–60.

———. *The Whole World Is Watching: Mass Media in the Making and Unmaking of the New Left.* Berkeley: University of California Press, 1980.

Graff, Gerald. "American Criticism Left and Right." In *Ideology and Classic American Literature* (see Bercovitch), 91–121.

Jameson, Fredric. *The Political Unconscious: Narrative as Socially Symbolic Act.* Ithaca: Cornell University Press, 1981.

Kessler, Lauren. *The Dissident Press: Alternative Journalism in American History.* Beverly Hills, Calif.: Sage Publications, 1974.

LaCapra, Dominick. *Rethinking Intellectual History: Texts, Contexts, Language.* Ithaca: Cornell University Press, 1983.

Lawler, Philip F. *The Alternative Influence: The Impact of Investigative Reporting Groups in America's Media.* Lanham, Md.: University Press of America, 1984.

Leamer, Laurence. *The Paper Revolutionaries: The Rise of the Underground Press.* New York: Simon & Schuster, 1972.

Lentricchia, Frank. *Criticism and Social Change.* Chicago: University of Chicago Press, 1983.

Lipsitz, George. *Time Passages: Collective Memory and American Popular Culture.* Minneapolis: University of Minnesota Press, 1990.

Mink, Louis O. "Narrative Form as a Cognitive Instrument." In *The Writing of History: Literary Form and Historical Understanding.* Edited by Robert H. Canary and Henry Kozicki, 129–50. Madison: University of Wisconsin Press. 1978.

Morgan, Richard. *Domestic Intelligence: Monitoring Dissent in America.* Austin: University of Texas Press, 1980.

Neier, Aryeh. "Surveillance as Censorship." In *Unamerican Activities: The Campaign Against the Underground Press,* coordinated by Geoffrey Rips, 9–17. San Francisco: City Lights Books, 1981.

Rome, Edwin P., and William H. Roberts. *Corporate and Commercial Free Speech: 1st Amendment Protection of Expression in Business.* Westport, Conn.: Quorum Books, 1985.

Schiller, Herbert I. *Culture, Inc: The Corporate Takeover of Public Expression.* New York: Oxford University Press, 1989.

Slotkin, Richard. "Myth and the Production of History." In *Ideology and Classic American Literature* (see Bercovitch), 70–90.

Trachtenberg, Alan. *The Incorporation of America: Culture and Society in the Gilded Age.* New York: Hill & Wang, 1982.

Tushnet, Mark. "Corporations and Free Speech." In *The Politics of Law: A Progressive Critique,* edited by David Kairys, 253–61. New York: Pantheon, 1982.

Urgo, Joseph. "Comedic Impulses and Societal Propriety: The Yippie! Carnival." *Studies in Popular Culture* X:1 (1987): 83–100.

Watson, Francis M., Jr. *The Alternative Media: Dismantling Two Centuries of Progress.* Rockford, Ill.: Rockford College Institute, 1979.

Yippie Book Collective. *Blacklisted News, Secret Histories . . . From Chicago, '68 to 1984.* New York: Bleecker Publishing, 1983.

Epilogue

Novels are not cultural ornaments. More than one historian has required on a syllabus a novel to exemplify or to illustrate a historical era, perhaps Sinclair Lewis's *Main Street* to capture, as it were, the American 1920s, or Tim O'Brien's *Going After Cacciato* to do the same for the Vietnam war. But this practice trivializes literary studies by turning the novel into a set piece, akin to a graph, a map, or a chart. It would be more productive to use *Main Street* as a way toward understanding Cincinnati's reaction to the Mapplethorpe exhibit, or to employ *Going After Cacciato*'s sense of mission as a critique of the space race (the race to the moon), which ran concurrent with Vietnam. Studies of the novel ought to free us from historical linearity in order to embrace and explore the associational qualities of the literary imagination.

One of the pleasures of the postmodern moment in academics, the disciplinary chaos that characterizes the university today, is that, for the moment, we are not bound to conventional structures of academic study. The inevitable backlash to this anarchy will eventually impose a pattern on scholarship and on the curriculum once again, but not before some discredited practices are either modified or abandoned. Postmodern freedom is the freedom to recombine, to take what *is*, regardless of form, and to place it next to something else that is. The result is some combination without precedent. As for the novel, literary studies can be enriched by forfeiting critical formalism, by removing the novel from the corporate artifice of a linear tradition of great works, lined up like dominoes with uniform bindings. The reader can then make arguments, as opposed to observations, about reality by looking not *at* the novel but *through* the novel. What is ultimately revealed will vary by who it is that does the looking, but in any case the novel will have proved useful, not merely ornamental.

A useful novel will display more than a perfectly enclosed narrative. All narrative enacts the problematic realm of human existence: the need for order. The need for order is not controversial, it is not political. However, the quality of order, of any order, is, of course, at the very core of politics—from society at large to the college curriculum. Even the anarchist cannot live without order; his quarrel is not with order but with establishment or the confusion of order with permanence. The making of the self into an object is a direct result of the necessary structuring of reality into something knowable. Because the novel is, by at least one definition, the transformation of chaos into a narrative structure, it requires close scrutiny. The novelist, far from writing "about" the real, is in effect written *by* the real, by her sense of what glues the self together as it moves about in time.

None of the pairings in this volume is definitive, but all are instead indications of an enormous amount of work that must be done to rescue the novel from its nearly invisible status in American culture. All readers of novels have had momentary flashes of recognition, where something in a novel brings to mind a historical event far removed from the literal subject matter of the text. We used to call this phenomenon evidence of the novel's classic status, but the very idea of a "classic" mitigated against its public use to understand something as ephemeral as reality. By reversing contextualism, so that the novel is not placed in historical context but provides, by itself, a literary context, critical study is both freed from control by the historians and enriched as a legitimate perspective on history.

INDEX

ABC World News Tonight, 40, 41, 45, 47, 48, 50, 51, 52, 53, 56, 58, 59, 60, 65–66, 67
Aaron, Betsy, 38–39, 48, 56, 65
Adams, Jacqueline, 63
Angus, Ian, 196
Appiah, Anthony, 8
Armstrong, David, 207
Armstrong, Louis, 11, 12, 14, 16, 55, 162
Atheide, David, 42, 64
Atwater, Lee, 63, 69

Baldwin, James, 16, 21, 22, 214–15
Barnes, Angela and Cliff, 61, 62–63, 64–65, 66, 67
Barth, John, 216
Baumbach, Jonathan, 16
Beal, Dana, 189, 190, 199
Bedell, George, 105
Benjamin, Walter, 185
Bentsen, Lloyd, 69–71
Berger, John, 116, 145
Berlin, Isaiah, 160
Bode, Ken, 57, 66
Bok, Curtis, 93
Boorstin, Daniel, 203
Braudel, Fernand, 184, 185, 194
Brokaw, Tom, 40, 46, 49, 64
Brooks, Tyrone, 65
Brownmiller, Susan, 81–82
Buell, Lawrence, 84
Burke, Kenneth, 16
Bush, George, 60, 62, 63, 65–66, 67, 68, 69–71, 195, 219
Butler, Thorpe, 12

CBS Evening News, 38–40, 47, 48, 50, 52, 53, 56, 57, 58, 59, 60, 61, 63, 64, 65, 66, 69
Cable, George Washington, 6
Callahan, John, 13
Carter, Jimmy, 42, 195, 198, 211
Cather, Willa, 157–60, 190, 195, 216, 218
    Works: Death Comes for the Archbishop, 166–67; A Lost Lady, 194, 202, 205, 214, 218; My Antonia, 163–65, 166, 185; Not Under Forty, 157, 186; O Pioneers, 162; The Professor's House, 163, 165; Sapphira and the Slave Girl, 159; Shadows on the Rock, 165–66
Chance, Mark, 207
Chancellor, John, 48, 54–55, 59
Chase, Rebecca, 40, 41
Chung, Connie, 48
Clark, James, 52–53
Clayton, Cassandra, 62, 65
Cohen, Barbara, 212
Cohen, Leonard, 196, 197, 217
Cohen, Sande, 161, 183–84
Conliff, Steve, 189, 193, 198
Conrad, Joseph, 9
Cornford, Francis, 164
Cosby Show, 12
Coward, Rosalind, 128

Darden, Clairbourne, 65
DeLeon, David, 208, 216
Dimen, Muriel, 78, 79
Donaldson, Sam, 58, 59
Douglas, Ann, 167

Douglass, Frederick, 23
Downing, John, 212, 214
Dukakis, Michael, 38, 39–40, 59, 63, 64, 65, 66, 67, 69–71
Dworkin, Andrea, 81, 82, 86, 118

Ellison, Ralph, 40, 42, 131, 159, 161–62; and invisibility, 27–29, 34–35, 40, 49, 55, 56, 60, 67, 68, 71, 79, 110, 132, 140, 148; and racial categorization, 5–10, 13–18, 54, 67, 68, 71, 216
Works: *Going to the Territory*, 7, 9, 10, 21, 25, 60, 67, 214; *Invisible Man*, 7, 43, 44–45, 46, 55, 67, 69, 71, 86, 158, 194; *Shadow and Act*, 9, 14, 15, 16, 22, 71

Faulkner, William, 35, 161–62, 216
Works: *Absalom, Absalom!*, 158; "Centaur in Brass," 105; *Light in August*, 105; *Requiem for a Nun*, 87–89; *Sanctuary*, 77, 79, 86, 117, 127, 148, 152, 158; *The Town*, 101; *The Wild Palms*, 105
Faw, Bob, 52–53
Fitzgerald, F. Scott, 29
Ford, Gerald, 195
Frazier, E. Franklin, 58

Gandolf, Ray, 51
Gans, Herbert, 44
Gates, Henry Louis, Jr., 7, 8, 9
Gentleman's Quarterly, 114, 115, 142
Gitlin, Todd, 190, 196
Glamour magazine, 7, 98, 159
Graber, Doris, 42, 50
Graff, Gerald, 196, 197, 203
Gravy, Wavy, 198
Gresset, Michel, 99
Griffin, Susan, 77, 79–81, 82, 84, 86, 94, 118

Harpers magazine, 15
Hart, Gary, 46
Hawthorne, Nathaniel, 158
Helmick, Evelyn, 167
Higham, John, 181
Hoffman, Abbie, 190–92
Horton, Willie, 57, 60–61, 62–68, 69–71
Hume, Brit, 56, 58, 59, 60

Hunt, E. Howard, 199
Hutchinson, Anne, 118–19

Jackson, Jesse, 15, 18, 31
Jackson, Michael, 45
Jacobs, Lynn, 213
Jameson, Fredric, 197
Jehlen, Myra, 123
Jennings, Peter, 40, 45, 47, 48, 59, 60
Jordan, Winthrop, 8, 66, 182
Judd, Jackie, 40, 48, 59

Kappeler, Susanne, 82, 86, 118
Kennedy, John F., 199
Kerr, Bob, 45, 68
Kibbey, Ann, 118
Kinder, Donald, 61–62
King, Martin Luther, Jr., 18, 41
Kirk, Paul, 58
Klotman, Phyllis, 11
Kolodny, Annette, 118–19
Krassner, Paul, 190

Lang, Amy Schrager, 118–19
LaCapra, Dominic, 83, 214, 215
Lawler, Philip, 212–13
Lederer, Laura, 81
Lennon, John, 192
Lentricchia, Frank, 133, 197, 203
Lewis, Sinclair, 223
Lipsitz, George, 213, 215–16
Lydon, Susan, 207

McCartney, Paul, 192
McClure, Robert D., 66
McGovern, George, 192
McLuhan, Marshall, 201
McPherson, James M., 19
Matefsky, George, 194, 209
Matthews, John T., 108
Miles, Margaret, 79, 101–02, 109–10, 116
Mink, Louis, 85, 185, 194
Mitchell, Andrea, 68
Mitchell, W. J. T., 182
Morton, Bruce, 39, 48–49, 52, 58, 66
Mudd, Roger, 212
Muhlenfeld, Elizabeth, 92
Munter, Carol, 117
Murphy, Dennis, 45, 46
Murphy, John J., 167

Muskie, Edmund, 55
Myers, Lisa, 62

NBC Nightly News, 40, 45, 46, 48, 49–
50, 54, 57, 58, 59, 62, 63, 66, 68
Nadel, Allan, 13
Neier, Aryeh, 210
Nichols, Grace, 193
Nixon, Richard, 53, 196

O'Brien, Sharon, 162–63
O'Brien, Tim, 223
Ohmann, Richard, 119
O'Meally, Robert, 24–25
Ostendorf, Brendt, 30

Page, Sally, 94
Palevsky, Max, 208
Patterson, Thomas E., 66
Pells, Richard, 7
Petit, Tom, 54
Playboy, 114, 115
Playgirl, 114, 115
Pornography, 77–78, 80–83, 85–87, 98,
108–09

Quayle, Dan, 71

Rather, Dan, 47, 52, 64, 69–71
Reagan, Ronald, 65, 66, 195, 198, 219
Reed, Adolph, 52
Robinson, Noah, 59
Rolling Stones, 77
Rome, Edwin P., 206–07
Rosowski, Susan J., 167
Rubin, Gayle, 85
Rubin, Jerry, 190–92

Schaub, Thomas, 12
Schiller, Herbert I., 200–01, 202–03,
205–06, 208, 214
Schlesinger, Richard, 60
Schwartz, Lawrence, 89, 92
Sears, David, 61–62
Self: objectified by culture, 7, 8, 17–18,
22–23, 26, 32, 33–36, 78–81, 85,
108–10, 123–24, 127, 137–40, 145,
147–48, 150–52, 158–60, 174, 183–
86, 198–200, 206, 215–16, 217, 224;
on television, 40–41, 55–56
Self, 114, 151
Slotkin, Richard, 118–19, 170, 171,
179, 203, 215
Smith, Valerie, 16
Snyder, Jimmy-the-Greek, 51–52
Spencer, Susan, 39, 58
Stahl, Lesley, 53, 64–65
Stepto, Robert, 13, 16
Strandberg, Victor, 96
Sturgis, Frank, 199

Tanner, Tony, 13
Television news, 42–44, 45–48, 49, 50,
52, 61–62, 64, 66
Thompson, Sharon, 101
Threlkeld, Richard, 45
Tichi, Cecelia, 84–85, 119
Time magazine, 15
Todorov, Tzvetan, 7, 9
Trachtenberg, Alan, 200
Tuchman, Gaye, 52
Tushnet, Mark, 201

Van Zandt, Peter, 39
Vance, Carole, 78, 82, 92, 115

Waggoner, Hyatt, 107
Walker, Alice, 216
Walker, Kenneth, 51
Walton, Anthony, 56, 60–61
Warhol, Andy, 145
Warren, Robert Penn, 216
Weaver, Paul, 43
Wenner, Jann, 207–08
Whitaker, Thomas R., 16
White, Hayden, 44, 68, 181, 183, 215
Wilson, Clint, 59, 62, 64
Wooten, James, 53, 58

Yippies, 19, 185; *Blacklisted News/Se-
cret Histories*, 189–90, 192–95, 197–
200, 207–09, 210, 216, 217–18; *Overthrow*, 190, 195, 200, 207, 209–14,
219
Yipster Times, 207

Zinn, Howard, 21–22, 183

Index   227